Disneyland Paris

Sightseeing in the area

The information contained in
the guide is correct at the time
of going to press, but may be
subject to variation because of
ongoing development of sights,
and changes in management
and the cost of living.

Contents

© Disney

At the Crossroads of Europe

Thanks to its location some 30km - 20 miles east of the French capital within the administrative limits of Marne-la-Vallée, one of the five new towns in the Paris region, Disneyland Paris occupies a special place at the heart of the European continent. The map below shows the **main routes** for travelling to the theme park from the major European cities. The estimated times displayed next to the distances in kilometres are inclusive, that is, they indicate total travelling time from the city centres to Disneyland Paris. The estimated times for air and train travel were also calculated on this basis.

If you **fly**, you will land at either Orly (south of Paris) or Roissy-Charles-de-Gaulle (north of Paris). Buses will then take you to Disneyland Paris.

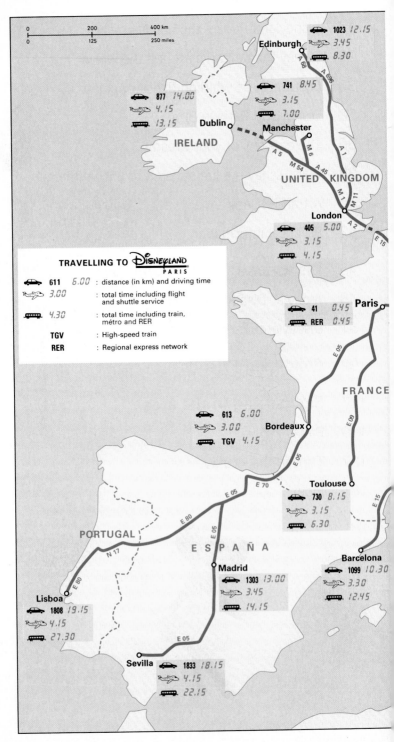

If you take the **train** to Paris you arrive either at the Gare du Nord, the Gare de l'Est, the Gare d'Austerlitz, the Gare de Lyon, the Gare du Montparnasse, or the Gare de St-Lazare.

From there you take the **métro** to Auber or Châtelet-Les-Halles stations, where you can change onto the eastbound **RER line A** (towards Marne-la-Vallée – Chessy). From the Gare du Nord you can also reach Châtelet-Les-Halles station by taking the B line of the RER (in the direction of Robinson or St-Rémy-lès-Chevreuse) or the D line, then take RER line A. From the Gare de Lyon you should take RER line A directly to the terminus (Marne-la-Vallée – Chessy station) and Disneyland Paris.

Since 1994 the **TGV** high-speed train has had its own station at the theme park. Disneyland Paris is thus at the hub of a high-speed train network with links to Lille, Lyon, Avignon and Marseille.

A stone's throw from Paris

Located on the plain of Brie, this entertainment and holiday complex (the theme park, six hotels, a camping and caravan site, Davy Crockett Ranch, a golf course and entertainment centre, Festival Disney) is very easy to reach via the A 4 motorway (Autoroute de l'Est) from Paris to Metz and Nancy. Follow the exit signs for "Disneyland" with a picture of Mickey (junction 14) about 30km - 20 miles from the capital. A long straight stretch of dual carriageway then leads directly to the Disneyland complex. Within the Ile-de-France region the A 104 and the N 104 (Francilienne) link the A 1 (Autoroute du Nord) and the A 6 (Autoroute du Soleil) motorways. The N 104 (Francilienne), passing to the south of Paris, links the A 10 motorway (L'Aquitaine) and the A 4 motorway (Autoroute de l'Est).

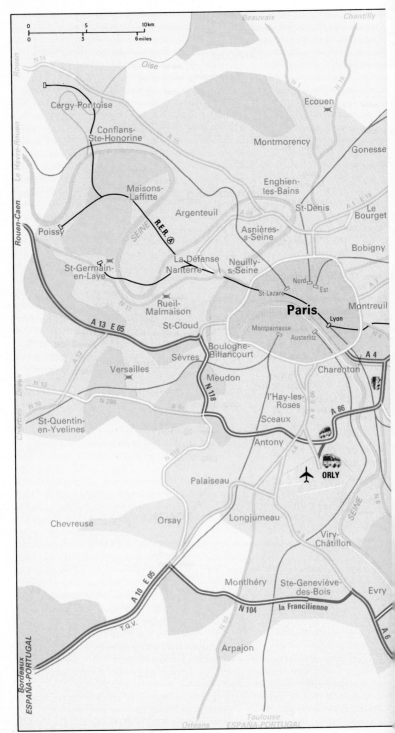

From the huge car park *(fee charged)*, a moving walkway in several sections leads visitors – for most of the way – to the entrance to the theme park and to Festival Disney. Already, jolly music in the background creates the mood for the fun ahead. The campsite and all the hotels have their own car parks reserved for their clients free of charge (tickets available from the hotel or campsite reception). A free yellow shuttle bus service to the theme park and Festival Disney is provided for clients of the five hotels which are set slightly apart from the theme park (the shuttle bus service runs between a clearly signposted bus stop at each hotel and the RER/TGV station).

Public transport: line A of the RER links Paris (Charles-de-Gaulle-Étoile, Auber, Châtelet-Les-Halles, Gare de Lyon and Nation stations) to the new town of Marne-la-Vallée and Disneyland Paris (Marne-la-Vallée – Chessy station). The buses from the airports arrive at the bus station near the RER/TGV station.

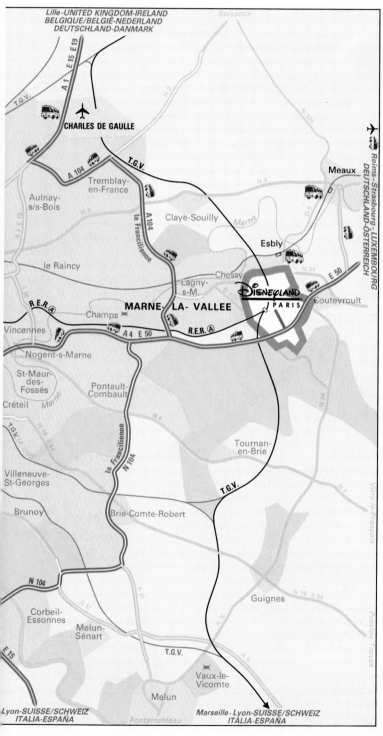

Disneyland Paris

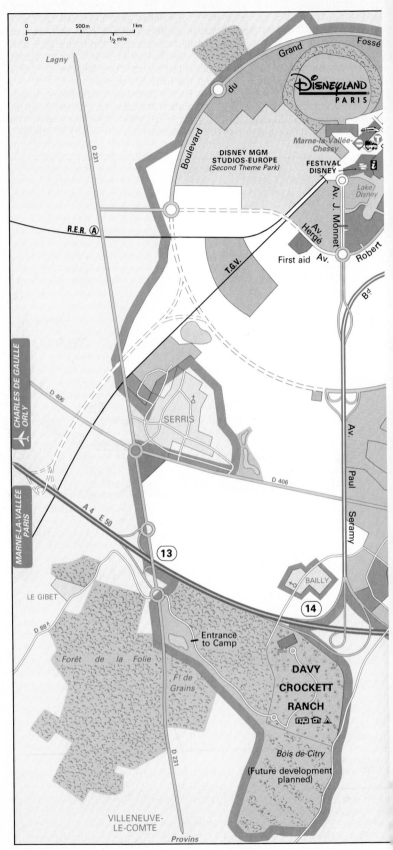

In 1992: total surface area 600 hectares - 1480 acres.

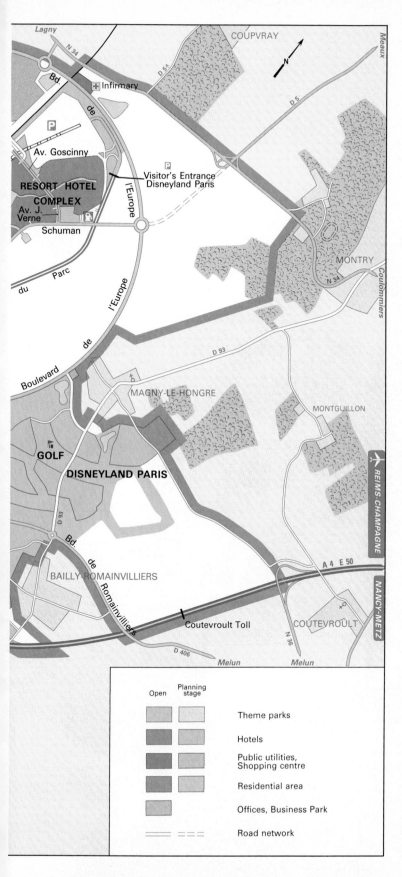

In 2017: total surface area 1943 hectares – 4800 acres.

Introduction

Disneyland Paris – the holiday resort

Disneyland Paris is a holiday complex designed for long or short stays, with a wide range of accommodation facilities and leisure activities. The coordinated design of welcome facilities, décor and activities make it a unique European holiday destination. The resort includes six hotels (three on the banks of Lake Disney, two beside the Rio Grande and Disneyland Hotel at the main entrance of the theme park) with a capacity of 5 200 rooms and a campsite with 97 pitches and 498 cabins. The architecture, landscaping and cuisine of each hotel evoke a particular region in the United States. The hotel staff's costumes, which differ widely depending on the staff member's function, recall various periods in America's history (1900, winning the West, etc.). The beautifully appointed rooms can accommodate up to four people and have private bathroom facilities, a colour television and a minibar (except Hotels Cheyenne and Santa Fé). A number of hotels have facilities for receptions, banquets, conferences and ballroom dances.

The restaurants and bars in the various hotels are open to the general public.

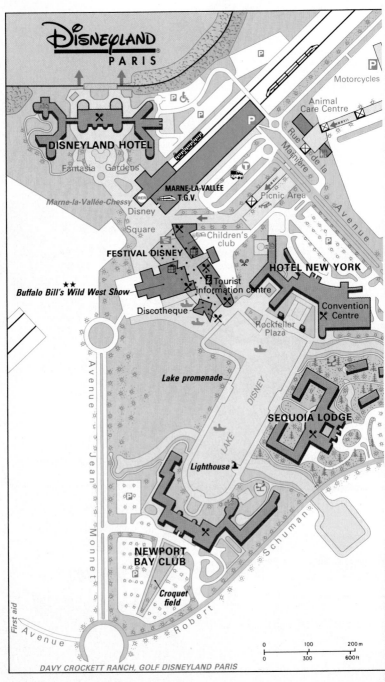

Lake Disney covers about 4ha - 10 acres and offers boating facilities *(rentals available at Festival Disney – Marina del Rey; types of boat for hire include battery-operated boats called "Toobies" and pedalos in the shape of giant swans).*

Three "rivers" run out of this lake, including the Rio Grande *(1)* which separates the Hotel Santa Fe from the Hotel Cheyenne. A landscaped promenade *(Lake Promenade)* around the edge of the lake connects the various hotels to the entertainment centre and the theme park. The landscape is designed to correspond with the theme of each hotel. In summer, old-fashioned buses run round the lake, linking Festival Disney, Sequoia Lodge and the Newport Bay Club. In addition to the six hotels and the campsite there is an entertainment centre *(Festival Disney)* and a golf course *(Golf Euro Disney)*.

---

(1) This North American river forms the border between the United States (Texas) and Mexico, where it is known as the Río Bravo. From its source in the San Juan (Rocky) Mountains in Colorado it meanders some 2.900km - 1 802 miles across New Mexico, watering its largest city, Albuquerque, before emptying into the Gulf of Mexico.

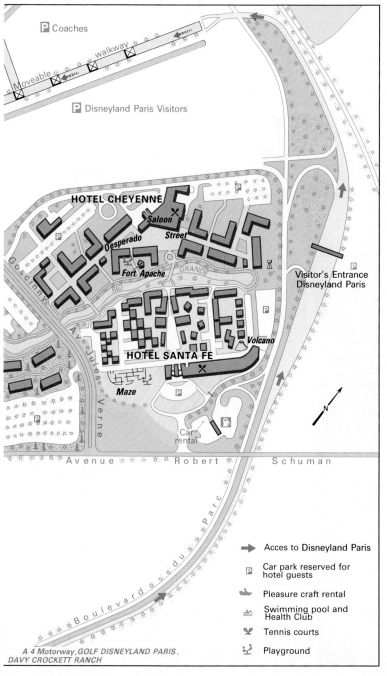

Disneyland Hotel

Luxury class, 479 rooms, 21 suites

This five-storey, luxurious hotel reflects the style and atmosphere of a turn-of-the-century Victorian palace found in the coastal towns of Florida and California. The rich and famous resided in palatial establishments carefully attended by a discrete and efficient staff. Splendidly appointed rooms and suites, plush salons and superb cuisine left the guests with indelible memories. Disneyland Hotel perpetuates this tradition.

The distinctive pink colour and outline of this hotel make it one of the most recognizable landmarks in the resort. The façades of the central building and wings are rhythmically composed with multi-faceted pavilions at intervals along them – a composition of infinite variety where pinnacles, gables, dormers and cupolas jostle for position. The colour scheme is a harmonious combination of pale pink timber walls and deeper pink – more burgundy – timber roofs. The two wings are reached through glazed-over passageways. The entrance drive brings cars up to a canopied porch. As soon as the car stops the car attendant, resplendent in his pink breeches and white collar and cuffs, hastens to open the door for the "guest". The entrance lobby is immense and most impressive. It is decorated in pale colours, with shiny white lacquer predominating on the walls, columns and two floors of arcades. The carpet on the floor has a floral pattern and blends well with the wicker, leather or fabric armchairs. Beautiful flower arrangements adorn several coffee tables. An enormous chandelier in the shape of leaves illuminates the centre of the

© Disney

lobby. The main staircase has two flights leading up to the first floor in opposite directions. The gallery here leads to the restaurants. At certain times of day, piano music can be heard playing in the background.

Guests in the Castle Club (50 rooms and suites) have their own private entrance and receive personalised service.

All Disneyland Hotel guests have access to the health club, indoor swimming pool, sauna, jacuzzi and video games arcade (Mad Hatter's Game Arcade).

Bars and restaurants

– **California Grill:** a smart restaurant with a seasonal menu. Guests can watch their meals being prepared. Wide selection of French and Californian wines.

– **Inventions:** a buffet offering specialities from the New World. Wide selection of wines. The restaurant is decorated with flying machines and early models of cars etc. – hence its name. Breakfast, also a buffet, is a show in itself. Several much-loved Disney characters, including a youthful Mickey, go from table to table greeting parents and their children, who are almost falling off their seats with impatience as they sit clutching their autograph books! Their little faces light up as the long-awaited character appears at their table... quick, get his autograph! Fond parents reach for their cameras and camcorders to immortalise the moment.

– **Café Fantasia:** snacks and hot drinks in a setting inspired by the animated feature film *Fantasia*. Breakfast served.

– **Main Street Lounge:** for a quick refuel. Wide selection of cocktails; piano bar; view of Main Street Station.

Shop

– **Galerie Mickey:** gift shop with Disney and other souvenirs on the hotel's theme.

Hotel New York

First Class, 539 rooms, 36 suites

This smart, imposing hotel reflects the varied architecture of different districts of Manhattan: Rockefeller Center, with five impressive eight-storey tower blocks mainly for business use, Gramercy Park with its rows of neat 19C, neo-Grec style town houses and the East Side with its brownstones (brown sandstone town houses built during the second half of the 19C); the town houses and brownstones form two lower wings on either side of the tower blocks.

The ornamental pool with fountain, on the lakeside on Rockefeller Plaza, doubles as an ice-skating rink in winter.

In front of the entrance a yellow New York taxi conjures up the atmosphere of this hotel from the moment you arrive.

The lobby, in granite and marble, and the various corridors contain several images evoking the "Big Apple" (as New York is nicknamed): a model of the Empire State Building and the Statue of Liberty, and a passing tribute to the famous Yankees baseball team and the equally famous Mets American Football team in the form of photographic souvenirs and two enormous team logos set into the floor.

The hotel is divided into different sections, each named after something to do with New York (Gramercy Park, Midtown, Brownstone, etc.).

Hotel facilities include, on the ground floor of Gramercy Park, a hairdresser's salon, a video games arcade (Times Square Game Arcade), and an Athletic Club with a swimming pool (part indoor, part outdoor), a fitness centre (gym, jacuzzi, sauna, Turkish sauna, massage parlour, sunbeds) and two tennis courts with lighting facilities for evening matches.

There is a children's recreation ground near the outdoor swimming pool with swings, slides and sandpits. Near reception, Peter Pan's Corner has cartoon shows.

Art Deco is the theme of the interior decoration. Each room has a surface area of 31sq m-334sq ft.

Guests at the Castle Club (130 rooms located on the sixth floor – Brownstone – with private entrance) enjoy personalised service and a private lounge where they are served free drinks and snacks.

© Disney

© Disney

Bars and restaurants

– **Manhattan Jazz Club Lounge:** drop in for a drink before or after dinner.

– **Manhattan Jazz Club:** a good place to finish the evening over a cocktail, listening to some of the best jazz in town in the style of the Harlem Cotton Club.

– **57th Street Bar:** cocktail bar with a view of Lake Disney.

– **Parkside Diner:** American food in Art Deco style surroundings, reminiscent of the "diners" of the 30s where people could go and eat uncomplicated fare in a convivial setting. Terrace in the summer.

Shop

– **Stock Exchange:** Disney and New York souvenirs.

Free shuttle bus to the theme park and *Festival Disney*.

The **New York Coliseum Convention Center** is located next to the hotel. It includes a *Grand Ballroom*, consisting of two to twelve independent modules, a ballroom called *Radio City Ballroom* that can be partitioned into three rooms and four conference rooms: *Wall Street, Columbus Avenue, Madison Avenue* and *Park Avenue*.

Newport Bay Club

Moderate, 1083 rooms, 15 suites

This hotel is named after the famous resort of Newport on Rhode Island and evokes New England at the turn of the century. The entrance to this luxurious hotel is distinguished by an imposing façade with a monumental colonnaded porch, overlooking green expanses of carefully tended lawns with colourful flower beds and trees here and there.

In the entrance lobby a globe illustrates epic sea voyages. The décor and the uniforms of the various members of staff continue the nautical theme, as do the names of the two sections of the hotel: port and starboard. On the lake side, rocking chairs have been arranged so that clients can sit and admire the lake and all the "Toobies" and pedalos bobbing around on it. The hotel buildings, covered with cream-coloured shipboard and topped by grey-green roofs, are laid out around a bay lit by a lighthouse. On top of this, an old sea-dog scouring the horizon with a telescope acts as a weather-vane.

The hotel has a croquet lawn and, near the lake, a lovely swimming pool (Nantucket Pool), part of which is covered (with a bar in the shape of a ship), and a fitness centre (gym, jacuzzi, sauna, Turkish sauna, UVA sunbeds). The hotel also has a conference room overlooking the lake.

Each room is very light (harmonious blue and white décor) and decorated in a nautical style (curtains and wall paper with yacht motifs). Children's facilities include a video games room (Sea Horse Club Game Room) and a playground near the swimming pool. There are cartoon shows in the entrance lobby.

Bars and restaurants

– **Cape Cod:** a buffet restaurant with a wide variety of dishes, including pizza, pasta, fish and meat, in the setting of an indoor garden. Every now and then the waiters and waitresses in their brightly coloured uniforms get together to do a little dance and sing along in mime to recordings of songs. Breakfast – continental or American-style – is served as a buffet.

– **Yacht Club:** a smart restaurant specialising in seafood. Fish and shellfish are on display on a fishmonger's slab, and there is a fish tank. Clients can watch their food being cooked. New England specialities on offer include the "clambake".

– **Fisherman's Wharf:** turn of the century style lounge aboard a cruiser. Piano bar, cocktails and view of Lake Disney.

Shop

– **Bay Boutique :** Disney and other souvenirs with a nautical theme.

Free shuttle bus to the theme park and *Festival Disney*.

Sequoia Lodge

Moderate, 997 rooms, 14 suites

Sequoia Lodge, with its long low forest lodges and stone and timber façades in a wooded setting overlooking Lake Disney, reflects the great American national parks *(1)*, such as the Sequoia National Park in California. Many of these parks, which consist of vast stretches of forest, are home to a variety of species, of which the most impressive are the giant sequoias that can live to be several thousand years old.

Visitors are greeted by a National Parks forester in uniform in front of the central pavilion which contains the hotel reception. The five forest lodges along the banks of the Rio Grande have been named after great American national parks: Yellowstone, Yosemite, Sierra, Monterey and Big Sur. The swimming pool (Quarry Pool, part of which is indoors) and the fitness centre (gym, jacuzzi, sauna, Turkish sauna, massage parlour, UVA sunbeds) are to be found next to the Big Sur Lodge. There is a children's playground near the swimming pool. Sequoia Lodge has two conference rooms, Buffalo and Coyote Rooms, and a video games room (Kit Carson's Arcade Game Room).

In summer, drinks are served on the terrace above the central pavilion, with a view of Lake Disney.

Each room measures 27sq m-290sq ft and is decorated in a rustic style.

© Disney

Bars and restaurants

– Redwood Bar and Lounge: very comfortable lounge with deep armchairs and a huge fireplace. This is a good place to relax on a winter evening over an American beer or a cocktail. Piano music.

– Hunter's Grill: this restaurant will go down well with lovers of spit-roasts - you can watch the spit turning over the open fire before you sit down for your meal. The décor is rustic. Each wooden table has a turntable on it on which various salads are offered as an hors-d'œuvres. A selection of spit-roasted meats still on the spit is brought and carved for each diner by a waiter dressed as a backwoodsman, armed with a sharp knife. Terrace in summer.

– Beaver Creek Tavern: barbecued ribs and chicken, etc.

Shop

– Northwest Passage : Disney and other souvenirs based on an American national park theme.

Free shuttle bus to the theme park and *Festival Disney*.

---

(1) A few of the American national parks:
Acadia National Park (Maine)
Grand Canyon National Park (Arizona)
Mammoth Cave National Park (Kentucky)
Redwood National Park (California)
Rocky Mountain National Park (Colorado)

Sequoia National Park (California)
Theodore Roosevelt National Park (North Dakota)
Voyageurs National Park (Minnesota)
Yellowstone National Park (Wyoming)
Yosemite National Park (California)

Hotel Santa Fe

Economy Class, 1000 rooms

A drive-in cinema screen marks the entrance (spot the famous Clint Eastwood stare). The hotel's theme is the American Southwest and especially New Mexico with its arid climate and sun-parched soil. Forty-two pueblos painted in subdued desert colours are laid out in four groups or trails: the Trail of Artefacts, the Trail of Water, the Trail of Monuments and the Trail of Legends.

Each trail uses symbols to illustrate the mythology and history of New Mexico (a giant cactus under glass, shells of cars buried in the sand, flying saucers, water – that highly valued resource, rocks, a dormant volcano)
The hotel has a video games room (Pow Wow Game Room) and a children's playground outside (Totem Circle Playground) built to look like the ruins of an ancient Central American Indian village – there is also a maze to unravel! Each room measures 21sq m-226sq ft and is decorated in the spirit of the American Southwest.

Bars and restaurants

– **La Cantina:** Tex-Mex food in the colourful setting of a New Mexico market place. Each stall has a particular dish to offer, and a small truck contains a selection of salads and crudités. Drinks are served from petrol pumps!

– **Rio Grande Bar:** there is a friendly atmosphere in this typical bar with its cosy fireplace. Tequila-based cocktails, margaritas, and beer are served, and on some evenings there is live country and western or Mexican music.

Shop

– **Trading Post:** Disney and other souvenirs based on a New Mexican theme.

Free shuttle bus to the theme park and *Festival Disney*.

Hotel Cheyenne

Economy Class, 1000 rooms

Across the Rio Grande from the Hotel Santa Fe is the Hotel Cheyenne which resembles a small frontier town from the Wild West. The Rio Grande is spanned by two wooden footbridges. The Wild West has been recreated with people in Western outfits ambling amidst brightly painted buildings with evocative names, such as Sitting Bull, Calamity Jane, Geronimo, etc. Turning a corner, you might even run into some trigger-happy characters. The street lights take the form of gallows... Children will love the canvas-topped wagons and, along the banks of the Rio Grande, the log fort (Fort Apache) and lines of Indian wigwams (The Corral).

Desperado Street, the main street with a name that says it all, runs through the centre of town. The hotel rooms are in the gaily painted two-storey buildings, on either side of the street. Each room measures 21sq m-226sq ft and is decorated in the style of the Far West (lamps shaped like cowboy boots).

Bars and restaurants

– **Chuck Wagon Café:** these surroundings would make any cowboy feel at home! You can eat at the bar, sitting on bar stools or saddles. The restaurant is self-service. Dishes are laid out on several stalls to look like a Texan market. Barbecued ribs etc., and salads.

– **Red Garter Saloon:** beer flows freely here and is sometimes even served in glasses shaped like cowboy boots. From time to time there are country and western music shows. There is always plenty of atmosphere.

Shop

– **General Store:** Disney and Western souvenirs. Near the store is a video games room (Nevada Game Room).

Free shuttle bus to the theme park and *Festival Disney*.

Davy Crockett Ranch (1)

498 cabins, 97 pitches for tents or caravans

Located in the woods of Citry, approximately 4.5km-3 miles from the theme park, this camping and caravanning site covering 56ha-139 acres brings back memories of the trappers, forty-niners and pioneers. It is divided into two distinct zones: one reserved for camping and caravanning and the other offering fully-equipped cabins that can accommodate up to six guests. *There is a free car park for residents.*

For sports enthusiasts, facilities include a fitness circuit, football, basketball and volleyball pitches, a tennis court, a gym and an area where you can play French *boules (pétanque).*

© Disney

Cabins: These rustic looking log cabins are distributed over several loops (Coyote Trail, Tomahawk Trail, Cherokee Trail, etc.). Each one covers 34sqm-366sq ft.

As in the hotels, the rooms are serviced daily.

They each have a fully-equipped kitchen with micro-wave oven, hot plate, fridge-freezer, dishwasher, crockery and cutlery; a living room with cable television and direct dialling phone; and bathroom. Some of the furniture may be made from trees that were cut down when the site was landscaped.

Each cabin has an outdoor barbecue, a picnic table and chairs and a parking space for your car.

Pitches – Each pitch, for both tents and caravans, is equipped with a water outlet and drain, an electrical outlet and a picnic table. There are separate blocks with toilet and washing facilities, washing machines, irons and ironing boards.

The village – This is at the heart of the Ranch. A central square, which hosts various forms of entertainment at certain times of the year, is surrounded by a number of timber (pine) buildings. Do not be surprised to meet two forest friends – Chip'n'Dale.

Davy's Farm – This little farm is a must for small children, who love to come and feed the little animals (chickens, peacocks, turkeys, ducks, rabbits, goats, miniature pigs). Children can also go for rides on ponies or in carts, while their parents go horse-riding.

Bicycles and electric cars can be hired from Bowie's Bike Barn.

Alamo Trading Post – This rustic "general store" is convenient for groceries and souvenirs of Disney or on a backwoodsman theme.

Saloon Bar – This cowboy-style bar is open in the evening during summer. Entertainment includes billiards, board games and karaoke, washed down by beer or cocktails.

---

(1) Davy Crockett (1786-1836), an American trapper born in Tennessee, was re-elected to Congress many times. He fought in the Creek Wars and was killed by the Mexicans at the Battle of the Alamo in 1836. His exploits are the stuff of legend.

Crockett's Tavern – Warm and pleasant décor entirely of wood, complemented by collection of tools used in the olden days by woodcutters and the early pioneers. Self-service restaurant: Tex-Mex dishes, chilli con carne, spaghetti, salad bar. Breakfast also served. Tavern overlooks the swimming pool though a huge plate-glass window. Videos and cartoons shown.

Blue Springs Pool – Superb indoor swimming pool (wooden décor). Water chutes, waterfalls, jacuzzi in a grotto, water canon, poolside bar, wooden footbridge and lookout tower (bathing supervised).

Indian Meadows – On certain evenings barbecues are organised round camp fires with country and western music in the background.

Festival Disney

Entertainment Centre

The eye-catching polished steel towers soar to 20m-66ft, well above the vast entertainment centre (about 18 000sq m-183 000sq ft) with its silvery façade. In the evening the centre is bathed in twinkling lights.

Festival Disney gives a glimpse of the way of life in an American town, and a good-humoured party spirit reigns in the main street leading down to the lake. On summer evenings, entertainments reach their height as the theme park shuts down for the night. Night owls can dance the night away in the

© Disney

discothèque. Shops, restaurants and bars are all humming with life. In the street itself, people test their skill on video games or other side shows, while jugglers, tightrope walkers, characters on stilts and musicians all vie for the applause of passers-by.

Shops

– **The Disney Store:** wide choice of Disney souvenirs and soft toys. Décor is on the theme of transport, with Mickey at the controls of a space ship and Scrooge McDuck and Pluto aboard an airship, the *Double Eagle II Transatlantic*. Three miniature trains – including a TGV – run round the shop.

– **Team Mickey:** for sports enthusiasts. Items on sale include sports wear and accessories (base-ball, golf, hockey).

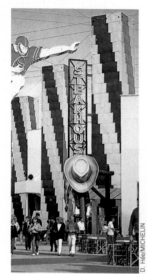

– **Hollywood Pictures:** all sort of items on the theme of the recent animated feature films *Aladdin* and *The Lion King*.

– **World of Toys:** Barbie doll is star of the show here, accompanied by cartoon characters such as Cinderella, Snow White and the Sleeping Beauty.

– **Buffalo Trading Co.:** evokes the "general stores" of the Far West. Cowboy outfits, denim jackets, shirts and jeans, boots, Stetsons and trappers' hats, Colts, groceries such as American and Mexican beer, tinned products (pâté, buffalo stew), spices and chilli con carne.

Bars and Restaurants

– **Annette's Diner:** fast food (sandwiches, burgers, salads, desserts) restaurant with cars as its theme. Admire the 50s style cars by the entrance. Old-fashioned juke boxes and waiters and waitresses on roller skates, who occasionally execute some fancy footwork on the bar itself, add to the atmosphere.

Nearby, some remote control American convoy trucks keep the children amused.

– **Sports Bar:** fast food, with a good selection of bottled beer and American and French beers on draught. The theme is American baseball and football: waiters and waitresses are dressed accordingly, photos of sports stars and famous teams adorn the walls and there are glass cases of sports trophies. Names such as the San Francisco 49ers, Boston Celtics, New York Giants, Chicago Bears and Giants may ring a bell...

– **Sandwiches New York Style:** what appears to be an old-fashioned grocer's store is in fact a Manhattan "deli". Old posters advertising New York entertainment (theatre, musicals) adorn the walls. Sandwich fillings include pastrami, corned beef and cheese, and bagels are also available.

– **Los Angeles Bar & Grill:** pasta, pizzas, salads and cakes in a Californian setting. Terrace overlooking the lakeside path.

– **Key West Seafood:** Florida and the sea are evoked by this seafood restaurant with a strong maritime atmosphere – staff dressed as sailors, fishing nets etc. You are even given a small mallet to get to grips with the more uncooperative shellfish... Specialities include crabs and clam soup. A covered terrace overlooks the lake.

– **Hurricanes:** lakeside discothèque with several bars. The cocktails will appeal to those with exotic tastes.

Nearby, the **Marina del Rey** offers remote control boats for youthful sailors and the opportunity to hire "Toobies" to take a trip round Lake Disney.

– **The Steakhouse:** a red-brick Chicago warehouse transformed into a classy restaurant for lovers of good meat and wine.

– **Billy Bob's Country Western Saloon:** cowboy's saloon for those who appreciate good beer. The saloon décor is of wood, with a large staircase, galleries and hunting trophies, and the waiters are dressed as cowboys, including the legendary Stetson. A band plays country and western dance music in a friendly relaxed atmosphere.

– **Rock'n'Roll America:** a rock'n'roll den with Elvis, the King, at the entrance. Music from the 50s and 60s includes names such as James Brown and Tina Turner. Some of the old-fashioned wireless sets which once played this crazy beat can be seen. You could be in New York, San Francisco or New Orleans. There is karaoke for the bolder visitors.

Buffalo Bill's Wild West Show

A wooden sculpture depicting a rodeo scene and a big poster remind you that Buffalo Bill is not far away...

Buffalo Bill, a legendary hero – William Frederick **Cody** (1846-1917), an American pioneer, took part in many adventures including the winning of the West, the Civil War, and the Indian Wars against the Cheyenne and the Sioux. During the construction of the Kansas-Pacific Railroad, William Cody, an unrivalled sharp-shooter, made his name hunting buffalo to supply meat to the work gangs. In 1869 he met a reporter, Ned Buntline, whose romantic tales about Buffalo Bill were enormously successful among newspaper readers. Buntline then convinced Buffalo Bill to go on the road. Thus was born Buffalo Bill's Wild West Show in 1883, in which Buffalo Bill acted out his own life story with the help of cowboys, Indians, horses, buffalo, etc. After touring the United States the troop made a big splash in Europe between 1887 and 1906.

Cookout Corral – This part of the Far West compound contains some of the animals which feature in Buffalo Bill's Wild West Show, such as quarter horses (among others), Indian Pinto ponies and Longhorn cattle. It is even possible to watch rehearsals for the show.

© Disney

The Dinner Show – Spectators are each given a straw cowboy's hat decorated with a coloured ribbon as they arrive, to get them into the spirit of things. They enter a replica of a ranch in the Far West which contains souvenirs of Buffalo Bill from the museum in Cody, a small mountain village founded by William Cody in 1901 in the state of Wyoming. Horses in their stalls complete the setting. Country and western bands entertain the spectators as they wait for the show to begin, perhaps taking a drink at the bar or looking round the shop.

The dinner show itself takes place in a large rectangular hall (40m by 20m – 130ft by 65ft) which can seat up to 1 000 people. The spectators are divided up into "ranches" according to the colour of the ribbon on their hat. The ranches compete against each other in the ensuing competitions. The master of ceremonies is the famous French impresario, Auguste Durand-Ruel. Buffalo Bill and his tough band of men, the Rough Riders, Annie Oakley, or "Little Sure Shot", and Sitting Bull and his braves bring the action-packed history of the Far West to life in a lively mounted show with background music, spectacular tricks and special effects. Jokes find their way into all the action as well. Horses, Longhorn cattle, buffalo, cowboys and Indians act out scenes from the best Westerns with shoot-outs, chases, hold-ups, US Cavalry charges and many more scenarios involving daring displays of horsemanship.

The traditional cowboy's supper is served on tin plates and includes chilli con carne, grilled chicken, sausages and spare ribs, corn on the cob, jacket potatoes, apple crumble and as much beer or Coca-Cola as you can drink.

Golf Disneyland Paris

This 90ha - 222 acre golf course has been beautifully landscaped to include rolling greens, lakes, rivers, waterfalls and a wide variety of trees (maples, sequoias, pines, spruces and elms). The course is the creation of Ronald Fream's, a company which specialises in golf courses (other courses it has designed include the Frégate Golf Club at Fréjus on the French Riviera and several clubs in California – in Santa Rosa – and Asia – in Bangkok). The 27-hole course can be broken down into 9-hole sections (par-36). The world of Disney is reflected in the names of the courses: The Hundred Acre Wood (with holes called Pooh, Piglet, Tigger, etc.), Wonderland (Alice, Cheshire Cat, White Rabbit) and Neverland (Peter Pan, Michael, Mr Smee). There is a 600sq m - 718sq yd putting green in the shape of Mickey Mouse's ears. The **Club House**, built by Gwathmey Seigel and Associates incorporates a bar, a restaurant with a roof shape like a golf ball and a shop called Goofy's Pro Shop, in which Goofy and Daisy, dressed for a game of golf, greet visitors (sports wear, golf accessories, Disney souvenirs).

© Disney

Disney theme parks around the world

North America: the United States

Disneyland (California) – The countryside around Anaheim in southern California was transformed into a recreational area in the 1950s. Opened on 17 July 1955, Disneyland, the first Disney theme park in the world, covers 30 hectares - 74 acres and eight individual "countries": Main Street, U.S.A.; Adventureland; New Orleans Square; Critter Country; Frontierland; Fantasyland, Mickey's Toontown and Tomorrowland. The Disneyland Hotel, accessible via the Disneyland monorail, is made up of three towers (the Sierra and Marina Towers, each with 11 floors, and the Bonita Tower, which is 14 storeys high).

Walt Disney World Resort (Florida) – Following the success of Disneyland, Walt Disney decided to build another theme park in the southeastern United States, an area blessed by a mild climate. The Walt Disney Company purchased more than 11 000 hectares - 27 170 acres of swampland near Orlando, Florida and transformed it into a fully equipped holiday resort. On 1 October 1971, Walt Disney World Resort opened for business, along with the Magic Kingdom, a new theme park spread over 43 hectares - 106 acres.
EPCOT Center opened in 1982. Looking towards the future (Future World) with its exhibits on technological progress, this park also includes the World Showcase, which illustrates many different countries. Its surface area is twice that of the Magic Kingdom.
In 1989 the movies were given the "best seat in the house" with the opening of **Disney-MGM Studios**. In addition to taking a trip through Walt Disney's productions, the visitor can watch spectacular special effects and discover the technique of animated drawing from the drawing board right up to the final film complete with sound. **Pleasure Island** (restaurants, shops and discos) and **Typhoon Lagoon** (a water theme park) were added to the site that same year. Walt Disney World Resort is also an immense complex of hotel and other accommodations and recreational activities that welcome enormous crowds all year round. There are a number of themed hotels, a campsite (Fort Wilderness), six golf courses, villas (Disney's Village Resort), and a shopping mall with restaurants and stores (Disney Village Marketplace).
All of the components of the Walt Disney World Resort are linked up by bus, boat and two monorails.

Asia: Japan

Tokyo Disneyland – Opened on 15 April 1983, this pentagon-shaped park (46 hectares - 114 acres) is located near Urayasu about 10km - 6 miles from the capital and like its predecessors covers many "countries": World Bazaar, Adventureland, Westernland, Fantasyland and Tomorrowland. World Bazaar was specially designed for the local climate. An enormous glass structure was erected over the shopping complex, beneath which visitors can stroll around in fair or foul weather.

Europe: France

Disneyland Paris – The first phase of Disney's European project was inaugurated on 12 April 1992 under the name of Euro Disney Resort. The resort was renamed Disneyland Paris in October 1994.

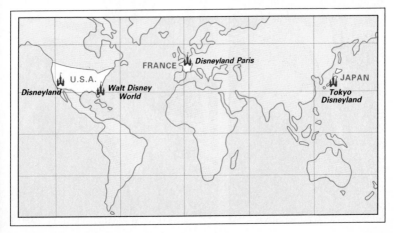

Costumes – a whirling dance of colour

Whether they be in the theme park, Festival Disney, the hotels or Davy Crockett Ranch, the costumes contribute as much as the plant life to the overall magical, exotic atmosphere of Disneyland Paris. Not only the Disney characters themselves but each member of staff has a role to play, and a costume which varies according to the season, so that visitors will feel all the more strongly that they have been swept off to a distant dream world.

© Disney

© Disney

© Disney

© Disney

Disneyland Paris in Brie

Disneyland Paris, which covers a surface area of 1 943 hectares - 4 800 acres (one-fifth of the area of Paris), is located in the Brie region of the Paris Basin. This low-lying area is linked to the North European Plain by Flanders, to the Rhône Basin by the Burgundy Gap and, beyond the Loire Valley, to the Aquitaine Basin by the Poitou Gap.

Geographical notes

The Brie region – Disneyland Paris lies in the northern part of this portion of the Paris Basin, which stretches westwards from the Grand Morin Valley. The Brie region is a limestone tableland, formed by lacustrine deposits, which rises gently from west to east. Further to the east, towards Reims, this tableland forms an escarpment called the "Côte de l'Ile-de-France" in the Champagne part of the Brie region.

In the Brie area the upper layers of decalcified limestone, known as millstone, are covered with a thick layer of fertile loess making this good agricultural land. The area was once heavily forested, but following the constant cutting and burning during the Middle Ages, all that is left are small woods, groves or other remnants such as the forests of Grains, Crécy or Ferrières in the vicinity of Disneyland Paris.

A varied industrial activity – The Brie region is primarily agricultural with large farms ranging in size from 250 to 400 hectares (620 to 1 000 acres). These highly mechanised farms practise intensive wheat and sugar beet farming. Tall grain silos located on the outskirts of a number of towns bear witness to this important activity, and the sugar refineries remind one of the industrial role played by the sugar beet.

The farms in this region are often isolated in the middle of a vast rolling landscape of open fields.

The region is also famous for its brie cheese. This is made exclusively from cows' milk and is recognizable by its circular shape. Brie cheeses can reach 40cm-16ins in diameter. Connoisseurs and gourmets prize in particular the subtle, creamy Meaux Brie, the less mature Coulommiers Brie, which is whiter, and the stronger-tasting Melun Brie, which has a firmer consistency.

There is also some industrial activity in the Brie region. The attentive traveller will notice pumping units or drilling rigs here and there which currently supply about 2 million tons of crude oil per year. The Grandpuits Refinery (northeast of Melun), which is also supplied by an oil pipeline from Le Havre, processes 4 million tons of crude oil per year.

The paper industry in the Grand Morin Valley and numerous food industries also contribute to the region's economic activity.

Historical notes

The cities located on the outskirts of the Brie region have always played a major role: Meaux, Coulommiers and Lagny during the Middle Ages, and Marne-la-Vallée today.

The fairs of Champagne – The Brie region has been the scene of considerable activity since the late Middle Ages. Abbeys such as Faremoutiers and Jouarre prospered in the area and contributed to the region's improvement. The cities of Meaux and Coulommiers also flourished and became active trading centres. The region, due to its central location, made its reputation and its fortune from the fairs which played an important role in developing trade throughout Europe. These commercial exchanges between northern and southern Europe were held according to an extremely exact schedule. In the course of the year two fairs were held in Troyes, two in Provins and one in Bar-sur-Aube. The year started out with the Lagny fair, 3km-2 miles west of the plain on which the Disneyland Paris is now located.

Cloth, silks and spices from the Orient as well as wines were traded at these fairs which attracted a host of merchants and traders to this part of the Brie region: Italian and German money-changers and merchants, as well as the merchants of Champagne.

These fairs remained prosperous till the early 14C, when the political and economic weight of Paris eclipsed the Champagne region.

Marne-la-Vallée – This is one of the five new towns in the Paris region (the others are Cergy-Pontoise, Évry, St-Quentin-en-Yvelines and Melun-Sénart). Construction began in 1972. The city has a population of 210 000 and is spread out along the Marne and other major communications routes, notably the A4 motorway and the A line of the RER.

In recent years a new vitality has been instilled into this community composed of older settlements and modern urban projects. The latter includes the Palacio d'Abraxas by the Catalan architect Ricardo Bofill and the Arènes de Picasso by Manual Núñez. Offices, housing, cultural and sports centres make it a city in its own right, despite its proximity to Paris.

Together with the Val d'Europe, Marne-la-Vallée now hosts Disneyland Paris. The reconstruction work carried out in sectors III and IV of Marne-la-Vallée have led to the setting up of a major archaeological project of great potential interest. Many sites have been discovered which contain valuable information on and evidence of human life in this area during the Gallo-Roman period and the Middle Ages.

A vast project

In 1984 the Walt Disney Company's management began seriously to consider creating a theme park in Europe (following the parks opened in the United States and Japan). Many countries were in the running: Britain, Germany, France, Italy and Spain. After visits to the site and studying a number of possible locations, the search was narrowed down to France and Spain. A thirty-year contract was signed by the Walt Disney Company and French authorities in 1987.

A new look – The portion of Marne-la-Vallée selected for the site overlaps into the towns of Bailly-Romainvilliers, Magny-le-Hongre, Coupvray, Chessy and Serris in a flat region of wheat and sugar beet production. Work on the site for the future park began in August 1988. Extraordinary efforts were made to transform this little corner of the Ile-de-France into a one-of-a-kind vacation resort in Europe: excavators, tippers, bulldozers and cranes began their daily ballet, which ended less than three years later.

Millions of cubic metres of earth were dug up, shifted, and hauled in. A lake (Lake Disney) and other stretches of water were created, tracks were laid for the RER and the TGV and foundations prepared for the new railway station. Roads were built, including a long dual carriageway access road to the park. More than 150 000 trees and bushes were planted, a third of them on the landscaped embankments formed around the theme park. For accommodation and recreational needs, six hotels, a campsite, a golf course and an entertainment centre were created on the site.

From 1992 to 2017 – The contract signed by the Walt Disney Company and the French authorities covers the development of the site until the year 2017. In addition to the construction of 13 000 additional hotel rooms, a conference centre, private homes, a second golf course and a water park, the future development will include the construction of a park on the theme of cinema.

Copper Beech

The trees in Disneyland Paris

The Brie region used to be covered with forests, but intensive farming of its rich soil has greatly reduced the forest cover.

When landscaping the site, an effort was made to recreate the original forest cover. Although the replantings include species native to Europe and especially to the Brie region, it has also been necessary to use trees from North America in order to create the best possible setting for the various themes of the hotels and the theme park.

Types of trees

These can be broken down into two categories: deciduous (oak, chestnut and larch), which lose their leaves in the winter, and coniferous (evergreen oak, pine and fir), which keep their leaves or needles all the year round.

Thus, among the various species of trees, we find:

Western Red Cedar (Giant Arborvitae) – This can reach 60m-200ft in height. Native to California and Alaska, it has a pyramidal shape and is resistant to moisture (so is widely used as timber).

Serbian Spruce – This sturdy conical tree grows slowly, up to 30m-100ft tall.

Colorado Spruce – This species is native to the Rocky Mountains. It is symmetrical, with bluish leaves and purplish-brown rough scaly bark.

Copper Beech – This majestic, wide-spreading tree has a rounded shape, a thick trunk and copper-brown coloured foliage.

White Fir – Native to the eastern Rockies, this conifer has wrinkly blackish bark. Its needles grow straight from the branch, and it has vertical cones.

Honey-Locust – Native to the eastern United States, this thorny tree has long, twisted, flat pods, which stay on the tree in winter, and its leaves are yellow-green. The Honey-Locust can reach 30m-100ft in height.

Eastern Hemlock – A tall (18-30m or 60-100ft) tree with a wide-spreading crown, heavy branches, dark green needles with white underneath and rough, blackish bark.

Silver Lime – A native of the Caucasus, this decorative tree with its greyish bark and leaves that are green on the top and whitish on the underside can reach a height of 30m-100ft.

Judas Tree – This native of the Mediterranean Basin often decorates parks and gardens. Its almost vertical branches sink down with age.

Pink Horse Chestnut – This dark-leaved tree is a hybrid of the chestnut and the clingstone peach tree, a North American tree with red blossoms.

Monkey Puzzle (Chile pine) – This slow-growing evergreen has a domed crown of spreading branches. Tough spiny leaves surround the stems. With its long straight trunk it can reach a height of 10m to 20m-35ft to 65ft.

Holm Oak – The Holm Oak has a short thick-set trunk with a wide-spreading thick dome. It stands up well under dry conditions and grows in thin limestone soils at less than 1 000m-3 280ft. It is an evergreen oak, the leaves of which remain a fine dark green.

Scots Pine – This is the most commonly found conifer in Ile-de-France and its flat needles are set in pairs along the russet-coloured twigs. The pine cones have hard, rough scales.

Common Yew – This tree with its indeciduous needles has purplish-brown, scaly bark. Its very hard wood enables it to survive for many years.

Cedar of Lebanon – This conifer, which originated in Africa and Asia, typically has massive, irregular spreads of branches growing from a large trunk with tufts of needles along the branches. Aromatic oil is obtained from its wood.

Western Red Cedar

Serbian Spruce

Colorado Spruce

Pink Horse Chestnut

Judas Tree

Giant Sequoia (Wellingtonia, Sierra Redwood, Mammoth or Big Tree) – A member of the cypress family, this conifer can grow to more than 100m-330ft high and live to over two thousand years old (making it the tallest and one of the oldest trees in the world). In the Muir Woods of California, a 112m-367ft high sequoia was discovered (equal to a thirty-storey building). The Giant Sequoia has thick, fibrous, reddish-brown bark and a pyramidal shape with drooping branches.

Cedar of Lebanon

Giant Sequoia

The gardens of your dreams★★★

Whether it be the theme park, the hotel complex, the campsite or the golf course, careful landscaping has made gardens an integral part of Disneyland Paris, reflecting the architecture and style of the theme park attractions, shops, hotels and restaurants down to the smallest detail. More than half the total area of the site (over 350ha - 865 acres) is covered by greenery or stretches of water. The theme park itself is surrounded by a "green belt" and divided into various lands with plant species on their particular theme, making the park essentially a collection of micro-climates. Besides new plants, Disneyland has introduced a number of new birds into the region.

Landscape gardeners tend the existing site and design fresh wonders to make visitors feel that they have entered a magic new world at Disneyland.

The gardeners at Disneyland Paris – These are true professionals, trained at horticultural college. Each gardener is put in charge of a particular section of the park, seeing to day-to-day garden care (to remove any wilting flowers or nasty weeds) and also choosing colour schemes, types of flowers, layout of flower

beds, ornamental displays etc. There is not a gardener in sight during the daytime at Disneyland. They emerge as soon as the park has closed and work through the night until opening time the following day. Their work includes regular jobs, such as trimming the 7.5km – 4.7 miles of hedge (top and both sides) which make up Alice's Curious Labyrinth, and seasonal jobs, such as renewing the flower displays in spring and autumn, which takes several nights as whole flower beds have to be dug up and replanted. In the winter some of the more delicate species have to be dug up to be put in greenhouses and replaced by more hardy plants, while others have a protective layer of straw put round them.

Spectacular flower beds – It took tons of peat and bedding compost to cover the heavy soil of the old beet fields. The moving walkway leading to the theme park is surrounded by cleverly harmonised, colourful flower beds. The Fantasia Gardens in front of the Disneyland Hotel are a magnificent spectacle; a landscaped park with lamps, summerhouses, lakes, streams and fountains unfolds to view. At the heart of the park is a splendid flower bed, 30m – 100ft in circumference, laid out to look like Mickey Mouse's head. It took over 2.500 flowering plants to create this floral composition, which changes colour with the seasons. Other flower beds blend in with one another, as well as with the colour scheme of the Disneyland Hotel itself. Each season has its own colour scheme, thus, in Main Street USA, particularly in Central Plaza, the red, green and white of winter gives way to brighter colours heralding the imminent arrival of spring and better weather. In Frontierland, cactuses grow on the banks of the Rivers of the Far West. In the winter they are kept in greenhouses. Adventureland is home to bamboo, eucalyptus and palm trees, giant rhododendrons, water plants and birds of paradise, which evoke the hot and steamy climate of the Caribbean. Fantasyland has softer, pastel shades and ornamental shrubs clipped into the shape of Disney characters which enhance its magical effect. Discoveryland takes us into the future with its sequoias and monkey puzzle trees.

Similarly, the hotels are set amidst vegetation appropriate to their theme. Walking from the Sequoia Lodge to the Hotel Santa Fe along the banks of Lake Disney and the Rio Grande, one sees a land-scape worthy of any national park.

A "garden" like this takes some watering. Two weather monitors (in the park and on the golf course) feed information into the computers which control the hoses in case there is not enough rainfall. To give you an idea, the electronic watering system installed in Disneyland includes 7 000km – 4 350 miles of hosepipe and 25 000 sprinklers.

Highlights of the gardens

Mickey's head (in summer: busy Lizzies; in autumn and winter: chrysanthemums)	Entrance to the park
Town Square, Central Plaza (in summer: begonias and busy Lizzies; in autumn: chrysanthemums and pansies; in winter: pansies)	Main Street, USA
Bamboo, tropical plants	Adventureland
The Cheshire Cat (in summer: begonias; in autumn: chrysanthemums)	Fantasyland (Alice's Curious Labyrinth)
Ornamental shrubs, lilies	Fantasyland

Frontierland's cactuses

This unique collection of cactuses (over 200) was donated by Mme Degueurce, a resident of Lagny. She and her husband had marked all the important events of their life by planting a new cactus. Friends of theirs who knew of this unusual hobby took over and added to the collection.

Walt Disney –
a life devoted to enchantment

1901 Walter Elias Disney, the fourth child of Flora and Elias Disney, is born on 5 December in Chicago, Illinois.

1906 The family moves to a farm near Marceline, Missouri.

1910 The family leaves Marceline for Kansas City. Walt is already showing a real talent for drawing.

1918 During the First World War Walt wants to join the army, but he is too young. Instead, he signs up the following year with the Red Cross and works in France as an ambulance driver.

1919-1921 In October 1919 he returns to Kansas City and does drawings for a small advertising agency. That is when he meets a young Dutchman, **Ub Iwerks**, who shares his love of drawing. A great friendship is born and they decide to pool their talents.

1922 Walt establishes Laugh-o-gram Films in Kansas City, but the company goes bankrupt after a year.

1923-1924 Walt sets out for Hollywood with only $40 in his pocket. Ub follows Walt to Hollywood and after many tries they succeed in producing a series of short films, called **Alice Comedies**, which combine animation and live action. Together with his brother Roy, Walt forms a company, The Disney Brothers Studio. At Roy's suggestion the name is changed and it becomes the Walt Disney Studio.

1925 On 13 July Walt marries Lillian Bounds.

1927 Following Alice, Disney is looking for a new character for his cartoons and hits on Oswald the Lucky Rabbit.

1928 On 18 November, Mickey and Minnie make their screen début in the film *Steamboat Willie*. The first animated film to use synchronized sound, *Steamboat Willie* represents a milestone both for Disney's cartoon technique and for his fabulous career. Needing a voice for the Mickey Mouse character, Disney does Mickey's voice himself.

1929 The Skeleton Dance marks the birth of a series of 75 *Silly Symphonies*, shorts where animals, insects and plants come to life. This series is shown at the same time as the Mickey series.

1932 First Academy Award for *Flowers and Trees*, a riotous symphony of colour.

1933 The movie *Three Little Pigs* enjoys tremendous success and wins an Academy Award. The film's theme song, *Who's Afraid of the Big Bad Wolf?*, is still popular more than half a century later.

1934 Created by Paul Winkler, *le Journal de Mickey (The Mickey Mouse Magazine)* appears in France.

1935 *The Band Concert:* first colour cartoon with Mickey.

1937 On 21 December, the first full-length animated feature film, **Snow White and the Seven Dwarfs**, premieres at the Carthay Circle Theatre in Los Angeles. It meets with resounding success.

1939 Child-star Shirley Temple hands Disney a special Academy Award: one full-sized and seven dwarf-sized!

1940 Premières of *Pinocchio* and *Fantasia*. Disney Studios continue to grow, employing a staff of over 1 000.

1941 *Dumbo* wins the Academy Award for Best Original Score.

1942 Première of the animated cartoon *Bambi*.

Walt Disney and his Norman ancestry

1066, an important date: the conquest of England by William the Conqueror, so magnificently depicted on the Bayeux tapestries *(see Michelin Green Guide Normandy)*. Two Norman soldiers, Hugues d'Isigny and his son Robert, natives of Isigny-sur-Mer, a small village located near the mouth of the Vire, decide to settle in England following the Conquest. Over the years the name d'Isigny gradually becomes "Disney" a more English-sounding family name. A branch of the Disney family emigrates to Ireland in the 17C. In 1834, Arundel Elias Disney and his brother Robert embark for North America with their families. They set sail from Liverpool and arrive in New York on 3 October after a month-long voyage. The American adventure begins.

1943 Release of *Der Fuehrer's Face* starring Donald Duck. A no-holds-barred portrait of Nazi Germany, this movie is extremely popular and wins an Academy Award for its theme.

1944 Mickey Mouse is used as a code word during the D-Day landings in Normandy.

1950 Disney produces his first Christmas television show. Success for *Treasure Island* (a film featuring live actors), and *Cinderella* (animation).

1951 Première of *Alice in Wonderland*.

1954 *Disneyland* goes on television and delights children throughout America. Release of the astonishing *20,000 Leagues Under the Sea*, which wins an Academy Award for its special effects.

1955 **Disneyland**, the world's first theme park, opens its doors on 17 July near Anaheim, California. Walt wanted to create "an enchanted little park where adults and children could enjoy themselves together". His dream was realized. Première of *Lady and the Tramp*. The *Mickey Mouse Club* debuts on television.

1961 Release of the animated feature film *One Hundred and One Dalmatians*.

1964 On August 29, *Mary Poppins* premières at Grauman's Chinese Theater in Hollywood. A mixture of animated cartoon and live action, the film wins six Academy Awards. Julie Andrews wins the award for Best Actress.

1966 On 15 December, the man who did all he could to bring dreams alive passes away, plunging children around the world into mourning. Faithful to Walt's ideas, Walt Disney Productions continues his work.

1970 Release of *The Aristocats*.

1971 On 1 October, **Walt Disney World Resort** opens near Orlando, Florida, with the new **Magic Kingdom** theme park.

1978 Mickey Mouse is 50 years old. A train crisscrosses the United States with the ever-youthful little mouse on board.

1982 **EPCOT Center** opens at the Walt Disney World Resort (EPCOT: Experimental Prototype Community of Tomorrow).

1983 On 15 April a new theme park opens in Japan, **Tokyo Disneyland.**

1988 On Mickey Mouse's 60th birthday the Walt Disney Company organizes festivities on a grand scale. The film *Who Framed Roger Rabbit*, which mixes animation and live action, collects four Academy Awards.

1989 Opening of **Disney-MGM Studios Theme Park, Pleasure Island** (restaurants, shops and discotheques) and **Typhoon Lagoon** (water park) at Walt Disney World Resort.

1990 Release of the animated feature film, *The Little Mermaid*, which wins two Academy Awards, for Best Original Score and Best Song.

1991 Walt Disney World Resort celebrates its 20th birthday with George Bush, President of the United States, in attendance. Release of the animated feature film, *Beauty and the Beast*.

1992 12 April: Inauguration of Euro Disney Resort, located east of Paris. Release of *Aladdin*.

1994 Release of *The Lion King*.

Art and Disney

The wonder of Disney animation

Animation is based upon the principle of **retinal persistence.** Like movies shot from real life, animated film is composed of many images which create an illusion of continuity when projected. The eye holds the effect of an image a fraction of a second, connecting it to the following image so that the images are perceived to be uninterrupted. A perfect illusion occurs when the images appear at the rate of 24 per second.

Fundamentals of animation – Numerous preparatory phases precede the actual drawing of the images which compose an animated film.

First, a **bible** containing information about the story to be filmed – place, time, characters with their physical descriptions, personalities, manners, etc. – must be created.

Then a **scenario** is written, detailing the order of action and the dialogue.

Next a reference board is designed for each character (the model sheet) presenting him or her from different angles (front, profile, back...) and in different positions (standing, sitting, bent over, running, sleeping...) and in different moods (amused, angry, afraid, proud or whichever moods the particular character needs). The background for each scene is designed in the same way. A reference board shows the background framing each scene from different perspectives and, if necessary, also shows the large backgrounds against which the characters move from place to place.

A colourist provides the final touch of colour to the various reference boards from which an entire team will work.

The storyboard – The story is broken down shot by shot. Camera movements (general and panoramic shots), character movements and special effects are outlined. The meticulous detailing of action is called the **storyboard.** Each picture is planned and any movements, dialogues or sounds, which may be needed, are recorded next to each picture. The timing in seconds and fractions of seconds for all the shots and dialogues appears on the exposure sheet.

Layout and animation – The layout is the pencil outline of the scene which is used by the animator to size his characters and action, and by the background artist for painting his background. The layout artist and the animator both work on paper with a pencil. Animators work on tracing paper placed on illuminated tables so that they can see the figures against the background. They are aided by assistants and inbetweeners who fill in the drawings in between the key poses drawn by the animators. The animators' pencil drawings are then transferred to celluloid sheets or "cels" by tracing in ink or by a Xerox process.

Colours are painted on the back of the celluloid within the outlines by artists in the Ink and Paint Department.

Filming – Each picture, composed of a background covered with "cels" of the character, is then photographed. The film takes form according to the detailed timing of the storyboard.

After the dialogues, music, sound and sound effects are recorded, the sound is mixed and added to the film.

Then the studios have finished their work and are ready to present a show for you!

Fantasia or music on film

According to Walt Disney, **Fantasia** was "the most exciting adventure" of the Disney creations, because it sprang from the idea of putting expressive images to great musical classics without recourse to words. The combination of music, painting, dramatic art and dance gave birth to an entirely new form of cinematographic art. The project began during the 1930s and the film was released in 1940.

To achieve his dream, Walt Disney collected particularly creative designers and worked very closely with Leopold Stokowski, conductor of the Philadelphia Orchestra, who helped choose most of the pieces. In the film we see Stokowski conducting his orchestra in Bach's *Toccata and Fugue in D minor*, Tchaikovsky's *Nutcracker Suite*, Paul Dukas's *The Sorcerer's Apprentice*, Stravinsky's *Rite of Spring*, Beethoven's *Pastoral Symphony*, Ponchielli's *Dance of the Hours*, Mussorgsky's *Night on the Bare Mountain* and Schubert's *Ave Maria*.

Between the segments, noted musicologist of the 1930s Deems Taylor, introduces each section of the programme. In the middle of the film we are introduced to the "sound track", a sensitive vertical line which vibrates, grows and changes colours in synchrony with the instruments, taking on highly suggestive shapes that follow the music.

Architecture

The Imagineers – True artists hide beneath this whimsical Disney term – artists and engineers who caused marvellous worlds to spring first from American, Japanese and now French soil.

To recreate one of the Monument Valley mountains, its slopes worn by time, to dig a mine where gold nuggets gleam, to build a fairy-tale castle inspired by a medieval manuscript illumination or a tropical banyan tree, or to construct the main street of a turn-of-the century American town, all on the plain of Brie, requires a bit of magic and the talent and technique of experts. The Imagineers' ideology may be summed up in three words: imagine, design and build. The design phase begins as soon as an idea is conceived and includes planning out the entire scenario as well as creating the drawings and the models necessary to visualize the project. Working with models is essential. Every detail, interior and exterior, is studied (layout, perspectives, landscapes, etc.) by the human eye and also by micro-cameras. The Imagineers research which are the best materials to give an impression of authenticity, which material or paint will evoke a certain stone or rock, which wood for a façade, how to create the leaves and branches for a giant treehouse... All these aspects are thoroughly studied with the weather in mind. When all of the plans and data have been gathered and approved, construction begins. And so it is that the Imagineers turn dreams into reality.

Renowned architects – Disney has long relied upon world-famous architects to design its resorts (hotels, golf courses and camp grounds) and offices. The California head office was designed by **Michael Graves**, and in Florida the casting center was designed by **Robert Stern** while the administrative center was designed by the innovative Japanese architect **Arata Isozaky**.

Disneyland Paris is again the work of Michael Graves (Hotel New York) and Robert Stern (Hotel Cheyenne and Newport Bay Club), both post-modernists like **Antoine Grumbach** (Sequoia Lodge), all of whom react against the excessive use of the right angle and the purity of line which have characterized modern architecture since the 1920s. **Antoine Predock** with his Hotel Santa Fe remains faithful to his constant preoccupation with Southwest America, the desert, the mystique of the Native American, and the meeting of the heavens and the earth (with the remains of a UFO as evidence). **Frank Gehry** demonstrates his adherence to deconstructivism with Festival Disney, the entertainment centre. Sculptor as well as architect, he treats his works like art before tackling their architectural function. He loves dislocated and uneven forms, readily excludes straight lines, favours raw materials like iron, wood and cement, and uses colour generously. He also designed the American Center at Bercy.

Gwathmey Siegel and Associates have built a Club-House for the golf course, in which colours are skilfully blended or contrasted with the surroundings.

Audio-Animatronics©

Figures – in human, animal or plant form – were the invention of Walt Disney himself. During a visit to Europe, Walt had been fascinated by a small mechanical whistling bird, which he took back to the United States. That was the beginning of the system which brings the art of animation to three-dimensional figures and combines and synchronizes mechanical movement and sound effects. The latest generation of Audio-Animatronics© figures includes the sleeping dragon, the pirates and ghosts.

Practical information

Access *See also pp 6 to 9.*

Bus services from Roissy and Orly Airports – Follow signs for "VEA Navettes Disneyland Paris". Departures every 30-45 min from 08.30 to 22.30 (19.45 out of season); price: 75F, under-3s free; ☎ (33 1) 64 30 66 56.

TGV - Eurostar – A direct link from London to Disneyland Paris will be provided by Eurostar via the Channel Tunnel (journey time: 3 hours, including change in Lille). Ask for details at local travel agents or stations.

RER – Return ticket from Paris: 74F including the métro. Tickets are available from all métro and RER stations.
On the A line of the RER the journey from the centre of Paris to Disneyland Paris at Marne-la-Vallée-Chessy station takes approximately 35 minutes. The first train from Paris to Disneyland Paris stops at Charles-de-Gaulle-Étoile at 05.16 and there is a train every 10 or 30 minutes thereafter, according to the time of day. For the return journey, consult the timetable in Marne-la-Vallée-Chessy station. The last train leaves at 00.22.

Disneyland Paris *For details of the holiday resort see pp 14-28*

Hotels

The price of a room *(sleeps up to four people)* varies according to the category of the hotel and the season: high season 550F to 2 490F; out of season 300F to 2 150F.

Davy Crockett Ranch

Cabins: *(up to six people)* May to October 440-770F per night. The rest of the year, deals available for 3, 4 or 7 night stays.
Pitches: for tents, caravans and camping cars 300F all the year round.

Reservations

Telephone:
United Kingdom and Republic of Ireland: 01733 33 55 65
Netherlands: 06 0789
Denmark, Norway and Finland: (33 1) 60 30 60 70
Sweden: 020 795 555
France: (33 1) 60 30 60 53 or (33 1) 60 30 60 30

The company's own tour operator, Disneyland Vacances, offers special terms for stays of several nights, including entrance to the theme park. Ask your tour operator or travel agent for further details.

Buffalo Bill's Wild West Show

Dinner show *(drinks included):* adults and children (12 and over) 325F, children (3-11 years) 200F. Reservations: ☎ (33 1) 60 45 71 00.

Golf Disneyland Paris

Open from April to October, except on Wednesdays and Thursdays. For further details: ☎ (33 1) 60 45 68 04. Equipment can be hired on site.

Post Office

In Festival Disney. Open daily from 10.45 to 12.00 and from 15.00 to 18.30 (19.00 on Saturdays, 18.00 on Sundays). NB Opening times may vary according to the season. ☎ (33 1) 60 43 31 31.

Tourist Information Centre

The **Maison du Tourisme d'Ile-de-France - Seine et Marne** is in Festival Disney. Open in summer daily from 09.00 to 23.00, in winter daily from 09.00 to 21.00 (23.00 on Fridays and Saturdays). ☎ (33 1) 60 43 33 33. Video presentation with special laser effects and relief models of the region's scenic treasures.

Animals

Pets, with the exception of guide dogs, are not allowed inside Disneyland Paris. Pets may be boarded at the Animal Care Center, located between the Disneyland visitors' car park and the main entrance to the theme park. Rate per day including food: 50F, overnight: 75F.

Disneyland Paris Theme Park

Opening times – The park is open all the year round: in July and August from 09.00 to 23.00; the rest of the year from 09.00 to 18.00 or 20.00, depending on the season. For further information ☏ (33 1) 64 74 43 00.

Car park – Cars: 40F; caravans: 60F; motorcycles: 25F; camping cars: 60F (150F for 24 hours).

Disneyland Paris Passports – The **one-day passport** gives a day's unlimited access to all the theme park's attractions, except the Rustler Roundup Shootin' Gallery. It is possible to leave the theme park and return the same day (you must get your hand stamped before leaving and keep your Disneyland Paris passport for re-admission).
Admission charges: *Free for under-3s, price for 3-11 year olds given in brackets.*
One-day passport: In season: 195F (150F), out of season: 150F (120F).
Two-day passport *(need not be consecutive)*: In season: 370F (285F), out of season: 285F (230F).
Three-day passport *(need not be consecutive)*: In season: 505F (390F), out of season: 390F (310F).
Annual passports are also available.
Guided tours: apply at City Hall in Town Square, Main Street, U.S.A.

Attractions – Certain attractions such as Big Thunder Mountain, Indiana Jones et le Temple du Péril, Star Tours, Space Mountain and Autopia are not advisable for people with a heart condition, back or neck problems and for children under three (special boarding restrictions enforced). Very young children may also be frightened by scenes in some attractions – check at each entrance.

Useful information

Disney information centre: Information on the theme park and entertainment programmes from City Hall (Main Street, U.S.A.).
Left luggage - coin-operated lockers: outside the main entrance and under Main Street Station. 15F and 10F.
Bank services: automatic teller machines on Main Street, U.S.A.
Currency exchange: main entrance, City Hall and at kiosks in Adventureland and Fantasyland. Most of the shops and restaurants accept credit cards, travellers cheques in French francs, Eurocheques as well as French cheques.
Lost and found: City Hall (Main Street, U.S.A.).
Camera rentals: both still and video cameras are available at Town Square Photography, Main Street, U.S.A.
First aid: Next to Plaza Gardens Restaurant, Main Street, U.S.A.
Public telephones and letter boxes: These are available throughout the theme park. Phone cards and stamps are on sale in all the shops.

Children

Stroller rentals: Town Square Terrace. 30F plus a 20F deposit.
Baby Care Center: changing facilities and bottle warmers are available on Main Street, U.S.A. beside Plaza Gardens Restaurant.
Lost children: Next to Plaza Gardens Restaurant on Main Street, U.S.A.

Disabled – A brochure, *Guest Special Services Guide*, is available at City Hall, Main Street, U.S.A. Many attractions, shops and restaurants are accessible to the disabled.
Car park for the disabled: beside Disneyland Hotel.
Wheelchair rental: Town Square Terrace. 30F plus a 20F deposit.
Blind/impaired vision: portable tape recorder and audio-cassettes are available from City Hall.
Deaf/impaired hearing: a special telephone device is available at City Hall.

Restaurants – The theme park has a wide choice of counter-service or table-service restaurants, offering a selection of cuisine from many different countries. Only table-service restaurants are licensed to serve alcohol. Eating places are listed under each land's heading ("Anyone for a snack or a drink?" and "For a special treat") in the section on the Disneyland Paris attractions.

Picnic Area – Visitors may not bring their own food and drink into the theme park. There is a picnic area situated between the main car park and Disney Square.

Disneyland
Paris

Disneyland Paris Theme Park

Surrounded by grass-covered embankments, the Disneyland Paris theme park, inspired by the work of Walt Disney, covers more than 55 hectares - 136 acres and five lands, each with its own special theme:

- **Main Street, U.S.A.**, the main street in an American turn-of-the-century town;
- **Frontierland**, the Far West;
- **Adventureland**, adventure, far-off lands and pirates;
- **Fantasyland**, the world of fairy tales;
- **Discoveryland**, the world of discovery and the future.

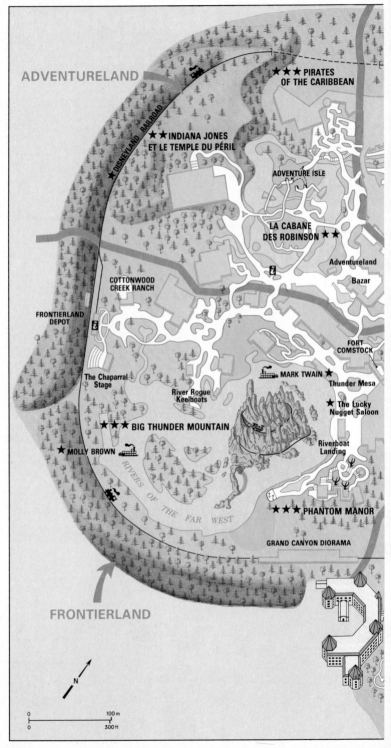

In addition to the most sophisticated attractions, veritable marvels of technology that rely on *Audio-Animatronics®* (robots that look like animals or people) in remarkable settings, as well as ongoing events and shows, each land also offers a large number of shops, snack-carts or trolleys (ice cream, popcorn and beverages) as well as restaurants and snack bars for every taste and pocket.

After leaving the car park reserved for visitors (11 500 parking spaces) or the RER/TGV railway station, the visitor reaches the theme park by passing under the Disneyland Hotel past the magnificent floral composition in the shape of Mickey Mouse's head.

The main entrance has several ticket booths with additional booths reserved for currency exchange.

Special access facilities are provided for the disabled.

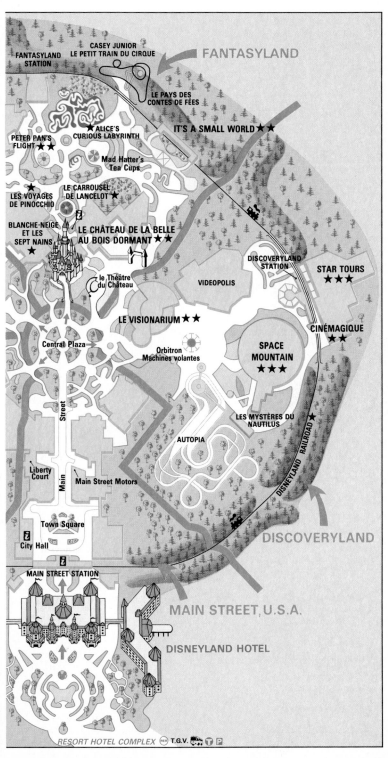

A day at Disneyland Paris

You will need two full days to visit the Disneyland Paris theme park and see all the attractions and shows.

For families that can only spend **one day** at Disneyland Paris, we have planned two programmes, each one aimed at a different age group. Thus, the first tour does not include attractions that could frighten small children. Children under 3 are not allowed on the following attractions: Big Thunder Mountain, Indiana Jones et le Temple du Péril, Space Mountain, Star Tours and Autopia. The second programme is for those who are looking for thrills.

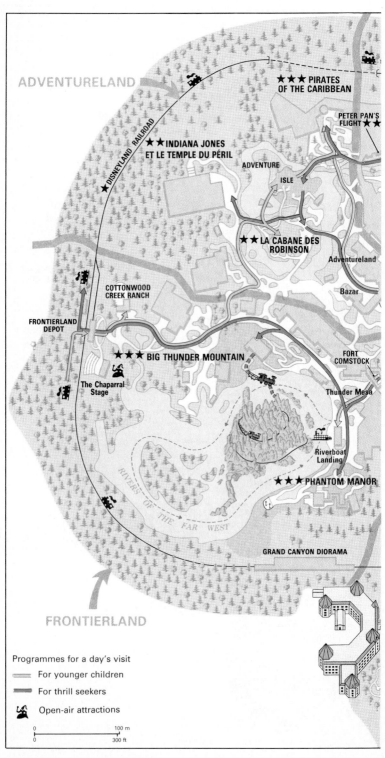

ADVENTURELAND

★★★ PIRATES OF THE CARIBBEAN

PETER PAN'S FLIGHT ★★

DISNEYLAND RAILROAD

★ ★INDIANA JONES ET LE TEMPLE DU PÉRIL

ADVENTURE ISLE

★★ LA CABANE DES ROBINSON

Adventureland

Bazar

COTTONWOOD CREEK RANCH

FRONTIERLAND DEPOT

★★★ BIG THUNDER MOUNTAIN

FORT COMSTOCK

The Chaparral Stage

Thunder Mesa

Riverboat Landing

★★ ★PHANTOM MANOR

RIVERS OF THE FAR WEST

GRAND CANYON DIORAMA

FRONTIERLAND

Programmes for a day's visit

⎯⎯ For younger children

⎯⎯ For thrill seekers

🐎 Open-air attractions

0 ___ 100 m
0 ___ 300 ft

When you go on one of the two tours, don't miss taking in at least one of the musical shows which take place at various spots in the theme park.

The daily parade, **La Parade Disney★★** (**1**) provides the perfect end to a dream-filled, magical day.

In summer when the theme park is open late, the highlights of the evening are the **Main Street Electrical Parade★★** (**2**) (a glittering procession of floats and performers) and **Fantasia in the Sky★** *(Fireworks)* (**3**).

Plan for at least a couple of stops during the day in order to rest, have a refreshing drink or something to eat, and don't forget to wear comfortable shoes.

Show times are available from the cashiers and at City Hall on Main Street, U.S.A.

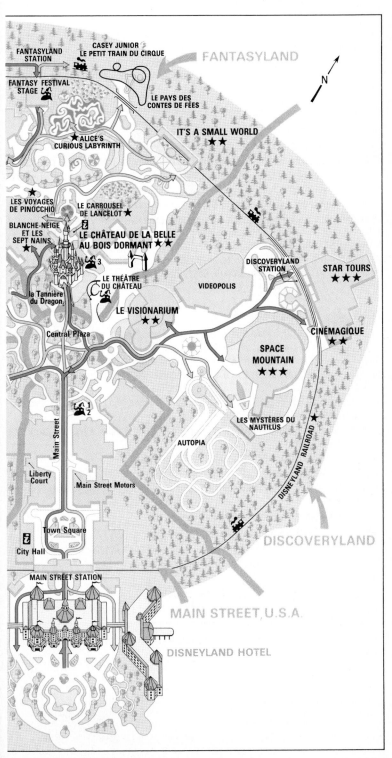

Tour 1: for younger children

From **Town Square** take a bus or taxi trip or walk up **Main Street, U.S.A.** to **Central Plaza** (where the children can have their photo taken with Mickey).

The bridge leading to **Le Château de la Belle au Bois Dormant**★★ will take you into **Fantasyland,** the land of fairy-tales. There, a variety of merry-go-rounds and attractions will carry you into the world of dreams:

– **Le Carrousel de Lancelot**★ with its gaily painted horses;

– **It's a Small World**★★, a trip with children from around the world;

– **Le Pays des Contes de Fées,** a magical cruise through the canals of Storybook Land;

– **Casey Jr., Le Petit Train du Cirque,** see Storybook Land aboard a little circus train;

– **Alice's Curious Labyrinth**★, a scene from Alice's Adventures in Wonderland;

– **Peter Pan's Flight**★★.

At **Fantasyland Station** take the **Disneyland Paris Railroad**★ to Frontierland - land of cowboys and Indians. After the train passes through the **Grand Canyon Diorama,** get off at Frontierland Depot.

Visit **Cottonwood Creek Ranch,** a Far West ranch, then head for **Adventureland,** where adventure is the keyword:

– **La Cabane des Robinson**★★, an ingeniously furnished treehouse;

– **Adventure Isle,** with its buried treasure;

– **Pirates of the Caribbean**★★★, where the Caribbean is swarming with pirates.

Return to Central Plaza via Adventureland Bazar. From there, you have the choice of two alternatives:

– **Discoveryland** with **Les Mystères du Nautilus** or **Autopia;**

– **Frontierland,** where you embark on a **paddle-wheel riverboat**★ (the *Molly Brown* or the *Mark Twain*) at Thunder Mesa Riverboat Landing for a restful, well-earned trip down the Rivers of the Far West.

– From Central Plaza return to **Main Street, U.S.A.** with it wide variety of shops (giant lollipops on sale at **Boardwalk Candy Palace**).

Tour 2: for thrill seekers

From **Town Square** take **Main Street, U.S.A.** to **Central Plaza.**

Then make for **Frontierland** via Fort Comstock. The shivers will start running down your spine in **Phantom Manor**★★★, a haunted house filled with weird happenings. The train from the **Big Thunder Mountain**★★★ mine will take you on a wild ride.

At Frontierland Depot, take the **Disneyland Paris Railroad**★ to Fantasyland Station. Turn into **Adventureland** on your right:

– **Indiana Jones et le Temple du Péril**★★, headlong rollercoaster race through the ruins of a temple;

– **Pirates of the Caribbean**★★★, the world of buccaneers;

– **La Cabane des Robinson**★★, an ingeniously furnished treehouse.

From Adventureland Bazar, return to Fantasyland and its marvellous, make-believe world.

– **Peter Pan's Flight**★★ across London at night;

– **Mad Hatter's Tea Cups,** for a crazy whirl!

– **Le Château de la Belle au Bois Dormant**★★ and **La Tanière du Dragon** (Dragon's Lair).

Yet more excitement awaits you in Discoveryland:

– **Le Visionarium**★★, a 360° voyage;

– **Space Mountain**★★★, take a trip to the moon;

– **Star Tours**★★★, a space voyage on board a cosmic spacecraft;

– **CinéMagique**★★, with Michael Jackson on another planet.

From Central Plaza return to **Main Street, U.S.A.** to browse round the wide variety of shops.

How about breakfast with a real, live Disney character,
as soon as the park has opened?

Hurry along to **Plaza Gardens Restaurant** *in Main Street, USA,*
where Minnie Mouse, Alice, the Queen of Hearts, Captain Hook, Mr Smee, Pluto
and many others are waiting to see you...

DISNEYLAND PARIS ATTRACTIONS

Adventure Isle

ADVENTURELAND – MAP P 52

A giant tree, an ominous Skull Rock, a pirate ship, an enormous mass of rock, luxuriant vegetation, and waterfalls greet the visitor who can reach the island via a number of different bridges.

Adventure Isle is in fact two separate islands linked by the swinging bridge, **Pont Suspendu**, and the floating barrel bridge, **Pont Flottant**, which span the shipwreck **L'Épave (A)** *(p 59)*. One of the two islands is inspired by the novel *Swiss Family Robinson (p 58)*, while the other is based on *Treasure Island*. In 1950 Disney made this novel, written by the Scotsman **Robert Louis Stevenson** (1850-1894), into a film. It recounts the adventures of young Jim Hawkins, who went off to sea in search of Captain Flint's fabulous treasure. Before giving up the ghost, this bloody freebooter gave Jim a map showing the island on which the treasure was buried. Accompanied by Dr. Livesey and Squire Trelawney, Jim embarks on a vessel commanded by Captain Smollett. That's when the adventures really start and who could ever forget the ship's cook, Long John Silver, inseperable from his parrot; the mutiny; Treasure Island and its buried booty; the pirates' attack and the bravery of young Jim Hawkins.

Captain Hook's Galley – Captain Hook's pirate ship, which proudly boasts three masts and a figurehead on the prow, has cast anchor in Cannonball Cove. A play area on the vessel's top deck will delight would-be pirates, who can ring the ship's bell, among other things.

Le Rocher-Qui-Bascule (Teetering Rock) – A play area that will delight adventurers of all ages.

Skull Rock (B) – The sight of this sinister hillside can only mean one thing – the villainous Captain Hook is nearby.

You can walk inside and discover mysterious caves and grottoes which overlook Cannonball Cove.

Ben Gunn's Cave (C) – In this large mass of rock several entrances offer a different route (Ambush Alley, Davy Jones's Locker, Dead Man's Maze, Spyglass Pass, Hook's Hideout and Keelhaul Caverns), in the search for hidden treasure. A spooky atmosphere reigns in a series of gloomy tunnels that lead up to the treasure chamber. Mysterious sounds accompany "explorers" who, depending on the path they take on their way to the treasure trove, will encounter waterfalls, crevices, menacing eyes glowing in the darkness,

© Disney

stalactites and stalagmites, a bottomless pit, bats, and a skeleton chained to the walls... no doubt the remains of a pirate who was foolish enough to challenge Ben Gunn.

Spyglass Hill (D) – The pirates needed their own lookout point – **Pirate Lookout**– so they could be warned in case of approaching vessels. Two telescopes at the top of this wooden tower on Spyglass Hill afford a view of Adventure Isle.

The nearby swinging bridge (Pont Suspendu) leads the bravest visitors to the neighbouring island and the treehouse, La Cabane des Robinson.

★★La Cabane des Robinson (Swiss Family Treehouse) – *P 58.*

Adventureland

MAP BELOW

Step from Central Plaza into the exotic atmosphere of the Adventureland Bazar, a desert fortress topped with colourful onion domes.
Adventureland offers the adventure of exotic, faraway lands, including Arabia, land of a Thousand and One Nights, Africa, and the Caribbean, kingdom of pirates.

Adventure on the high seas

Treasure Island, The Buccaneer, The Red Corsair, Blackbeard the Pirate, All Aboard, Pirates – each film evokes adventures on the high seas. But who were these adventurers and plunderers, given to carousing, whose exploits are the stuff of legend?

Pirates and buccaneers, corsairs and privateers, old sea-dogs all! – Unlike corsairs and privateers who were hired by their governments, pirates were unscrupulous adventurers who would pillage any merchant ship that sailed

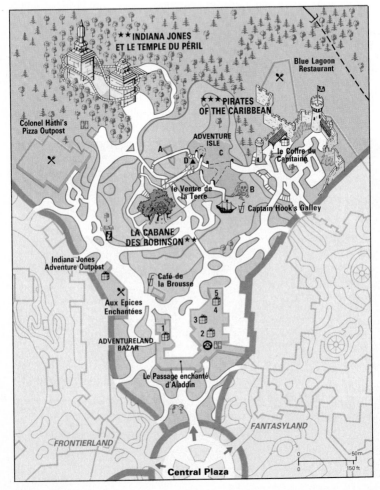

the seven seas. History shows that maritime powers sometimes hired seasoned sailors to wage merciless trade wars! The first Mediterranean pirates appeared during Antiquity, and Greece, with its many isles situated on the trading routes, was the place of choice for marauders of the sea. On the Mediterranean and the Aegean Seas, Aetolians and Cretans harried the laden merchant vessels.

The Romans also had to deal with pirate ships attacking boats loaded with wheat bound for Rome. In 67 BC the Roman general, Pompey the Great, started a campaign against the pirates who had infested the Mediterranean. With 5 000 galleys and 120 000 men he waged total war and in three months achieved his goal.

From the 11C the pirates of the Barbary Coast plundered the Mediterranean and supplied North African slave markets.

In the Baltic Sea, the 13-15C Hanseatic League, a maritime and commercial association of north German cities, had to struggle with the Vitalien pirates. The rival maritime republics of Venice and Genoa, with their far-spread trading posts and strong fleets, were greatly plagued by piracy.

From the 16C, American gold excited greed in Europe, especially in Spain. This century marked the rise of Spain's maritime influence and the establishment of her Caribbean colonies. Galleons loaded with gold and goods became the prey of pirates and buccaneers, who operated from Tortuga Island in the 17C.

The term **buccaneer,** dating from this period, originates from the French word *boucan* for a rig made out of branches upon which meat was smoked to preserve it. Also known as the "Brethren of the Coast", these adventurers operated mainly in the Caribbean Sea, resupplying ships and pillaging storm-wrecked vessels.

The Indian Ocean and the China Sea were not spared and pirates ransomed the East India Company's boats, as well as the modest merchant ships travelling the sea routes. In Asia pirate activity was associated with the opium trade until the Europeans eliminated piracy and took over the lucrative trade themselves.

Many pirates, buccaneers and corsairs have become legendary: the Barbarossa brothers reigned over the Barbary Coast in the 16C; Sir Francis Drake, the celebrated admiral and privateer of the Elizabethan age; Sir Henry Morgan, the 17C Welsh buccaneer; the two French privateers, Duguay-Trouin and Surcouf; and last but not least, Edward Teach, nicknamed Blackbeard, that formidable 18C figure who operated in American waters and inspired rumours of great buried treasure.

Attractions

Anyone for souvenirs?

Adventureland Bazar

Five boutiques, four of which open onto a covered courtyard, lure visitors to a marketplace of far-off lands. Craftsmen at work on copper, wood or leather in the narrow, winding streets add to the atmosphere, not unlike that of a souk.

La Girafe Curieuse (The Curious Giraffe) (1) – In front of this shop, there is a Land Rover buried in sand at the foot of a palm tree. In keeping with its theme of the wide expanses of Africa, the shop offers all the necessary clothes and accessories for a safari, under the watchful eye of the giraffe peering over the wall.

© Disney

La Reine des Serpents (The Serpent Queen) **(2)** – This mysterious creature, with the head of a woman and the body of a snake, comes from the tales of the *Thousand and One Nights*. Stuffed animals, statuettes and trinkets.

Les Trésors de Schéhérazade (Scheherezade's Treasures) **(3)** – The story of Sinbad the Sailor from the *Thousand and One Nights* is the theme of this boutique. Various souvenirs illustrate Sinbad's travels in Egypt, Morocco, Persia and India. Dolls, lanterns, wrought-iron objects. Also leather clothing and articles from North Africa.

L'Échoppe d'Aladdin (Aladdin's Shop) **(4)** – Aladdin and his magic lamp of the *Thousand and One Nights* is the theme here. A carpet with such passengers as a tiger and three monkeys floats above the entry. Jewellery, clothes and other objects on the theme of Aladdin on sale.

Le Chant des Tam-Tams (The Song of the Tom-Toms) **(5)** – Inside this African hut, the decor is inspired by an East African tale of a caterpillar with special powers. Pottery, sculpted wood objects, willow and raffia baskets, clothes and accessories on the theme of *The Jungle Book*.

Indiana Jones Adventure Outpost – Clothing, jewellery and souvenirs for adventurers.

Le Coffre du Capitaine (The Captain's Chest) – Decorated like a pirate's den with buried treasure. Various objects with a nautical theme.

Anyone for a snack or a drink?

Besides the various snack-carts:

Colonel Hathi's Pizza Outpost – Pizzas, salads and Italian specialities in a jungle setting. In the centre of the room, parrots *(Audio-Animatronics®)* flutter in a tree.

Aux Épices Enchantées (Enchanted Spices) – Fake elephants' tusks mark the entrance to this restaurant with dried mud walls, which features a decor straight from the Congo. Safari trophies and souvenirs, masks, shields and lances line the walls. Shish Kebab, lamb curry and African specialities.

Café de la Brousse (The Bush Cafe) – A thatched African hut by the water's edge with a view of Adventure Isle with la Cabane des Robinson. Refreshments, mint tea, coffee, chips and oriental pastries.

Captain Hook's Galley – You can get drinks and various kinds of cookie (macaroons) through the portholes on the port side. Also, sandwiches, hot-dogs and apple doughnuts.

For a special treat

Blue Lagoon Restaurant – In this Caribbean paradise of sandy beaches, palm trees and thatched huts beneath the light of a permanent moon, one can dine on exotic fish and Caribbean specialities while the boats from the Pirates of the Caribbean attraction glide past. Wine list.

Music, dancing and laughter

Les Tam-Tams Africains (African Tomtoms) – Near the restaurant, Aux Épices Enchantées, or the Temple du Péril, Africa comes alive through the rhythmic beat of drums played by musicians in costume.

Alice's Curious Labyrinth★

FANTASYLAND – MAP P 68

Nearby, strange "frisky fountains" raise many an eyebrow. This attraction is based on a scene from Lewis Carroll's story *Alice's Adventures in Wonderland (p 101)*, later made into an animated film by Walt Disney. After leaving the Mad Hatter's Tea Cups, the visitors find themselves in a strange forest filled with confusing signs pointing every which way. The Cheshire Cat isn't much help in pointing the way to the Queen of Hearts' Castle.

The labyrinth is a topiary maze of giant thuyas and ivy, dominated by the Queen of Hearts' Castle. On one side a floral design depicts the Cheshire Cat grinning broadly. Watch out for those rolling eyes and that grin, especially at night!

After having crossed the threshold, which is decorated with a profusion of hearts, the visitor, like Alice, "falls" down a rabbit hole and suddenly finds himself in a world of greenery filled with strange figures. The way to the castle does not look like it's going to be easy. Various scenes follow in rapid succession, filled with encounters that hearken back to episodes from Lewis Carroll's tale: the hookah-smoking Caterpillar, the Dodo Bird, the man-size playing cards who are painting the roses red in honour of the Queen and finally the **Queen of Hearts' Castle** with playing card soldiers guarding the entrance.

This strange purple castle, topped by five towers, is definitely worth a visit. There is a good view of Fantasyland from the roof. But beware of the Queen of Hearts!

Autopia

DISCOVERYLAND – MAP P 63

Countless science fiction writers have dreamed up futuristic cities and metropolises in the most extraordinary shapes and sizes, crisscrossed by highways and byways packed with speeding vehicles piloted by humans – or humanoids.

The setting of Autopia recalls "another world" with its stacked saucer-shaped buildings and long, thin spires jutting toward the heavens.

Jump behind the wheel of your 50s-style sports car, in bright fluorescent colours, to speed off down the Magic Highway of the Future, through breathtaking natural surroundings.

Big Thunder Mountain★★★

FRONTIERLAND – MAP P 74

Surrounded by the Rivers of the Far West, Big Thunder Mountain rises to a height of 33m-108ft and recalls the rocky, wind-scoured peaks of Monument Valley *(p 73)*.

The barren red rock attests to the dryness of the climate. To reach the mines of Big Thunder Mountain visitors board a runaway mine train that leaves from the mainland to re-emerge on the island.

Big Thunder Mountain Railroad – The weatherbeaten stone and wood buildings belong to the Big Thunder Mining Company. They recall a time and an industry long gone. Authentic mining and hoisting equipment, a coal furnace, a mule pen and a quay for the boats complete the picture.

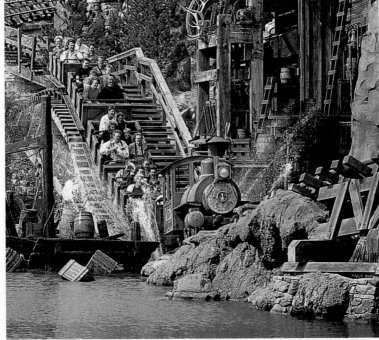

In the old sawmill where travellers wait to begin their trip, the sounds of a water pump and an air compressor add to those of the trains constantly rumbling in and out of the station. Tip trucks, a waterwheel, and a steam tractor can also be seen in the surrounding area.

Each train is made up of a locomotive and five carriages. Once the passengers are safely installed in their seats (with safety bars), the train sets off and the thrills begin.

The train crosses under the Rivers of the Far West through a pitch-black tunnel on its way to the mountain. Once on the island, the train moves at a dizzying speed along tracks with steep rises, followed by plunging falls and banked curves. The driverless train has to cross the bridge before floodwaters wash it away. The wild ride continues through a mine explosion of collapsing rocks and an unholy din, with flashes of light revealing rock streaked with shining seams of gold. The train shoots out into daylight, only to plunge again into a cave filled with bats emitting high-pitched squeaks. The train finally pulls into the mining company station. Despite all the dangers, everybody makes it back safe and sound.

Blanche-Neige et les Sept Nains★

(Snow White and the Seven Dwarfs)

FANTASYLAND – MAP P 68 – CHILDHOOD FRIENDS P 114

The façade of the building in which this attraction is housed was inspired by the castle of the Wicked Queen. The Queen may appear above the entrance, drawing back a curtain to gaze at the visitors below.

© Disney

A Wondrous Tale – The brothers Grimm created Snow White, a gentle princess with skin as white as snow. Her father the king remarries and his new wife turns out to be a jealous woman. Each day the Queen gazes into her mirror and intones "Mirror, mirror, on the wall, who is the fairest one of all?".

One day, while Snow White is busy drawing water from the well, she meets the prince of her dreams and she falls in love immediately. Meantime in the castle, the queen's mirror tells her that Snow White is fairer than she. Crazed with rage, she calls a trusty huntsman and orders him to take Snow White off into the forest, to kill her, and bring back her heart. But the man's heart is softened by the innocence of the young girl and he lets her escape into the forest, which is soon wrapped in the dark cloak of night. When dawn comes she is surrounded by the animals of the forest who have come to help her. All set off towards a humble cottage inhabited by seven dwarfs who earn their living working in a diamond mine. But the Queen learns from her mirror that Snow White is hiding in the forest and she decides to kill Snow White herself. She swallows a devilish potion which transforms her into a hideous, wrinkled old hag. To carry out her evil designs, she drips a few drops of poison into an apple in the hope that Snow White will want to bite into this appetizing fruit.

In the forest, Snow White has changed the Dwarfs' way of life for the better and a joyous atmosphere reigns in their small cottage. One day, while the Dwarfs are away working in the diamond mine, an old hag raps on the window pane. Moved by pity for the old woman, Snow White accepts an apple as a gift. The Witch savours her victory. Warned of the danger by the forest animals, the Dwarfs come running to Snow White's rescue. The horrible old hag takes to her heels when she sees them coming, but they set off after her. Following a wild chase through the forest, the cursed Witch disappears into a gulley.

Back at the cottage the Dwarfs find Snow White lying lifeless. Deeply grieving, they make a beautiful glass coffin in which she will lie in the forest for all eternity. Only a kiss can bring her back to life – that of the handsome Prince Charming, no doubt...

The attraction – All aboard the Dwarfs' mine train! The Grimm brothers' tale comes alive again in a series of alternately charming and disturbing scenes that you will discover while riding through the attraction.

An atmosphere of merriment, music and song fills the cottage under the bemused eye of Snow White and the forest animals. Your encounter with the Wicked Queen and her frightful raven on the way to the mine certainly spells trouble.

Throughout the rest of the trip, in which you'll discover the Wicked Queen's castle and the terrifying forest, the Witch is everywhere at once and can spring out at any moment, at any turning in the road. Fortunately, Prince Charming sees to it that each visitor finishes up this turbulent ride with a smile.

Snow White and the Seven Dwarfs also make an appearance at Le Théâtre du Château.

La Cabane des Robinson★★

(Swiss Family Treehouse)

ADVENTURELAND – MAP P 52

A giant banyan tree planted square in the middle of a small island is the setting for La Cabane des Robinson.

Swiss Family Robinson, a novel written by **Johann David Wyss** (1743-1818) and published later in the 19C by his son Johann Rudolf, inspired this attraction. The family left Switzerland and boarded a vessel bound for the New World. A storm of rare violence sank the ship. The family was washed up on an uninhabited island, where they built their home in a tree and then began all sorts of exciting adventures.

In 1960 Walt Disney made their story into a film called *The Swiss Family Robinson*. The story is not without similarities to Daniel Defoe's Robinson Crusoe. The Robinsons and their three sons (Fritz, Ernst and Francis) sail off to New Guinea but are shipwrecked on a island following a violent storm. Lucky to have salvaged some of their equipment and belongings from the wreck, they gradually build a treehouse and adapt to life in this marvellous paradise. The island has several surprises in store for them.

La Clairière (The Glade) – A small peaceful, shady clearing for those who wish to sit and relax.

A Truly Amazing Treehouse – The lifelike banyan tree (the only artificial tree in Disneyland), a fig tree native to India, is 27m-89ft high and has a tangled mass of roots at its base. The root cellar, **Le Ventre de la Terre,** is used both as a storage cellar and as a place of refuge in time of danger.

© Disney

This charming and highly original tree-top house is built on four levels reached by staircases winding up through enormous branches covered in leaves.

As you climb the stairs you will discover the various rooms in the home. An ingenious system of pipes, bamboo buckets and water wheels is used to supply all the rooms with running water from a fresh brook.

Each room is ingeniously furnished and decorated: the kitchen which doubles as a dining room, with a sink, volcanic stone fireplace and utensils; the observation post, from which you can discover **Pegleg Point,** the most remote point on the island, and the Temple du Péril; the library, filled with books rescued from the wreck, to nurture the mind; the living room where the family used to listen to the lively music of the organ; the parents' bedroom and the children's comfortable room – the magpie nest– perched at the top of the tree, which they finished building on the first anniversary of the shipwreck. Signal flags float here and there, recalling their nautical origins.

L'Épave (The Shipwreck) (A) – The wreck of the Robinson's vessel lies split in two, spanned by the floating bridge, on the other side of the island. A few brief lines on a sign trace its sad story.

There is a lovely view from the poop-deck of the ship (platform). The luxuriant vegetation, the small beach of fine sand and the waterfall carry visitors off to the tropics. The Temple du Péril looms in the distance to the right.

Le Carrousel de Lancelot★

(Lancelot's Merry-Go-Round)

FANTASYLAND – MAP P 68

The age of knights and jousting comes back to life in the form of a merry-go-round of wooden horses where noble steeds carry their horsemen on a ride worthy of the Knights of the Round Table. The brightly-coloured mounts, carved from poplar or lime wood, have caparisons adorned with heraldic devices.

© Disney

Lancelot of the Lake – Lancelot was brought up by Vivien, the Lady of the Lake. He is one of the knights of King Arthur, the legendary Celtic king who made his name in the early 6C in the Celtic wars against the Anglo-Saxons. At King Arthur's court Lancelot falls in love with Guinevere, Arthur's queen. A prime example of the courtly lover, he must withstand many trials for the love of his lady.

Chrétien de Troyes' (1135-1183) early 12C romance recounts the adventures of Lancelot in *Lancelot* or *The Knight in the Tumbril*. This skilled narrator interwove courtly love, adventure and honour. Chrétien himself may have been influenced by Wace's translation of tales by Geoffrey of Monmouth.

Casey Jr., le Petit Train du Cirque

FANTASYLAND – MAP P 68

All aboard this jolly little circus train, with its brightly coloured carriages, inspired by the story of *Dumbo*, for a trip through Storybook Land!

The Chaparral Stage

FRONTIERLAND – MAP P 74

Consult the entertainment programme.

Hillbilly Hoedown – An open-air stage, cart wheels, bales of straw and barrels all set the scene for a Western show. Anticipation gradually builds up among the rows of seats as a group of cowboys plays country and western music. The musicians are then joined by a troupe of dancers, including Chip'n'Dale, dressed – *de rigueur!* – in cowboy hats. By the time the hero Davy Crockett appears, accompanied by the huge Hillbilly Bears Wendell and Dig-Al, excitement has reached fever pitch.

Look out for Chip'n'Dale if you're camping at the Davy Crockett Ranch!

Le Château de la Belle au Bois Dormant★★

(Sleeping Beauty Castle)

FANTASYLAND – MAP P 68 – CHILDHOOD FRIENDS P 113

The castle lies at the very heart of the Disneyland Paris theme park. Its outline rises at the far end of Main Street, overlooking the other lands in the theme park from its 45m-148ft. This dream castle was based on the tale of *Sleeping Beauty* by Charles Perrault. Its architects also found inspiration in the *Duke of Berry's Book of Hours (see below)*.

The fairy-tale – A little princess named Aurora is born in King Stephen's castle. A great celebration is organized for her christening. Trumpets blare and bells peal. A festive crowd of nobles and peasants gathers to pay their respects to the child. The guests are entertained by jousting knights. King Hubert and his son Prince Phillip have come from the neighbouring kingdom and the three good fairies Youth, Wisdom and Kindness (named Flora, Fauna and Merryweather in the Disney version) are also present.

They weave a web of spells around the cradle with a stroke of their magic wands, promising the baby a life filled with happiness. Before Kindness has a chance to give the baby the gift she has brought, Maleficent, the wicked fairy, suddenly appears in a flash of lightning. Furious that she wasn't invited to the celebration, she threatens the baby in the cradle, predicting that before she reaches the age of 16 she will prick her finger on the spindle of a spinning-wheel and die.

Fortunately, Kindness is able to reduce this heavy sentence. Instead of dying, Aurora will fall into a deep sleep from which she can only be awakened by the kiss of a prince on her forehead. Back at the castle the King orders that all the spinning-wheels in the kingdom be collected and burned. The good fairies decide to hide Aurora until she has reached the age of 17, in order to protect her from Maleficent. They transform themselves into peasants and go off into the forest to raise their "orphaned niece". The days turn into months and the months into years and soon it is time for Aurora to return to her parents.

At the palace, preparations are underway for her birthday. But the wicked fairy Maleficent has managed to find Aurora. Aurora pricks her finger on the spindle that Maleficent hands her and falls into a deep sleep. Maleficent plans to capture Prince Phillip, who has grown up to be a handsome young man, because she thinks he is the only person who has the power to awaken Aurora. Phillip is captured and after many adventures succeeds in slaying the horrible fairy, who had transformed herself into a dragon. The Prince returns to the palace to awaken the Princess with a kiss and as in many fairy-tales, the couple marries and lives happily ever after.

The Duke of Berry's Book of Hours (Les Très Riches Heures du duc de Berry) – The third son of John II the Good, King of France, **Jean de Berry** (1340-1416) was a great nobleman and generous patron of the arts. He made Bourges his capital and transformed it into a renowned centre of the arts in the late 14C and early 15C, rivalling the Duke of Burgundy's court at Dijon and the papal court at Avignon *(see the Michelin Green Guide to Berry Limousin in French)*. His extremely refined tastes attracted many talented artists: painters, silversmiths, potters, master glaziers, sculptors, etc. A great admirer of illuminations (colourful illustrations used to embellish manuscripts), Jean de Berry commissioned a number of manuscripts, like the manuscript illuminated by the Limbourg brothers in the 15C, *The Duke of Berry's Book of Hours*, a copy of which is on display in the Château de Chantilly, north of Paris. This masterful work magnificently illustrates the work of the twelve months of the year. In the background, both dominating and guarding the surrounding countryside, loom castles and monuments from the Middle Ages right up to the Renaissance. You will recognize Dourdan, the Louvre, the Sainte-Chapelle, and Vincennes among them.

★★Le Château de la Belle au Bois Dormant

This colourful fairy-tale castle is the centrepiece of the theme park. Cross the moat and drawbridge to reach the fortified entrance. Above the pink castle walls and decorative grey stonework are sixteen turreted towers with decorative gold cresting, pennants and weathervanes. Above the entrance is a 'polage' window, which continually changes patterns, from a rose to that of two doves.

Interior – In the great hall, illuminated by torchlight and with Tchaikovsky's ballet music playing in the background, an 11.5m-36ft-high vaulted ceiling rests on massive tree-shaped stone columns. A spiral staircase leads to the **Galerie de la Belle au Bois Dormant,** where Aubusson tapestries, stained-glass windows and illuminated manuscripts depict numerous scenes from the fairy-tale *Sleeping Beauty:* the good fairies bringing their gifts, the wicked fairy Maleficent casting her spell, the spinning-wheels being consumed by fire and Prince Phillip waking the Princess Aurora with a kiss. There is a good view of the whole of Fantasyland from the ramparts.

Aubusson tapestries – The tapestries in the Château de la Belle au Bois Dormant as well as in the Auberge de Cendrillon were made for Disneyland Paris by the Aubusson tapestry workshops following traditional methods.
Aubusson tapestries are traditionally woven on a horizontal loom (**low warp** or *basse lisse*), rather than on a vertical loom (**high warp** or *haute lisse*) as at the Gobelins workshops in Paris, for example. In either case, the tapestry is woven by stretching longitudinal (warp) threads on a loom and interlacing different coloured cross (weft) threads following the shapes on the design (cartoon) to make the pattern or image required.
The interlacing of these two sets of threads is done by separating the odd and even threads of the warp to allow a shuttle (or a bobbin, on high warp looms), around which the weft thread is wound, to pass from side to side between them. To separate the threads on a low warp loom, cotton threads *(lisses)* are looped round each warp thread corresponding to an odd number and fastened to a cylinder underneath the tapestry, and similarly loops encircling the warp threads corresponding to even numbers are attached to another cylinder beneath the tapestry. The cylinders are connected to treadles, so that weavers can move all the odd threads or all the even threads with their foot, leaving both hands free. On high warp looms, there is only one set of loops, encircling every other warp thread, attached to a single cylinder above the weavers' heads, which they can move by hand.
Once the weft threads have been interlaced with the warp, they must be pulled tight and pushed close up together with the rest of the weft using a special comb or other device. Weavers work from the reverse side of their tapestry, using a mirror to check the progress of their work. Weaving a tapestry by these traditional methods is quite slow work; it takes an expert on average a month to produce 1sq m – 11sq ft of tapestry. *(For further details, see the Michelin Green Guide to Berry Limousin in French).*

La Tanière du Dragon (The Dragon's Lair) – In the depths of the castle a great scaly creature, 27m-89ft long and weighing over two tons, slumbers in an ill-lit, smoky dungeon. The sleeping dragon twitches, snorts and blinks his eyes strangely. Woe betide anyone who dares to wake the dragon!

Renew acquaintance with your childhood friends at La Parade Disney★★
a riot of colours and costumes
which makes its lively way through Fantasyland and down Main Street USA every day.

CinéMagique★★

DISCOVERYLAND – MAP P 63

In an auditorium built to seat 695, a musical in 3-D (special glasses are supplied at the entrance) brimming with rhythm and special effects recounts the adventures of **Captain EO** in the person of Michael Jackson.

On a distant planet a tyrannical queen reigns over an ugly, black, frightening world. Captain EO embarks for the planet aboard a spaceship. Will he be able to transform this sinister world into a world of light through music and dance? Such famous names in the film-world as George Lucas and Francis Ford Coppola joined with Disney to create this festival of sight and sound.

Previous examples of this type of attraction are to be found in Disneyland, California and at EPCOT Center in Florida.

Michael Jackson, the outstanding star of "Thriller" – The youngest member of the Jackson Five, the group he sang with until 1984, Michael is without a doubt the child prodigy of the family. Born in 1958, he recorded his first solo at the age of 13 and rapidly grew to be an accomplished singer, songwriter and dancer. On stage his showmanship is electrifying as he stupefies his audience with his moonwalks, flash-frame poses, spins, kicks, glides and other fancy footwork.

His jerky, frenzied music relies heavily on synthesizers and electronic percussion. Besides the album *Thriller*, which along with its video was a hit around the world, his greatest successes include *Someone in the Dark* (score for the film *E.T. The Extra-Terrestrial*), *She's Out of My Life, Say, Say, Say*, which he sings with Paul McCartney, and *The Man*. He has also sung with Mick Jagger and Diana Ross. In 1984 *Thriller* was awarded eight Grammy Awards earning Michael an invitation to the White House from the then President of the United States, Ronald Reagan.

Cottonwood Creek Ranch

FRONTIERLAND – MAP P 74

Located near Frontierland Depot, this typical western ranch brings to life all aspects of traditional farming in the Far West.

At the entrance, visitors can watch a craftsman carving wooden animals in the **Woodcarver's Workshop.**

Chickens and ducks wander freely among the visitors in the **Critter Corral.**

A few sheep and one or two goats graze peacefully on the slopes of **Goat Hill.** Not far from the ranch the sails of a windmill turn slowly in the wind, while ducks paddle about on a pond.

Dapper Dan's Hair Cuts

MAIN STREET, U.S.A. – MAP P 84

Got a few days' growth of beard? Hair too long? Whatever the problem, the barber will take care of it here in this exact replica of an old-fashioned corner barber shop! The interior features mahogany furniture, marble counter tops, comfortable tilt-back chairs for the customers, old mirrors, period posters and a collection of shaving mugs, giving an authentic, turn-of-the-century atmosphere. An old 1910 telephone recalls the days of "party lines", when several households shared the same telephone line. You could call people up and chat for hours...

The **Main Street Quartet** performs here several times a day.

MAP BELOW

The world of discovery and invention is portrayed here through the use of futuristic structures and high technology.

This land pays homage to great European inventors and writers like Leonardo da Vinci, Jules Verne and H.G. Wells, visionaries in their own time, whose tales and inventions showed that imagination can become reality.

Great Visionaries

Leonardo da Vinci, a universal genius (1452-1519) – Born in Vinci, Tuscany, this creative genius whose "vision was four centuries ahead of its time" displayed a gift for drawing, painting and the sciences quite early in life. In 1469 his family moved to Florence, where he learned to paint from the old master, Verrocchio. The Tuscan city did not offer him an opportunity to develop his many talents, however, and in 1482 he left for Milan. There, his patron was a member of the Sforza family, Ludovico il Moro, for whom he exercised a wide variety of professions: painter, sculptor, civil and military engineer, hydraulics engineer, urban planner, musician, organizer of shows, etc. At the same time, he continued his study of the human anatomy, water, air, the flight of birds, physics and mechanics.

The fall of Ludovico il Moro in 1499 forced da Vinci to leave Milan. It was not until 1516 that he again found a suitable patron in the French King, François I. In the interval he returned to Florence, then moved in 1507 to Milan before leaving for Rome in 1513 where he served Julian de Medici, the pope's brother. Upon arrival in France in 1516 the king settled him in the manor house of Le Clos-Lucé (*see Michelin Green Guide Châteaux of the Loire*) where he died in 1519 aged 67.

His eventful life was incredibly productive. Art, of course, benefited enormously from his genius. An unequalled painter, he invented the renowned technique of *sfumato*, an airy mist that gave remarkable relief and depth to

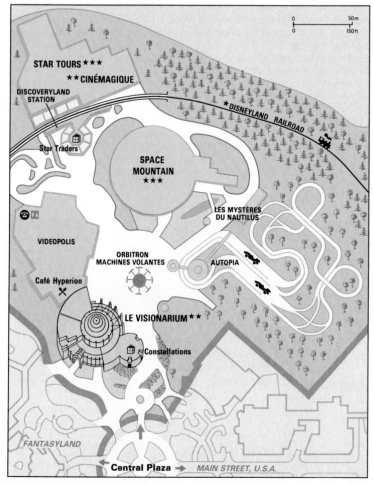

all of his figures and landscapes, clothing their surface in velvet light. The painter of the *Mona Lisa* (*La Joconde* – now in the Louvre) was also an architect and was credited with designing the double spiral staircase in the Château de Chambord. Leonardo da Vinci, a prolific and visionary engineer, did not live to see many of his inventions built. It was not until the 20C that most of his ideas took shape and finally became reality. As early as the 15C, da Vinci had already invented the parachute, helicopter, aeroplane, tank, machine-gun, swivel bridge, paddle-wheel boat, power hammer... and even the projection of pictures with a lantern.

Jules Verne, creator of visionary works of science fiction (1828-1905)

– Born in Nantes, Jules Verne was educated to follow in his father's footsteps in the family's legal practice. While studying law in Paris he met Alexandre Dumas and began spending most of his time in the tightly-knit world of the theatre and the stage, writing plays, operettas and comic operas. Having tried his hand at writing, he had no trouble finding sufficient material for his fertile imagination in childhood memories of the port of Nantes, his unslaked thirst for voyages to far-off lands, and his taste for the fantastic literature of Edgar Allen Poe and Hoffmann. Even in his earliest novels, he wrote of voyages. This theme quickly became an occasion for wild adventures, as in *Mysterious Island* or *Around the World in Eighty Days;* or for marvellous voyages of exploration, such as the exploration of the earth and its depths (*A Journey to the Centre of the Earth*), as well as the depths of the sea (*Twenty Thousand Leagues Under the Sea*) and outer space (*From the Earth to the Moon*).

Jules Verne's dreams did not become reality until a century after he had imagined them. He himself studied geography, physics and mathematics in order to make them seem as realistic as possible. Amazing machines (spaceships, submarines, bathyscaphes, atomic bombs, etc.) sprang from his imagination, exciting the wonder of his sceptical contemporaries. He believed that "other men will be capable of building anything that a man can possibly imagine". His prolific writings bear this out, since most of his visions have become reality. What is more, the United States Navy paid homage to Jules Verne by christening its first atomic submarine the *Nautilus*, the name of Captain Nemo's submarine in *Twenty Thousand Leagues Under the Sea* – and one of the craters on the moon bears the name: Jules Verne.

Herbert George Wells, a master of fantasy (1866-1946)

– Born in Bromley, England, into a family of modest means, Wells was apprenticed at 14 years to the drapers' trade. At the age of 17 he became a pupil-teacher and won a scholarship to study science in London. There he met Thomas Henry Huxley, the eminent naturalist and friend of Charles Darwin. Three years of study had a strong impact on the rest of his life. The subjects of Wells' novels came from his romantic view of science, combined with his writer's imagination.

Before becoming an unchallenged master of the futuristic novel, Wells contributed to numerous newspapers. His literary works include: *The Time Machine* (1895); *The Island of Doctor Moreau* (1896); *The Invisible Man* (1897); *The War of the Worlds* (1898), the radio adaptation of which in 1938 by Orson Welles created a wave of panic in the United States; and *The First Men in the Moon* (1901). Since works of the imagination do not rule out humour, Wells wrote *The History of Mr. Polly* (1910) and *Kipps* (1905), where he used his own experience of life to bring to the fore his feelings of rebellion.

Attractions

★★★**Star Tours** – *P 93*

★★★**Space Mountain** – *P 92*

★★**Le Visionarium** – *P 96.*

★★**CinéMagique** – *P 62*

Les **Mystères du Nautilus** – *P 87.*

Videopolis – *P 96.*

Autopia – *P 56.*

Orbitron- Machines Volantes – *P 88.*

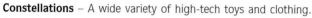

© Disney/Lucasfilm Ltd

Anyone for souvenirs?

Constellations – A wide variety of high-tech toys and clothing.

Star Traders – You will find toys, games, and gifts in this shop built to look like a space station.

Anyone for a snack or a drink?

Besides the various snack-carts:

Café Hyperion – This cafe is located in the same building as Videopolis, under the enormous floating dirigible Hyperion and adjacent to the amphitheatre. The menu includes hamburgers, sausages, sandwiches, salads, pizzas and pasta.

Music, dancing and laughter

The Discovery Hitmen – Rhythm and Blues music.

Les Percussions Galactiques – In front of Videopolis, four entertainers from a far off planet give an astounding percussion performance.

Robomime – What on earth can this strange metallic apparition greeting visitors be?

Stickman – This person dressed as Mandrake the Magician plays a stringed instrument.

Discoveryland Station

DISCOVERYLAND – MAP P 63

There is an impressive view of Space Mountain from this station, which is decorated in the futuristic style of the 1890s. The outlandish flying machines of Orbitron can be seen circling in the sky in the distance. The next stop down the line is Main Street Station.

Disneyland Paris Railroad★

MAIN STREET, U.S.A.; FRONTIERLAND; FANTASYLAND; DISCOVERYLAND – MAP PP 46-47

Late 19C America is brought back to life by four trains, each made up of a steam locomotive and five passenger coaches. Starting in the 1850s, the conquest of the wide open spaces of the American West led to the appearance of a new means of transport, the "Iron Horse" *(p 72)*.

The trains chug around the park, stopping at four stations: Main Street Station, Frontierland Depot, Fantasyland Station and Discoveryland Station. The trains are just like old-fashioned steam-trains, with their whistles, bells, cattle shield and, on two of them, a diamond shaped chimney. They really are steam driven, and Frontierland Depot is where they refuel.

After pulling out of Main Street Station, the train enters the American West by passing through the **Grand Canyon Diorama** *(p 77)*. Between Frontierland Depot and Fantasyland Station it skirts Adventureland, and even passes through the **Pirates of the Caribbean** attraction *(p 91)*. After Fantasyland Station travellers discover the unique landscape of Discoveryland, following which the trip continues back to Main Street Station.

The train ride is a pleasant way to see the magic world of Disneyland and its marvellous variety of plants from land to land.

Each locomotive is a different colour; the *Western* is green, the *Holliday* red, the *Presidential* blue and the *California* grey. Three of them are called after a famous American hero: **W. F. Cody**, better known as Buffalo Bill *(see p 27)*; **C. K. Holliday** (1852-1900), a powerful figure in the history of railroads and the person responsible for Topeka being chosen as the

capital of Kansas; and **G. Washington**, hero of the American War of Independence and the first President of the United States of America, elected in 1789. The fourth locomotive is called **Eureka**.

Each coach has glass windows, a sound system and luxurious interior decoration, and each is named after an American city or other particular sight: Denver, Atlantic City, Niagara Falls, Boston, Philadelphia, San Francisco, Los Angeles.

Dumbo the Flying Elephant

FANTASYLAND – MAP P 68 – CHILDHOOD FRIENDS P 104

This cute little elephant with his enormous ears and shy smile will take all comers on a ride high over Fantasyland under the watchful eye of Timothy, the protective mouse.

You can make the "Dumbo" vehicle fly high or low.

Fantasia in the Sky★

(Fireworks)

On summer nights and on certain days in other seasons when the park is open late **fireworks** light up the sky above Lake Disney. Their brilliant flashes and bursts of colourful light illuminate Disneyland Paris and signal the end of a day spent in a world of magic and wonder.

The spectacle is a magnificent one when viewed from the banks of the lake, Fantasia Gardens or Main Street, U.S.A.

Fantasy Festival Stage

FANTASYLAND – MAP P 68

Consult the entertainment programme (subject to variation).

C'est Magique★ – This lively musical revue *(half an hour long)*, which takes the form of a series of tableaux from each Disney land, is performed several times a day near Fantasyland Station. It includes many dancers, as well as some of the famous characters created by Walt Disney. During the show, you will recognise Goofy dressed as a cowboy, Chip'n'Dale as Indians, King Louie (King of the Monkeys from the *Jungle Book*) and his jazz band of merry monkeys, and of course the inseparable Mickey and Minnie. The show ends in a shower of confetti.

Fantasyland

PLAN OVERLEAF

Identifiable by Le Château de la Belle au Bois Dormant, this land is the kingdom of legends and fairy-tales written by many famous European authors like Charles Perrault, the Grimm brothers and Lewis Carroll *(p 101)* whose unforgettable stories were brought to the screen by Walt Disney.

Fantasyland, land of the imagination, resembles the old villages of many European countries. In the streets it is not unusual to encounter famous Disney characters merrily greeting visitors, posing for photographs with the children or signing autographs.

Attractions

★★Le Château de la Belle au Bois Dormant – *P 60.*

★★It's a Small World – *P 79.*

★★Peter Pan's Flight – *P 89.*

★Blanche-Neige et les Sept Nains – *P 57.*

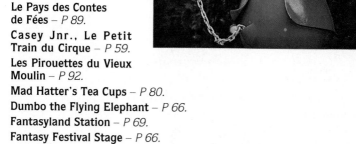

★Les Voyages de Pinocchio – *P 97.*

★Le Carrousel de Lancelot – *P 59.*

★Alice's Curious Labyrinth – *P 55.*

Le Pays des Contes de Fées – *P 89.*

Casey Jnr., Le Petit Train du Cirque – *P 59.*

Les Pirouettes du Vieux Moulin – *P 92.*

Mad Hatter's Tea Cups – *P 80.*

Dumbo the Flying Elephant – *P 66.*

Fantasyland Station – *P 69.*

Fantasy Festival Stage – *P 66.*

Le Théâtre du Château – *P 94.*

Anyone for souvenirs?

La Boutique du Château (The Castle Boutique) (1) – On the ground floor of Le Château de la Belle au Bois Dormant, this boutique with its barrel-vaulted ceiling is decorated in Gothic style. On one wall, a stained-glass window represents two characters from the tale, King Stephen and King Hubert. Christmas decorations and decorative objects are offered for sale.

Merlin l'Enchanteur (Merlin the Magician) – Also located on the ground floor of the castle, Merlin's den, with strange inventions hanging on the walls, reflects his eccentricity. Even the goods lift seems to have sprung from his imagination. Accents of medieval music add to the enchantment. Pewter and crystal figurines as well as toys are for sale.

The magical Merlin was a character of the Breton cycle like Lancelot of the Lake *(p 59)*. During the Middle Ages, the Norman trouvère Robert de Boron recounted Merlin's adventures in a prose romance, *Merlin*. In 1963 Walt Disney adapted the legend of King Arthur and produced an animated feature film, *The Sword in the Stone (p 69)*.

La Confiserie des Trois Fées (The Three Fairies Candy Shop) (2) – Here we find the three good fairies, Flora, Fauna and Merryweather, surrounded by sweets in their thatched cottage.

La Chaumière des Sept Nains (The Seven Dwarfs' Cottage) – Games, toys and clothing for children.

Sir Mickey's – Mickey's admirers will find soft toys and clothing amidst a giant bean stalk.

La Ménagerie du Royaume (The Kingdom's Menagerie) (3) – A large choice of soft toys.

Le Brave Petit Tailleur (The Brave Little Tailor) (4) – Clothing and other ideas for presents based on Mickey as the Brave Little Tailor.

La Bottega di Geppetto (Geppetto's Workshop) – The 'workshop' offers wooden objects such as marionettes, cuckoo clocks and music boxes for sale.

La Petite Maison des Jouets – Soft toys and souvenirs of Disneyland and Paris.

Anyone for a snack or a drink?

Besides the various snack-carts:

Pizzeria Bella Notte – Italian décor based on an eatery in *Lady and the Tramp*. Choice of pizzas and pasta.

Fantasia Gelati – Mouth-watering Italian ices.

Au Chalet de la Marionnette (The Marionette's Chalet) – Northern Italian and German atmosphere and cuisine, under the watchful eye of host Pinocchio. The menu includes roast chicken and sausages. For dessert: Black Forest gâteau, apple strudel and Linzertorte.

Toad Hall Restaurant – From the other side of the English Channel comes this half-timbered inn. The interior is inspired by Kenneth Grahame's story *The Wind in the Willows* (1908), whose captivating animal characters – Mole, Rat, Badger and Toad – have appealing human traits. This work was brought to the screen by Walt Disney in 1949, under the title of *The Adventures of Ichabod and Mr. Toad*.
Very British fast food: fish and chips, pork pies and steamed puddings.

March Hare Refreshments – Just as in *Alice in Wonderland*, one should celebrate by eating "unbirthday cake!".

The Old Mill – This windmill, which recalls Holland, was inspired by the Academy Award-winning Walt Disney short film *The Old Mill*, made in 1937. Specializes in frozen and fresh yogurt with a variety of toppings.

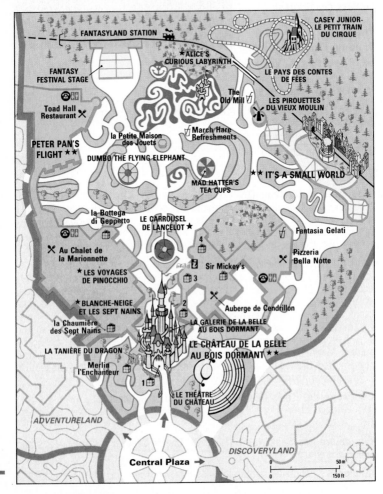

1 *The Castle Boutique* – 2 *The Three Fairies Candy Shop*
3 *The Kingdom's Menagerie* – 4 *The Brave Little Tailor*

For a special treat

Auberge de Cendrillon (Cinderella's Inn) — What could be more marvellous? You are greeted at the entrance by an attendant in a three-cornered, feathered hat, before enjoying a meal in romantic medieval surroundings inspired by the film *Cinderella* with several of its scenes illustrated on tapestries hand-woven in Aubusson.

In one of the rooms the glass carriage glitters. Choose from guinea fowl with bacon, ham, scallops and grilled salmon, which could be washed down by a little treat from the wine list. Desserts include chervil crepes, and flaky pear pastry and fresh fruit.

© Disney

The Cinderella fairy-tale — Cinderella had become no more than a servant to her cruel Stepmother and her ugly Stepsisters and she longed to escape from her life of drudgery.

An invitation to a ball was to change her fate. The king was eager to find a suitable bride for the Prince and he had invited all the eligible maidens in the kingdom to a grand ball a the castle. Would the Prince find the bride of his dreams?

Cinderella's Fairy Godmother made sure that she went to the ball.

Everyone remembers the ball gown, the magic of the pumpkin coach pulled by mice, the glass slipper and the happy ending.

Music, dancing and laughter

Excalibur — Merlin the Magician searches the audience for an apprentice gifted with magic powers, capable of lifting Excalibur — the sword of the future King Arthur — from the anvil in which it is stuck. The lucky young man who is picked out will be proclaimed king and given a royal mantle, crown and sceptre.

Medieval Fanfare — Heralds, sound your trumpets! A medieval fanfare is played by musicians with long trumpets decorated with pennants.

T-Bone Brothers — These gaily dressed trombone players play swing or Disney numbers for your entertainment.

Fantasyland Station

FANTASYLAND — MAP OPPOSITE

After pulling out of Frontierland Depot the **Disneyland Paris Railroad** (*p 65*) steam train stops at Fantasyland Station to give travellers a chance to visit this land of fairy-tales. Next stop: Discoveryland Station.

The décor for this station is taken from scenes of *Peter Pan* representing London in the Victorian era. And it wouldn't be a train station without the picturesque clock on the façade ticking off the hours!

A theatrical wardrobe for a cast of 12 000

Over 400 000 separate costumes are required to dress the Disneyland Paris cast.
These specially designed costumes range from 14C royal attire and Victorian gowns to cowboy gear and space suits (see pp 30-31 for some examples).

Fort Comstock

From Central Plaza and the castle, stockade-style towers flank the entrance to Frontierland. This is **Fort Comstock**, an outpost of the American West built to "protect" the town of Thunder Mesa, home of the pioneering gold-diggers.

Legends of the Far West – The tour of the fort of the famous US Cavalry begins in the tower on the left as you enter, the US Cavalry Quartermaster's quarters. As you follow the tour, you will see scenes and characters evoking the history of the Far West. The **Forty-Niner,** joining in the gold rush; the **Outlaw** in his cell, lounging around on his mattress with playing cards in his hand; the **Lawman,** wearing his star-shaped badge of office, the fastest draw in town and unwavering upholder of public order; the **Frontiersman,** actually Davy Crockett himself, the famous lord of the wild frontier regions. The Wilderness Trail leads to a **Native American camp,** three wigwams containing a display of authentic Cheyenne craftsmanship. Sometimes, the Indians themselves are there, in their striking feather headdresses. In the courtyard of the fort, the **Showman** completes this evocation of the legends of the West. This is of course Buffalo Bill with his famous Wild West Show which drew spectators by the hundred *(p 27)*.

Frontierland

MAP P 74

Viewed from Central Plaza, **Fort Comstock** *(see above)* marks the entrance to Frontierland. Here visitors are transported into the Far West with its fantastic landscapes, typical boom town of Thunder Mesa, legends and folklore.

Two islands rise from the large river (Rivers of the Far West) in the heart of Frontierland. A majestic mountain looms above the larger island, the arid **Big Thunder Mountain,** which seems to have come straight out of Monument Valley (Arizona and Utah). The smaller island, **Wilderness Island,** is an uninhabited, sparsely forested area. On the "mainland" shore old Joe casts his fishing line into the water while his dog barks at the passing boats.

Rivers of the Far West – This calm river flowing through Frontierland recalls the western rivers which played an important role during the Gold Rush – the Rio Grande of New Mexico, the Colorado which crosses Colorado, Arizona and California and the Sacramento of northern California.

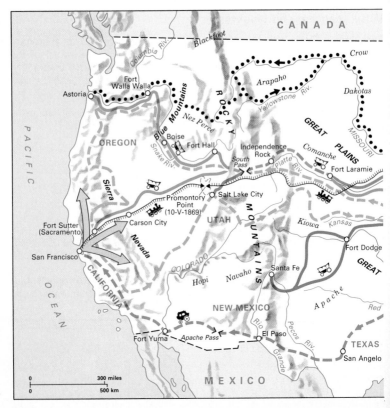

A little history

Conquest of the West – The West was the favoured territory of trappers like Smith and Walker who discovered the South Pass and found a way through the Rockies. Later they blazed the Oregon Trail in the North and the California Trail near San Francisco *(map below)*.

It all began in Paris on 30 April 1803, when, for a paltry 15 million dollars, Napoleon sold Louisiana to the Americans. The territory extending from the Gulf of Mexico to Canada blocked the route to the West. The Lousiana Purchase doubled the size of the United States, greatly strengthened the country materially and provided the impetus necessary for the westward expansion.

In that same year, President Jefferson entrusted **Meriwether Lewis** (1774-1809), his special adviser, with a mission to explore the area above the Mississippi and to search for a passage linking the Atlantic and the Pacific Ocean.

Lewis, accompanied by his friend, **William Clark** (1770-1838), threw himself into the adventure which took them two years (1804-1806) and was later known as the Lewis and Clark Expedition. Leaving from Saint Louis, the expedition reached the Pacific coast after a trip of more than 12000km - 7460 miles across unknown territory inhabited by Indians and divided by the formidable Rocky Mountains. Their detailed reports stressed the fertility of the regions they crossed.

Pioneer Era – In 1842, in response to a request by the Army's topographic service, John Charles Frémont led a new expedition into the heart of the Rockies accompanied by Kit Carson, the guide, and the German topographer, Charles Preuss. In the lyrical report of the journey that he read before Congress in 1843, Frémont presented the West as a veritable paradise. Until then, Americans, with the exception of some trappers, had ignored the West, but for decades thereafter the West would excite passions, changing forever the

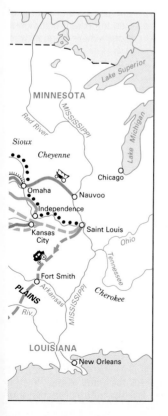

CONQUEST OF THE WEST

● ● ● ● ● ● Lewis and Clark Expedition (1803-1806)

— — — Charles Frémont Expedition (1842)

⟹ The California Gold Rush (1848)

🛒 Trek West (1845-1880)

▬▬▬ Oregon Trail

▬▬▬ Mormon Trail

▮▮▮▮ California Trail

▬ ▬ ▬ Santa Fe Trail

🚘 Butterfield Overland Trail

🚂 "Transcontinental Railroad"(1863-1869)

⊥⊥⊥⊥⊥ Union Pacific Railroad

⊤⊤⊤⊤⊤ Central Pacific Railroad

The boundaries shown between the United States, Mexico and Canada represent the present-day boundaries

71

history of the United States. For many years the masses of Europeans attracted by the New World and by the gold that lay buried in its soil would contribute greatly to the population and development of the West.

The new immigrants drove their wagon trains along one of four trails *(pp 70-71)* westwards towards the Promised Land. This became the era of pioneers, the era of wide open spaces, of Indian territories, of mountains and of rivers. This period of history, which is illustrated by numerous Westerns, has become legendary.

The wagon trains were made up of entire families in groups of hundreds or even thousands of people, travelling in covered wagons drawn by horses or oxen. When night fell, the wagons gathered in a circle, a corral, with the animals in the middle. Men stood guard not only to protect against Indian attacks, but also against attack by outlaws.

In 1862, despite the Civil War raging in the United States, politicians showed a keen interest in the western territories and passed the Homestead Act. All heads of a household were entitled to receive 160 acres in return for the right to live on the land for five consecutive years. This measure accelerated economic expansion in the West.

The Iron Horse – During the 1850s politicians and businessmen believed that settlement and development of western territories were being inhibited by the difficulty and slowness of communication. The Butterfield Overland Company coaches or the Pony Express riders protected important shipments of goods, passengers and mail crossing hostile regions where danger was constant.

The idea of building a railroad to link the East and West was not a sudden decision. The colossal enterprise required funding, materials and labour – and there was also the problem of the Rockies. In January 1863 work began on the Central Pacific Railroad in Sacramento, followed by the Union Pacific Railroad in Omaha. The latter was directed by General Dodge, Civil War hero and a hero of the war against the Cheyennes. On 10 May 1869, Eastmet West in Promontory Point as the first transcontinental line was finished. Other lines would follow, and the railroad promoted settlement of the Great Plains.

The Gold Rush – On 24 January 1848, James Marshall, worker in a California saw mill, discovered a gold nugget in the waters where he was working, completely by chance. He was greatly excited, and the news spread quickly.

1848 was a crazy year in California as people poured west. During this year and the following years, gold prospectors arriving by land and by sea invaded this new Eldorado. Camps sprung up and towns grew, gold was everywhere, and hysteria as well.

The first prospectors explored the river beds with rudimentary tools like the wash-trough (a sort of frying pan to wash the sand and gravel), the cradle (a sort of sieve), the axe and the pick. But quickly it became evident that there were veins of gold in the mountains. The individual prospectors gradually gave way to mining companies which controlled the gold-bearing regions by the middle of the 19C.

Miners lived in camps, modelled after army camps. These camps bore names evoking the nationality or place of origin – French Flat, Missouri Bar, etc. The trading posts provided food, drink, tobacco, clothes and tools. In the beginning, order reigned in the mining regions, but the influx of immigrants

Ch. Boisvieux

in 1850, the arrival of adventurers and ruffians, and the lack of sites increased conflict and violence in the gold mining communities. The ten commandments of the miner, written by J.M. Hutchings were formalized by an Act and adopted in 1853.

The great California Gold Rush lasted until 1856, although the most feverish years were between 1849 and 1852. Today this period has entered into folklore.

Those amazing landscapes

Monument Valley – Lying on the border between Arizona and Utah, this extraordinary natural phenomenon is characterized by fantastically shaped landforms. The weathering of horizontally layered rocks – with varying degrees of resistance – has resulted in an angular landscape dominated by isolated tablelands known as mesas, such as Sentinel Mesa and Thunderbird Mesa, and smaller remnants or buttes.

The even smaller outliers or chimney rocks – such as Totem Pole – are impressive as they rise hundreds of feet into the air. These variously shaped and coloured monoliths create a supernatural landscape.

When the Navaho Indians settled in this extensive valley they turned to farming, herding and weaving to earn their livelihood.

It is hardly surprising that famous film directors chose this territory as the ideal setting for their Westerns, such as John Ford in his memorable film *Stagecoach*.

Grand Cányon – *P 77.*

Attractions

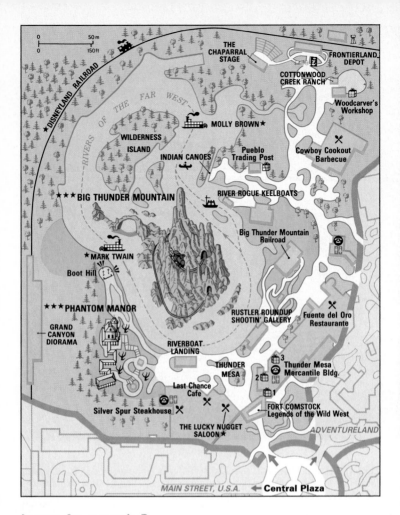

Anyone for souvenirs?

Thunder Mesa Mercantile Bldg – This rustic wooden store houses several shops:

Tobias Norton & Sons – Frontier Traders (1) – Leather is the speciality – hats, boots, belts, wallets and other items.

Bonanza Outfitters (2) – "Cowboy" clothes and Indian articles.

Eureka Mining Supplies and Assay Office (3) – In an abandoned mining cabin, toys and sweets.

Pueblo Trading Post – This adobe building overlooking the Rivers of the Far West houses Indian crafts.

Woodcarver's Workshop – In Cottonwood Creek Ranch, a wood sculptor carves various objects.

Anyone for a snack or a drink?

Besides the various snack-carts:

Last Chance Cafe – Barbecue sandwiches and salads in a dining room decorated with "WANTED" posters!

The Lucky Nugget Saloon★ – The lunch menu offers a choice of sandwiches and salads, while chicken and pork ribs or prime rib are served during the evening show, **Lilly's Follies.**

Fuente del Oro Restaurante – A Mexican atmosphere with typical Tex-Mex dishes such as chilli con carne, fajitas (meat or chicken with vegetables) and tacos (meat tortillas).

Cowboy Cookout Barbecue – A very western atmosphere reigns in this solid wooden barn with its menu of barbecue favourites: hamburgers, spare ribs, chicken and chilli con carne. Real cowboys perform country and western music at various times throughout the day.

For a special treat

Silver Spur Steakhouse – Across from Thunder Mesa Riverboat Landing, this table-service restaurant with a comfortable and elegant interior offers T-Bone steaks, spare ribs and grilled chicken breast. There is a wine menu and a choice of beers.

Music, dancing and laughter

The Lucky Nugget Saloon★ – *P 80.*

The Country Band – Country-and-western or cajun music at the Cowboy Cookout Barbecue or the Cottonwood Creek Ranch performed by a western quartet.

The Card Shark – Don't trust that card player – he's a professional cheat!

The Dixieland Band – At the Thunder Mesa Riverboat Landing, a group of six musicians dressed in brown and yellow play Dixieland music.

Johnny Guitar – Called after the 1953 film, this cowboy armed with his trusty guitar sings traditional songs.

Hillbilly Trio – Three very strange gold diggers, who can be seen near Fort Comstock. They play a banjo, a guitar and a highly original instrument called the *Wash Tub Bass*, actually a single-stringed double bass with a broomstick as its neck and a wash tub as its body.

The Frontier Brass – A brass ensemble plays theme music from famous westerns.

Wild West entertainment

Buffalo Bill's Wild West Show★★ – This action-packed show is to be found in the entertainment centre, Festival Disney *(p 27)*.

Some western expressions

Boot Hill: where men killed in brawls were buried with their boots on.
Bowie knife: large-bladed pioneer knife, named after James Bowie, friend of Davy Crockett. Both men died at the Alamo.
Brand: identifying mark burned onto livestock with a red-hot iron.
Bronco: wild horse.
Chaparajos or Chaps: leather protection cowboys wore over their trousers to protect themselves from sagebrush, cactus and mesquite.
Chaparral: thickets of brush and cactus.
Chuckwagon: kitchen on wheels.
Colt: revolver, named after its inventor Samuel Colt.
Corral: for pioneers, a circle formed by wagons to protect themselves against attack. In Texas, an enclosure for animals.
Gambler: card player.
Gringo: pejorative Mexican term for an American.
Longhorn: breed of cattle known for its long horns and descended from animals introduced by the Spanish in the 17C.
Marshal: responsible for order in a town.
Maverick: an unmarked animal, named after Samuel Maverick, a rancher who did not brand his animals.
Outlaw: a fugitive from justice.
Ranch: property, with all its lands and outbuildings.
Roundup: one of the cowboy's jobs, gathering in the cattle caught earlier with a lasso.
Sachem: Indian tribal elder or chief.
Saloon: bar and gaming establishment.
Squaw: Indian woman or wife.
Tomahawk: Indian battle axe.
Trading post: store with basic provisions, clothes, ammunition and tools.
Trail: path or track.
Vaquero: stockman.
Winchester: repeating rifle.

Famous Westerns

Stagecoach by John Ford (1939)
My Darling Clementine
by John Ford (1946)
Red River
by Howard Hawks (1948)
High Noon
by Fred Zinnemann (1952)
The Big Sky
by Howard Hawks (1952)
Johnny Guitar
by Nicholas Ray (1953)
Vera Cruz
by Robert Aldrich (1954)
The Man From Laramie
by Anthony Mann (1955)
The Searchers by John Ford (1956)
Gunfight at the O.K. Corral
by John Sturges (1957)
Rio Bravo by Howard Hawks (1959)
Last Train From Gun Hill
by John Sturges (1959)
The Magnificent Seven
by John Sturges (1960)
The Alamo by John Wayne (1960)

The Man Who Shot Liberty Valance
by John Ford (1962)
A Fistful of Dollars (Per un Pugno
di Dollari) by Sergio Leone (1964)
For a Few Dollars More
(Per Qualche Dollari in Più)
by Sergio Leone (1965)
The Good, the Bad and the Ugly
(Il Buono, il Brutto, il Cattivo)
by Sergio Leone (1966)
Once Upon a Time in the West by
Sergio Leone (1969)
Butch Cassidy and the Sundance Kid
by George Roy Hill (1969)
The Wild Bunch
by Sam Peckinpah (1969)
Little Big Man by Arthur Penn (1970)
Pale Rider by Clint Eastwood (1985)
Silverado by Lawrence Kasdan (1985)
Dances With Wolves by Kevin Costner
(1991)
Unforgiven by Clint Eastwood (1992)
Maverick by Richard Donner (1994)
Wyatt Earp by Lawrence Kasdan (1994)

After visiting, go to **Billy Bob's Country Western Saloon** *in Festival Disney:
country music, western atmosphere.*

Frontierland Depot

FRONTIERLAND – MAP P 74

This rustic wooden station from an old western town is one of four stops on the Disneyland Paris Railroad line. The train pulls in with a toot of its whistle and a burst of steam cloud, before moving on to the land of fairy-tales, Fantasyland.
The station's traditional double-sloped slate roof is flanked by covered wings to protect arriving and departing passengers from inclement weather.
Inside, train timetables and routes are posted. The pot-bellied stove and stationmaster's office, with its telegraph and ticket office window, recreate the atmosphere of an old backwoods train station.
On the other side of the platform are the goods warehouse and a water tower ready to supply the steam engine with enough water for a few more excursions around the perimeter of Disneyland Paris.

Grand Canyon Diorama

FRONTIERLAND – MAP P 74

From Main Street Station, Disneyland trains chug off towards the American West. The first adventure encountered is an 80m-262ft-long tunnel in which the varied and awesome beauty of the Grand Canyon is recreated. The magic of special lighting effects and the background music of Ferde Grofé's *Grand Canyon Suite* help bring an Indian summer day in the Grand Canyon to life. The attraction is only visible from the Disneyland Paris Railroad steam trains.

Grand Canyon: two billion years of earth's history – The Colorado River rises in the Colorado Rocky Mountains, then runs 2300km-1440 miles southwest to Mexico where it plunges into the Gulf of California. In Arizona it has created an erosional feature considered to be one of the wonders of the natural world. This gigantic cleft with its dizzyingly high walls extends for 450km-280 miles. Its width varies from 6.5km-4 miles to 29km-18 miles and its average depth is 1600m-5280ft or a mile. The main agents of erosion, the Colorado River and its tributaries, have gradually eroded the various strata and although the canyon was created in the Cenozoic Era – roughly 6 million years ago – the rocks which make up the canyon are much older.

Visitors can read the canyon's complex geological history by looking at the different strata. At the bottom of the canyon, the river flows through a V-shaped gorge carved out of Pre-Cambrian gneiss and schist. These ancient and resistant rocks form the walls of the Inner Gorge. Above rises 300m-984ft of soft sandstones and clays. As the gorge opens out alternating hard and soft layers of dark-coloured hard Cambrian sandstone, green shales and limestones are followed by the massive Carboniferous limestone layer known as Redwall. This in turn is topped by 300m-984ft of red clay, which when eroded gives its red colour to the rocks below. Hard sandstones and limestones crown this layer. The immensity of the horizons as well as the ochre and red colours of the rocks give the Canyon a phantasmagoric allure which takes on extraordinary dimensions at sunrise and sunset.

Horse-Drawn Streetcars

MAIN STREET, U.S.A. – MAP P 84

Three streetcars *(San Francisco, St-Louis* and *Saratoga)* drawn by sturdy Percheron draught-horses and driven by liveried coachmen transport visitors from the Town Square to Central Plaza and the castle and back. The leisurely drive up scenic Main Street, lined with picturesque storefronts, also offers a taste of a small American town in another era.

© Disney

The Percheron, "Always Ready to Pitch in and Pull" – As its name indicates, this horse is a native of Perche, a hilly region between the Paris Basin and the mixed woodland and pasture land of Normandy. Strong and tough without being too heavy, the Percheron was in vogue at a time when almost all vehicles were drawn by horses. Farmers relied heavily on the Percheron draught horse to pull all sorts of carts, sleighs, rollers, harrows, and later, mechanical mowers, reapers and threshers. The Percheron was also the king of road hauling, although in the mid-19C the expansion of railroads undermined this position, especially when it came to carrying the mail. Numerous "White Horse" inns bear witness even today to the importance of these famous horses. They remind us that each team included a white horse so as to be more visible at night.

The Percheron quickly adapted to pulling the omnibuses and streetcars that began to appear in the greater Paris region at that time. The fame of these powerful horses soon crossed the Atlantic and the breed was raised in Michigan, Illinois, Minnesota and Canada, whose cities also had their horse-drawn omnibuses. This "urban hauler" was also adopted by firemen and the army, which put the Percheron to work pulling heavy artillery, ambulances, field kitchens and sutler's carts.

Indiana Jones et le Temple du Péril★★

ADVENTURELAND – MAP P 52

Not your average archaeologist... – *Raiders of the Lost Ark, Indiana Jones and the Temple of Doom* and *Indiana Jones and the Last Crusade,* directed by Stephen Spielberg, chronicle the breathtaking adventures of archaeologist Indiana Jones, or Indy to his friends, as he overcomes all sorts of hideous and life-threatening dangers, emerging triumphantly intact with his incorrigible grin and battered old hat.

The attraction – The façade of a ruined temple, guarded by two sphinx-like lions, appears through the jungle foliage. You pass an abandoned archaeologists' camp, with rusting jeeps and equipment scattered on the ground. How long has that washing been drying on the line? Past the camp, the foliage becomes thicker again. You get to the site of the dig, but this too looks as if it has been abandoned. Boxes of artefacts uncovered during the dig lie around, near a van which is falling to pieces and, further off, another jeep. A map has been spread out in front of one of the tents. Where have the archaeologists got to?
The only way you find out more is to climb up the steps between the two guardian stone cobras, jump into a little cart and set off on a mad careering journey round the site of the excavations to... who knows where? The cart rockets along crazily at dizzying speed, even turning upside down! After nightfall, the whole scene is swathed in mystery in the flickering torchlight, and the journey takes on a whole new dimension.

© Disney/Lucasfilm Ltd

Indian Canoes

FRONTIERLAND – MAP P 74

A landing stage on the banks of the Rivers of the Far West, not far from the Pueblo Trading Post, offers a lovely view of the river. There the athletically inclined can paddle a canoe around Wilderness Island, Big Thunder Mountain, and among the rock formations and caves. The *Mark Twain* and *Molly Brown* steamboats and the *Raccoon* and *Coyote* keelboats also cruise on the Rivers of the Far West.

Disneyland Paris in the making...
360 000 trees and shrubs have been planted on the site.
68 000 cubic metres of artificial rocks have been created
using 9.5 million kg of cement
and 500 000 litres of paint.

It's a Small World★★

Just beside Fantasyland Station, a brightly coloured façade representing world-famous monuments (the Eiffel Tower, Big Ben, the Taj Mahal and others) marks the entrance to a classic Disney attraction, which celebrates the joy and innocence of children around the world. Originally designed by Disney for the New York World Fair in 1964-65, It's a Small World has been adopted by all Disney parks – Disneyland, the Magic Kingdom in Florida and Tokyo Disneyland.

Note the giant cuckoo clock which springs to life on the quarter of every hour – the hands move, the doors open and toy soldiers announce the arrival of children who parade by and then disappear.

© Disney

The attraction consists of a cruise in small boats which glide slowly over dreamy blue waters. Hundreds of *Audio-Animatronics*® children in national dress dance and sing against backgrounds decorated to represent their native countries. As the boats pass through the various countries, the joyous theme song resounds in the language of the country. During the grande finale all boundaries disappear and the children come together in a jubilant display of universal friendship in a dazzling setting of blue-white costumes and décor.

On the way out of the attraction, **The World Chorus** features the children once again, this time in a miniature "world city" setting. Their voices ring out, thanks to the latest technology in the world's telecommunications systems which makes distances seem minimal, enabling people all over the world to communicate with one another (telephone, fax, video etc.).

Liberty Court

As part of Liberty Arcade, a covered passageway running parallel to Main Street, U.S.A., Liberty Court pays homage to the "grandest lady in the world", who has welcomed travellers to New York harbour for more than a century. **The Statue of Liberty Tableau** recreates the inauguration on 28 October 1886 of "Lady Liberty", complete with American President Grover Cleveland, French sculptor Auguste Bartholdi and cheering crowds.

Liberty lighting the world – *See the Michelin Green Guide to New York City.* The statue stands 46m-151ft tall, with a head measuring 5.2m-16ft by 3m-10ft. The right arm is 12.8m-43ft long with a diameter of 3.6m-13ft, while the index finger measures 2.4m-8ft.

The universal symbol of New York City was a result of France's idea to offer a monument commemorating the friendship between the two nations, a friendship which dated back to the American War of Independence. Édouard de Laboulaye, jurist and historian, an expert on the United States and admirer of its institutions, proposed the project during a dinner one summer night in 1865 at which **Frédéric Auguste Bartholdi** (1834-1904), a sculptor from the French city of Colmar, was also present.

New York Harbour was elected as the site and Bartholdi commissioned to create the monument. He designed a giant figure of Liberty presenting a flaming torch of liberty to light the world with the promise of freedom and justice for all.

Work began in 1874. The French engineer **Gustave Eiffel** was associated with the project and oversaw the construction of the sturdy steel frame. Twelve years later, Bartholdi unveiled the statue by removing the French flag which covered the statue's crowned head.

In preparation for her 100th birthday, "Miss Liberty" underwent extensive restoration over several years. In 1986, she stood resplendent as the French and American Presidents met together once more in New York for a celebration in her honour.

The Lucky Nugget Saloon★

FRONTIERLAND – MAP P 74

Dinner-show or drinks.

Every Far West town had a saloon, and Thunder Mesa is no exception to the rule! Inspired by Frederick Remington's paintings of the Old West, the horse shoe-shaped interior is richly furnished with mahogany and oak furniture, red velvet curtains with fringes and brass chandeliers.

© Disney

The saloon belongs to Miss Lil, who became rich after she found her "lucky nugget." The nugget certainly changed her life. Today, her wardrobe is full of silk dresses. During a visit to Paris and the Moulin Rouge she met Pierre Paradis, who gave her the idea of opening an establishment with a musical revue and can-can dancers. Miss Lil managed to bring both a troupe of dancers and Pierre Paradis back with her to Thunder Mesa, where she bought a saloon, transformed it and baptised it *The Lucky Nugget*.

Lilly's Follies – Led by Miss Lil herself the spectacular show features Pierre Paradis, six lovely dancers, performing all-American songs and the famous can-can for the grande finale to music played by the Lucky Nugget Boys.

Mad Hatter's Tea Cups

FANTASYLAND – MAP P 68

This merry-go-round, inspired by Lewis Carroll's story *Alice's Adventures in Wonderland (p 101)*, recreates the table of the Mad Hatter, that great lover of tea parties and "un-birthday" celebrations.

Here, gigantic tea cups spin in every direction at a furious pace, making the riders a little dizzy!

Main Street Electrical Parade★★

FANTASYLAND – MAIN STREET, U.S.A. – MAPS PP 68 AND 84

During summer evenings, and certain evenings out of season, a glittering procession of floats and performers winds through the park at nightfall!

The electrical parade, which for 15 years has entertained visitors to the Magic Kingdom in Florida with its multi-coloured lights, cos-tumes and music, includes about 20 floats decorated with 700 000 light bulbs. More than 100 famous characters representing Walt Disney's world, as well as amusing snails and glow-worms, participate in the spectacular, fairy-tale-like parade as it makes its way from Fantasyland and down Main Street, U.S.A.

Main Street Motors

MAIN STREET, U.S.A. – MAP P 84

Along the pavement, a petrol pump from another era draws attention to the "garage", now transformed into a clothes and sports wear shop, where two vintage cars are on display:

–E.M.F. Gentleman's Roadster: this 30-horsepower convertible had a cruising speed of 60-70kmph - 37-43mph. The aim of the company formed by Barney Everitt, William Metzger and Walter Flanders was to produce well-engineered, high-quality cars. The present model which dates from 1908 is a good example of their work. The company closed down in 1912 despite the success of the E.M.F.

–Oakland: this 1911 model was built by the Oakland Motor Car Company of Pontiac, Michigan. The company produced cars between 1907 and 1931. The model on display has the steering wheel on the right, like all the Oakland cars which were built prior to 1915. The Oakland has always been considered as one of the better American cars.

You can have your photo taken in front of this car, dressed in old-fashioned costumes – either as a driver or passenger at the turn of the century.

Original posters, number plates and various mechanic's tools are included in this exhibition on the theme of the car.

Main Street Station

MAIN STREET, U.S.A. – MAP P 84

From this turn-of-the century station located just inside the entrance to the theme park one can board the Disneyland Paris Railroad which circles the park, stopping at Frontierland Depot in the land of cowboys and Indians, at Fantasyland Station, the land of fairy-tales, and at Discoveryland Station, near the land of technical innovation.

Entertainment Disney-style!

La Parade Disney (p 88); Main Street Electrical Parade (p 81); Fantasia in the Sky (p 66); Fantasy Festival Stage (p 66); The Lucky Nugget Saloon – Lilly's Follies (p 80); The Chaparral Stage (p 59); Videopolis (p 96); Le Théâtre du Château (p 94); Buffalo Bill's Wild West Show (p 27).

Main Street, U.S.A.

MAP P 84

Beyond Main Street Station, the main street of a turn-of-the-century American town ushers you into Walt Disney's enchanted kingdom. In the distance is the majestic outline of Le Château de la Belle au Bois Dormant.

Main Street really bustles! A streetcar pulled by Percheron horses and vintage cars carry a never-ending stream of visitors from Town Square to Central Plaza, the centre of the Park.

On either side, Main Street is lined with boutiques and restaurants whose Victorian façades recall the America of yesterday. The signs, gaslights, lampposts, fire hydrants, and mailboxes add an authentic touch.

All along the street, where wandering balloon sellers (Mickey and Minnie balloons) make the street glint silver, picturesque groups of musicians transport visitors into turn-of-the-century America with their melodies.

Not far from Casey's Corner, on the border of Frontierland, long queues build up at certain times of day at a little, elevated square – it's Mickey himself, and one by one visitors can have their photo taken with him and shake his hand. Similarly, at 17.00 Minnie and her friends drive up to Central Plaza in a car, for **Minnie's Tea-Time** in front of the Château de la Belle au Bois Dormant.

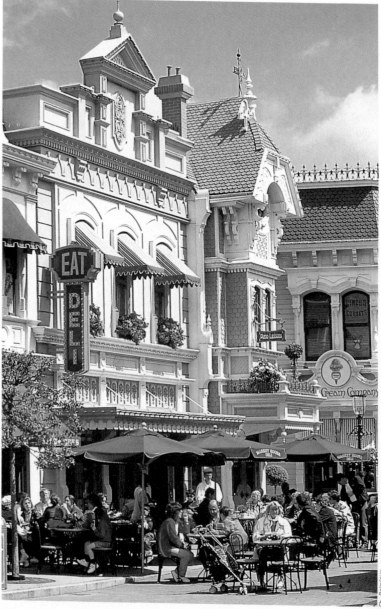

Ch. Boisvieux

In season, there is the **Good Morning Main Street** parade about an hour after the theme park opens. Mickey, Minnie and their friends from the shops and restaurants greet visitors as they process up Main Street to Central Plaza, accompanied by a troupe of dancers.

America in music

Ragtime – This blend of popular black music and airs imported from Europe, like military marches or dances such as the mazurka and the polka, appeared in the United States in the 19C. Played on the piano, ragtime is by definition jerky, characterized by an unevenness of rhythm between the two hands.

Often played on dance-hall pianos as accompaniment for cabaret or bar dancers, ragtime allowed the dancer to demonstrate virtuosity and sometimes to tap out the rhythm with his or her feet (as in tap dancing). Ragtime arrived in the industrial cities of the North with black immigration and became especially popular in New York where it influenced jazz.

With James Scott (1886-1939) and Joseph Lamb (1887-1960), the most famous and prolific composer of ragtime was **Scott Joplin,** called the "King of Ragtime." Although he was primarily self-taught, he was influenced by a German musician of European tradition, a fact which explains why classical ragtime has a rigid form.

Joplin worked as a bar pianist in Missouri for many years before moving to Chicago and then New York. He composed the renowned *Maple Leaf Rag, The Entertainer* and the *Magnetic Rag.*

Jazz – It was born between 1890 and 1910 in New Orleans (Louisiana) and has its roots in black popular music (negro spirituals and blues). **New Orleans jazz** is based on collective improvisation and a two-beat rhythm. Its best representatives are Jelly Roll Morton, **Sidney Bechet,** King Oliver and **Louis Armstrong.** This type of jazz was dominant until 1929 when King Oliver and Jelly Roll Morton retired.

During the **middle jazz** period, soloist improvisation and orchestral composition held sway, preparing the way for the big bands. During this period the Cotton Club in Harlem became the hot spot for jazz with **Duke Ellington** (1928), **Cab Calloway** and Jimmy Lunceford (1934). The **Count Basie Orchestra,** formed in 1936, illustrated a similar current in Kansas City. During the 1930s this period became known as the "Age of Swing," and clarinettist **Benny Goodman** became known as the "King of Swing."

At the beginning of the 1940s a new style appeared which altered the rhythm. **Be-Bop** entered the scene at *Minston's Playhouse,* represented by **Fats Navarro, Miles Davis,** and **Charlie Parker.**

During the 1950s a generation of black musicians created **hard-bop** in reaction to the **cool jazz** of Gil Evans, Gerry Mulligan or pianist Lennie Tristano. Hard-bop, which advocated a return to the roots of jazz, was characterized by its fervour, and was represented by Art Blakey, Horace Silver and Cannonball Adderley.

During the 1960s, the creative **Charles Mingus,** Ornette Coleman, and **John Coltrane** gave jazz a new tone, leading to **free jazz,** a jazz liberated from the older models. Cecil Taylor, Albert Ayler, and Archie Shepp were among the musicians of free jazz.

From the 1970s on, jazz has evolved in a number of different directions, variously drawing its inspiration from the music of other continents and other styles.

Dixieland – This style of jazz was born in the American South at the beginning of the 20C. Performed by small groups, it allowed for broad improvisation. It is sometimes associated with the music played by white orchestras, especially in the 1920s in Chicago, and was inspired by black jazz musicians from New Orleans.

Attractions

Main Street Station – *P 81.*
Horse-Drawn Streetcars – *P 77.*
Main Street Vehicles – *P 87.*

Dapper Dan's Hair Cuts – *P 62.*
Liberty Court – *P 79.*
Main Street Motors – *P 81.*

*Don't miss **Main Street at Christmas**, with the giant Christmas tree decorated with tempting titbits, the bright and festive shop windows, the sparkling arches of coloured lights and the Christmas parade with Santa on his sleigh drawn by reindeers all the way from Lapland...*

Plaza West Boutique (1) – *On Station Plaza (Disneyland Hotel)*. Film and Disney souvenirs.

Plaza East Boutique (12) – *On Station Plaza (Disneyland Hotel)*. Films and Disney souvenirs.

Discovery Arcade – To the right of Main Street this covered arcade lined by shops leads from Town Square to Central Plaza. An exhibition illustrates the inventions of man and displays futuristic posters of major American cities.

Liberty Arcade – This second shop-lined arcade runs down the left side of Main Street and makes a good alternative in times of bad weather. A series of shop windows contains a display on the Statue of Liberty and how it was designed and built.

Town Square Photography (11) – In this turn-of-the-century boutique you can find photo and video equipment and rentals.

Silhouette Artist (11) – With paper and scissors you have your silhouette as a souvenir!

He can also be found in Fantasyland near Excalibur, when the weather permits.

Boardwalk Candy Palace (10) – Atlantic City, a New Jersey seaside resort and its boardwalk for those who like to eat giant lollipops, candy, etc. Pastel-coloured décor.

The Storybook Store – This store offers a wide selection of Disney books, albums and cassettes.

Ribbons and Bows Hat Shop – In this Victorian hat shop you can buy monogrammed hats and other headgear.

Emporium – A large turn-of-the-century store with many departments, including **The Toy Chest** (toys and games) and **Bixby Brothers** (clothing, hats and jewellery).

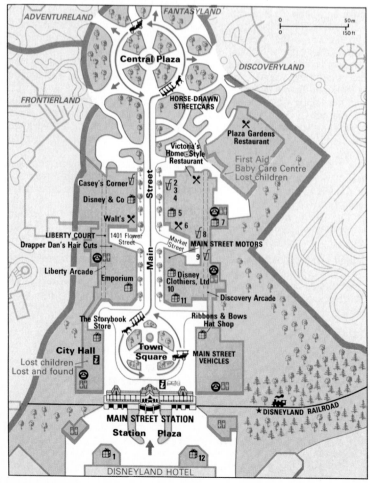

85

Disney Clothiers, Ltd – Disney clothing, for fun or fashion, in an elegant Victorian-era boutique.

Harrington's Fine China & Porcelains (5) – This boutique breathes elegance with its Chinese porcelain, crystal and cut-glass objects, and jewellery boxes.

Disneyana Collectibles (7) – Lithographs, ceramic figurines and rare books.

Disney & Co – Around a magnificent multicoloured carrousel you will find stuffed Disney toys, clothing, and decorative articles.

Glass Fantasies – Blown-glass art objects made right before your very eyes.

Anyone for a snack or a drink?

Besides the various snack-carts:

The Ice Cream Company (9) – Large selection of ice creams and sorbets.

The Coffee Grinder (8) – Coffee house with its unmistakable aroma and selection of coffees. Pastries.

Market House Deli (6) – Atmosphere of a small town grocery store of days gone by. Hot or cold giant sandwiches and salads.

Cookie Kitchen (3) – Beverages and all manner of cookies for those with a sweet tooth!

Cable Car Bake Shop (4) – The mouth-watering aroma of cakes fresh from the oven fills this shop decorated to evoke San Francisco and its famous cable-cars. Continental breakfast is available in the morning.

Victoria's Home-Style Restaurant – Pot pies – beef, chicken, vegetable and seafood – are the specialities in this late 19C family boarding house.

The Gibson Girl Ice Cream Parlour (2) – Fruit-flavoured ice cream, banana splits and milk shakes.

Casey's Corner – The setting is inspired by the American national sport: baseball. Authentic gear, pictures of old-time teams like the Brooklyn Dodgers and Chicago White Stockings, as well as famous players such as Babe Ruth and Lou Gehrig.
There is a choice of hot dogs, chilli con carne. A peanut vendor sells his wares just like at the stadium. Musical atmosphere *(see below)*.

Plaza Gardens Restaurant – In a corner of Central Plaza, this comfortable, Victorian-style establishment offers a sumptuous buffet, including cold and hot dishes such as smoked salmon, assorted cheeses, scrambled eggs and ham steaks.
In the morning, breakfast is served in the company of Disney characters. As in the Disneyland Hotel, children wait wide-eyed with excitement for their favourite character to come and sign their autograph book. Their eyes open even wider when Captain Hook, Mr. Smee, Alice and Tweedledee and Tweedledum burst in on the scene.

For a special treat

Walt's – an American Restaurant – This stylish restaurant is decorated in homage to Walt Disney. The menu is like a photograph album, containing several pictures of his life. The first floor has been divided into small, elegant dining rooms. In this peaceful atmosphere, well prepared American specialities – meat and fish dishes – are served. The dessert trolley is a feast for the eyes as well as the stomach... There is a good wine list.

Music, dancing and laughter

The Main Street Quartet – Four men in straw boaters on a weird-looking bicycle also give rousing renditions of Barber Shop numbers up and down Main Street. They sometimes perform in the nearby barber's shop.

Main Street Patrol – As in the silent movies of **Mack Sennett** (1884-1960), one of the pioneers of American burlesque cinema, the saxophone sextet (from soprano to bass) demonstrates its musical and comic talent.

The Dixieland Band – This group of musicians greets visitors on Town Square as the park opens. See also Frontierland.

Ragtime Jack – Ragtime fans can listen to and watch a musician dressed like a turn-of-the-century baseball player. He plays and leads sing-alongs inside Casey's Corner.

I've lost my mummy...
She can find me at **City Hall** *on Town Square, Main Street, USA.*

Main Street Vehicles

MAIN STREET, U.S.A. – MAP P 84

From Town Square four vintage vehicles, that look like they come straight out of an old film, cruise up Main Street to Central Plaza, carrying young and old alike. Choose from a double-decker omnibus, a police van or "paddy wagon", a fire engine or a limousine.

Les Mystères du Nautilus

DISCOVERYLAND – MAP P 63

Jules Verne's novel *Twenty Thousand Leagues under the Sea*, published in 1869, was adapted and screened by Richard Fleischer in 1954 for the Walt Disney Studios. The film contained some remarkable special effects and enjoyed a huge success at the box office. The adventures of Ned Land (played by Kirk Douglas), the submarine *Nautilus* under the command of the mysterious Captain Nemo (played by James Mason) and the attack by the giant octopus gave rise to some memorable film shots.

The first *Nautulus*, which later became the *Nautilus*, was the creation of Robert Fulton, who built a propeller-driven submarine in France in 1798. Jules Verne borrowed the name for the submarine in his novel. The first ever nuclear submarine, named the *Nautilus*, was launched by the American Navy on 21 January 1954.

The Submarine – A strange metal creature bristling with saw teeth and with bulging eyes floats on the bubbling water of a lagoon – this is the *Nautilus*, the enigmatic Captain Nemo's submarine. From the lighthouse, a stairway leads down into the very entrails of the monster. You hear the voice of the captain, and the guided tour begins. Gold and precious stones, and Ned Land's banjo made from the shell of a turtle are to be found in one of the rooms. The captain's cabin, the card room, the ship's bridge and the diving chamber with diving suits follow one after the other. Then the visit takes you into a huge, opulently decorated chamber, the Grand Salon. Bach's well-known Toccata in D minor is being played on the organ in the background. Through the porthole you can see the depths of the ocean... and, suddenly, some enormous tentacles! The submarine is being attacked by a giant octopus! Action stations! Will the powerful electric shocks from the submarine be enough to finish the monster off?

Orbitron – Machines Volantes

DISCOVERYLAND – MAP P 63

In the heart of Discoveryland, Orbitron is a ride with self-piloted flying machines you can fly up or down as you wish!
The small rocket ships of the Orbitron circle in space around stylized planets.

La Parade Disney★★

FANTASYLAND – MAIN STREET, U.S.A. – MAPS P 68 AND P 84

The first **Disney Parade** was held in 1955 at Disneyland Park, in California. That year, it so happened that Thanksgiving Day was the occasion of the parade. The origins of this American holiday date back to 1621, when the *Mayflower* pilgrims who had survived the first harsh winter in the New World, thanked the Lord for their survival and their first harvest. Today this holiday is a chance for American families to gather together around a festive meal of roast turkey.

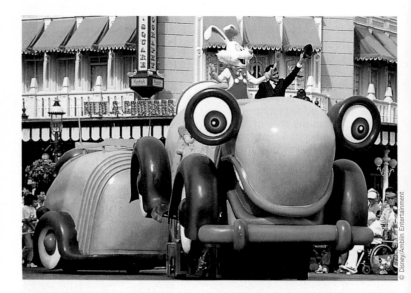

© Disney/Amblin Entertainment

The purpose of the first parade was to entertain as many visitors as possible at any one time and create a festive holiday atmosphere. The original parade was such a hit that these parades have become daily features at all the Disney theme parks since then, and regardless of whether you are in France, the United States or Japan it's a sure crowd puller. Over 200 actors take part in this carnival parade, as it wends its merry way through Fantasyland and down Main Street U.S.A. Mickey and Minnie Mouse wave at spectators from an aeroplane, which heads a long procession of floats, each on the theme of a particular Walt Disney animated feature film. Each gaily decorated float carries several Disney characters and is a festival in itself of music, lights and colour. Jugglers, dancers, horsemen and more Disney characters weave in between the floats. Films represented include *The Sleeping Beauty, Pinocchio, Snow White and the Seven Dwarfs, Cinderella, Dumbo, Peter Pan, The Jungle Book, Who Framed Roger Rabbit, The Little Mermaid, Beauty and the Beast, Aladdin* and *The Lion King*.

Looking for thrills?

Don't miss:

Big Thunder Mountain★★★ *(Frontierland)*
Indiana Jones et le Temple du Péril★★ *(Adventureland)*
Star Tours★★★ *(Discoveryland)*
Space Mountain★★★ *(Discoveryland)*

Le Passage Enchanté d'Aladdin

ADVENTURELAND – MAP P 52

Several scenes from the film *Aladdin* are reproduced along corridors decorated with precious stones. The evil Jafar and his awful parrot are to be found lurking here, but also the magic lamp and the good Genie, and finally Princess Jasmine and Aladdin, or Prince Ali, on their magic carpet.

© Disney

Le Pays des Contes de Fées

FANTASYLAND – MAP P 68

A huge open book, gondoliers and a cruise through the magical world of Storybook Land. The pastel-coloured barges, which have familiar names (Tinker Bell, Beauty, Wendy, Alice, Cinderella, Aurora etc.), glide slowly through delightful miniature landscapes – each with background music – which evoke several fairy stories or cartoons: *Snow White and the Seven Dwarfs, Hansel and Gretel, The Little Mermaid, Peter and the Wolf, Aladdin, Merlin the Magician, Beauty and the Beast* and *The Wizard of Oz.*

© Disney

Peter Pan's Flight★★

FANTASYLAND – MAP P 68 – CHILDHOOD FRIENDS P 110

A group of half-timbered cottages, such as one finds in the English countryside, house this attraction inspired by Sir J. M. Barrie's tale and by the Walt Disney animated feature film, Peter Pan.

The story of the little boy who didn't want to grow up – The Darlings live in a comfortable London house. Their daughter, Wendy, amuses herself by telling her two little brothers, John and Michael, the story of Peter Pan, the little boy who refuses to grow up. One night Mr. and Mrs. Darling are invited over to their friends' house. Wendy, John and Michael stay at home alone. Wendy is convinced that Peter Pan is going to return to look for his shadow, which he forgot during his last visit. The miracle occurs, as Peter Pan flies down out of the sky and into their home, accompanied by his friend Tinker Bell. He persuades the children to fly away with him to Never Land (Never Never Land in J.M. Barrie's original tale). With the help of Tinker Bell and her "pixie dust", nothing could be simpler than teaching them to fly. They all soar off together and after several hours of flight arrive at their destination. There they must avoid the cannonballs fired from the evil Captain Hook's ship. Captain Hook has a score to settle with Peter Pan. A long time ago, Peter Pan cut off Captain Hook's hand in a duel. The hand was gobbled up by a hungry Crocodile, who has been trying to get at the rest of Captain Hook ever since. Everyone in this little world encounters dangerous situations, from which they all escape, of course. The Darlings return from their evening out and find their three children sleeping peacefully as if nothing had happened.

The attraction – Enter by the clock tower with the ominous pirate's ship perched at the top as a harbinger.... Visitors climb aboard small pirate ships and off they soar through the air to discover the wonderful world of Peter Pan, through a series of enchanting tableaux.

The ships fly over the rooftops of London and the clouds of smoke from the many chimneys. Then, it's a short visit to the Darlings, to meet Michael, John and Wendy, and last but not least Nana, the lovable St Bernard dog, who is the children's nanny. Next comes the journey to the stars and Never Land where the adventures really begin – the Indian camp, Captain Hook, the Crocodile and other fantasy-filled scenes.

Fifteen men on the Dead Man's Chest –
Yo-ho-ho and a bottle of rum!
More about pirates under Adventure Isle and Pirates of the Caribbean.

Phantom Manor★★★

FRONTIERLAND – MAP P 74

Is it really only coincidence that the café on the path leading to the Phantom Manor is called Last Chance Café, and that the last house in Thunder Mesa belongs to J. Nutterville, Undertaker and Cabinet Maker?

Standing high above the Rivers of the Far West this abandoned manor house is set in an eerie landscape of skeletal trees.

This imposing two-storeyed house with a large porch, steep mansard roofs and tall chimneys was once the comfortable home of one of the first families to settle in Thunder Mesa. Lured by the Gold Rush they had been lucky!

From the dilapidated state of the house – the windows and shutters are in poor repair and the wood ravaged by time – it would seem that no one lives there any more. But wait, is that not smoke coming from two chimneys?

Listen, as you approach the house, strange noises fill the air, the curtains stir and a light seems to glide from one window to the next. Take your courage in both hands and enter. Once in the hallway an eerie voice from beyond the

© Disney

grave invites visitors to tour the premises. It's too late to turn back, the heavy front door has groaned shut. We learn of the misadventure of the daughter of the house, abandoned by her future husband on her wedding day. Everything was ready and the house decorated to celebrate the happy event. The unfortunate girl's portrait hangs in the corner. The next room is both doorless and windowless and has more portraits, but wait they are becoming longer and longer and the ceiling is moving upwards! The haunted house has many such surprises in store for the visitor. The future bride invites the guest to board small black vehicles and then the journey into the world of darkness and gloom begins. Beware, as 999 ghosts already haunt the manor, and they may be looking for number 1 000! As the vehicles move from room to room the unsuspecting guests are assailed by macabre and sinister goings-on. The ride takes you to the ghost town of Phantom Canyon, where you will meet in another world, places and characters that you have already met in Frontierland.

On leaving Phantom Manor you pass through the family graveyard, **Boot Hill**, where strange tomb stones recall the deceased.

Pirates of the Caribbean★★★

ADVENTURELAND – MAP P 52

The very mention of the word Caribbean evokes sparkling, warm waters, hidden coves, stately galleons loaded with booty gliding past in full sail,... marauding pirates and booming cannons.

© Disney

Once aboard flat-bottomed boats the visitors should prepare themselves to relive the drama of adventure on the high seas. A sequence of lively scenes follows, marvellously animated by *Audio-Animatronics® (p 41)* with realistic and amazing effects. Watch out for those swashbuckling pirates and stray cannon-balls.

The Spanish port's main point of defence is the massive stone fortress, but wait, the Jolly Roger flies above the tower, leaving none in any doubt that the pirates are in command. A macabre atmosphere reigns in the basement of the fort; there are cells, and skeletons which have been there for goodness knows how long. Near the **Blue Lagoon Restaurant** *(p 55)* an octopus patiently explores the interior of a wrecked galleon.

Once inside the fort everything indicates a state of siege and pirates are swarming everywhere. Below in the harbour a pirate ship, broadside on, fires salvo after salvo. The ship's captain is shouting orders to his men.

We see the pirate attack on this Spanish port, the plundering and pillaging by the buccaneers, the capturing of some of the townspeople and their pleas for mercy as they are thrown into a well, and the auctioning of several maidens. The conquering pirates carouse while the plundered city is aflame and the arsenal becomes a burning inferno. Beyond there are glimpses of the pirates' booty, with golden pieces of eight aplenty, the captain's strange cabin and the ultimate fate of these rascally adventurers – three prisoners in a cell are desperately trying to reach the key to their freedom, which is hanging from a keyring in the jaws of dog tantalisingly just out of their reach.

Les Pirouettes du Vieux Moulin

FANTASYLAND – MAP P 68

The sails of the pretty Old Mill turn in the breeze. Behind the windmill, the big wheel is fitted with seats in the shape of giant wooden buckets, from which you can get a bird's eye view over Fantasyland.

River Rogue Keelboats

FRONTIERLAND – MAP P 74

The rustic keelboats *Raccoon* and *Coyote*, moored in shadowy **Smuggler's Cove**, recall a familiar 19C-style of river transport.
Guided by a pilot, these fast-moving keelboats glide along the Rivers of the Far West, affording a view of Frontierland, dominated by Big Thunder Mountain and the foreboding Phantom Manor.

Rustler Roundup Shootin' Gallery

FRONTIERLAND – MAP P 74

Bring along plenty of small change so you can play this game of skill.
Can you shoot as straight as Buffalo Bill? Test your skills at this Wild West shooting gallery, located opposite the Eureka Mining Supplies and Assay Office shop.
Despite its rustic appearance, the shooting gallery is high-tech and a "bull's eye" on any of the 74 targets results in the powder keg exploding, a vulture squawking or some other noise. If you miss your mark, the bullet ricochets loudly, so take your time and aim straight!

Space Mountain★★★

DISCOVERYLAND – MAP P 63

"Whatever one can dream, one can achieve."
This attraction from outer space draws on Jules Verne's novel *From the Earth to the Moon* (1873). This huge copper and bronze mountain, flanked by an enormous cannon pointing skywards, is there to be explored by those who dare...
In the novel, the *Columbiad* cannon shoots three "astronauts" towards the moon before they are ready. Modern "astronauts" willing to take the risk must take their seats aboard a rocket-train, which slowly bears them into the waiting cannon. There is a deafening explosion – hold onto your hats! The rocket-train is catapulted into outer space, embarking on a journey at supersonic speed through the dark and often hostile wastes of the cosmos. You just never know when the next errant meteorite or shooting star is going to pop up, and they must be avoided at all costs, using the most breathtaking acrobatic manœuvres, in order to return safely to Earth.

Star Tours★★★

All aboard a starspeeder for a journey to the moon of Endor and the galaxies beyond.

This attraction, a favourite at other Disney parks, is outstanding for its flight simulation and special effects. It was inspired by the film Star Wars and bears the signature of George Lucas.

Before taking a seat in the spacecraft, travellers enter an orbital station filled with intense activity: the two robots R2D2 and C3PO supervise a vehicle s repairs while humanoids prepare themselves for their next flight.

Take-off time approaches, the vessel's doors open, the time has come to board. Surprise! The pilot, a small robot named RX 24, also known as Rex, cheerfully warns travellers that this is his first flight.

Fasten your seatbelts, a breathtaking adventure is about to begin! The spacecraft leaves the station to plunge into starry infinity at a dizzying speed.

© Disney/Lucasfilm Ltd

Astroport Services Interstellaires – Having left the starship Starspeeder 3000, you can set off on another journey through the universe of interactive video games where everyone can join in the fun. Transform your face (with hilarious results!) with the **Photomorph** and have your picture taken. After this extraterrestrial trip, a short chat with the resident psychologist **N-Grid** – multilingual, luckily – can help you get to know the real you a little better. Aspiring pilots can take the controls of a space ship in **Star-Course**, following its course on a screen. Great skill is necessary as there is a constant risk of colliding with something. Asteroids and alien spaceships have a habit of appearing suddenly out of nowhere...

Star Wars – The film **Star Wars** was produced by **George Lucas** in 1977. This full-length science fiction film, with its innovative production techniques and special effects, marked a turning point in film history.

It was an extraordinary commercial success internationally and two characters, the friendly robots R2D2 (small and squat) and C3PO (tall, of human appearance with a body of gilded metal) became household names.

George Lucas drew upon *chansons de geste*, mystical tales, and swashbuckling adventure stories in creating his cosmic epic of the eternal struggle between the forces of good and evil.

For those seeking further adventures in outer space, try:

Space Mountain
Orbitron – Machines Volantes
Le Visionarium

Of course, there's always excitement at the other extreme, in the depths of the ocean, discovering **Les Mystères du Nautilus**...

Le Théâtre du Château

(The Castle Theatre)

FANTASYLAND – MAP P 68

Consult the entertainment programme (subject to variation).

Le Livre Magique de Mickey★ – Mickey appears on stage in the magician's costume he wore in the film Fantasia. He flourishes a magic wand, and the huge book opens. Out of its pages step characters from three famous fairy stories: Cinderella, Snow White and the Seven Dwarfs and Sleeping Beauty. The show begins, with colourful costumes, music, dancing and, as a grand finale, the releasing of doves.

From dreams to reality
Imagineers are the chief magicians of Disney Theme Parks.
With their own brand of "pixie dust" they make dreams
into reality by creating the enchanted world of Disney.

Thunder Mesa Riverboat Landing

FRONTIERLAND – PLAN P 74

At the landing stage in Thunder Mesa, two superb **riverboats**, the *Mark Twain* a sternwheel steamboat and the *Molly Brown*, her sister ship the sidewheeler, recall the grand epoch of steam navigation on the Mississippi.

These magnificent riverboats take passengers for a romantic cruise around Big Thunder Mountain on the Rivers of the Far West and provide a good chance to appreciate the rugged scenery of Frontierland.

The bell rings to signal the departure of the riverboat, which is also sometimes accompanied by music from the Dixieland Band. As the riverboat draws away from the jetty, the passengers leaning against the boat's rails can enjoy the sights of Frontierland as they glide past. The best view is from the upper deck. You see the mine, the mountain and the crazy runaway train, a pirates' lair in a cave, old Joe (who has never yet caught a fish) and his dog barking at the riverboat as it passes, caribou on the river banks, a crow on an abandoned wagon, geysers which every now

and then send their powerful jets shooting skywards, skeletons of dinosaurs, a coyote howling atop a rocky arch and finally the sinister outline of Phantom Manor.

"Mark Twain ..... mark three" – This is how the sounder loudly warns the riverboat captain of the depth of the Mississippi.

Samuel Langhorne Clemens who passionately loved this great river, synonymous with freedom and adventure, took his pseudonym from the sounder's cry.

Born in 1835, **Samuel L. Clemens** grew up in Hannibal, a small town on the banks of the Mississippi, north of Saint Louis in the state of Missouri. At the age of twelve the fatherless boy was apprenticed to a printer. But he was quickly attracted by the river of his youth which at that time separated the already developed East from the West, a vast territory populated with Indians where it was possible for anyone not afraid of adventure and danger to make a fortune.

At 18 he was apprenticed to a riverboat captain whose ship linked Saint Louis to New Orleans, a voyage of 4000km - 2485 miles fraught with difficulties: storms, fogs, rocks and shallows. In 1860 the Civil War put an end to his career as a captain. During the war years Mark Twain was struck with gold fever. But he met with absolutely no luck at all. So he turned to a career first as a journalist then as a writer.

His greatest success, *The Adventures of Tom Sawyer* (1876) and *The Adventures of Huckleberry Finn* (1884) brought him fame and he became known as the father of modern American literature. The exploits of Tom and Huck, the friendly rogues of his novels, were inspired by his childhood years. Through different characters who describe their surroundings, Mark Twain recounts the history of the American frontier, a history in which the Mississippi river plays a principal role. The author's house (Mark Twain House) in Hartford, Connecticut, is open to the public *(see the Michelin Green Guide to New England)*.

Disneyland (California), the Magic Kingdom at Walt Disney World (Florida) and Tokyo Disneyland (Japan) recreate the stories of Mark Twain and the territory of Tom Sawyer.

© Disney

Molly Brown – During the night of 14-15 April 1912, one of the greatest catastrophes known to man occurred: the sinking of the *Titanic* during her maiden transatlantic voyage. This luxurious brand-new British ocean liner left Southampton, its home port in southern England. While sailing south of Newfoundland it collided with an iceberg and sank. Approximately 1500 people perished in the icy waters of the Arctic Ocean.

Among the miraculous survivors was a rich American, Molly Brown. During the drama she proved her cool-headedness and extraordinary courage, throwing her energy into saving numerous human lives, at the risk of her own.

Don't forget, you can pilot your own boat on Lake Disney; ask at the Marina del Rey in Festival Disney about hiring "Toobies" or swan-shaped pedalos!

Videopolis

Hyperion, a colourful air ship 35m-115ft long, the product of Jules Verne's imagination, floats over the entrance and the **Café Hyperion** *(p 65).*
Consult the entertainment programme (subject to variation).

La Belle et la Bête★★ – This fairy story was written in the 18C by Jeanne-Marie Le Prince de Beaumont. Jean Cocteau took the storyline in 1946 and brought it to the screen with Josette Day as Beauty and Jean Marais as the Beast.
Next to the Café Hyperion, four giant screens show extracts from cartoons. When showtime arrives, the audience takes its seats in the amphitheatre in front a stage. A roving camera sweeps the audience, and – oh horror! – is that really your face on one of the big screens? The fairy story is brought to life in the form of a musical. As the curtain rises, strange and wonderful characters appear on stage: Lumière the candelabra-cum-manservant, Big Ben the pendulum-clock-cum-head-waiter, Miss Samovar the teapot-cum-cook and Zip the cup of tea. There is a party going on at the château; everyone is singing and dancing and having tremendous fun. The music sets everyone's feet tapping. Then a series of scenes, ranging from sinister to heartwarming, unfolds some of the great moments in history. The whole show is spectacular, with a marvellous array of costumes, colours, music and dance against a stunning background.

Le Visionarium★★

Inside this circular building you can take a journey through time where flying machines, and the most diverse, marvellous technological inventions blend in an explosion of light and sound.
A video screen lights up and the humanoid Timekeeper appears. While he is telling visitors that he has invented a fantastic machine which they will see in a time chamber, a robot suddenly appears. It is called 9-Eye because it is equipped with nine eyes or rather a camera with nine lenses. The sound of 9-Eye's voice leaves no doubt that she is a woman! Timekeeper and 9-Eye show inventions which have changed the world such as the motor car, the aeroplane, electricity, the telephone, etc.
After this introduction, Timekeeper and 9-Eye invite everyone to step into the time machine: a specially designed room where in spectacular Circle-Vision® on a 360° screen a film adventure, *From Time to Time* presents Europe past, present and future. During this action-packed journey through many European countries, the audience encounters famous characters such as Jules Verne (played by Michel Piccoli), Louis XV (Jean Rochefort), Madame de Pompadour (Nathalie Baye) and Leonardo da Vinci (Franco Nero).
A superbly produced show with realistic effects! As you are surrounded by theatre screens the impression is staggering – hold on to the railings as you may experience a strong sensation of being off balance.

Les Voyages de Pinocchio★

(Pinocchio's Travels)

FANTASYLAND – MAP P 68 – CHILDHOOD FRIENDS P 110

The setting for this attraction is a typical Italian town. Les Voyages de Pinocchio was influenced by Carlo Collodi's tale and the Walt Disney cartoon.

The marvellous story of the wooden marionette – In his workshop Geppetto sculpts wooden objects, including Pinocchio, a marionette. Geppetto has two friends (the kitten Figaro and the goldfish Cleo), but his dearest wish is to have a real little boy, instead of a wooden marionette. So before he goes to sleep, he wishes upon a star that his dream might come true. Jiminy, a friendly cricket who has taken shelter in Geppetto's house, watches astonished as the Blue Fairy comes down from the sky. She goes to the stand where the puppet sits and with a touch of her magic wand brings him to life. Pinocchio becomes a real boy. But all human beings must have a conscience and Jiminy seems perfect for this role. Another touch of the magic wand transforms Jiminy, first dressed in rags, into an elegant cricket wearing a frock coat, top hat and carrying an umbrella. After all, a conscience needs to be properly dressed!
Escorted by his "conscience," Pinocchio throws himself into life, but like all other little boys he runs into thousands of temptations and his own innocence plays tricks on him. He even lies and each time he lies his nose grows longer. The adventures Pinocchio experiences! He meets Honest John and Gideon, two rascals who sell him to Stromboli the travelling puppet-maker, who in turn sells him to a fat coachman who buys children and takes them to Pleasure Island where they are turned into donkeys to work in the mines, and finally Monstro the whale, who swallows Geppetto on his raft when he is in search of Pinocchio....

The attraction – It begins in Pinocchio's home village. Small cars carry the audience past a series of beautifully designed animated scenes including such characters as Geppetto, Jiminy Cricket, Stromboli, Monstro...and the marvellous story of Pinocchio unfolds before their eyes as well as in their memories.

© Disney

PLUTO
It found please return to
MICKEY MOUSE

Childhood
Friends

The familiar characters immortalized by Walt Disney in his comics and cartoons have given countless hours of pleasure to children and adults the world over! Many of these characters originated in Disney's imagination, but others – Snow White, Pinocchio or Peter Pan – were found in European fairy-tales and novels.

During your visit to Disneyland Paris you will meet many of these characters "in person" as they come to shake your hand, pose for a souvenir picture with you, or sign your autograph book!

The "year of birth" of the characters described below refers to the year they first appeared in a Disney production in the United States.

The Beauty and the Beast

Aladdin

Year of birth: 1992 in the animated feature film *Aladdin*.

Origin: One of the heroes of *A Thousand and One Nights*, a collection of stories from the Orient written over several centuries by anonymous authors.

Profile: This young street urchin from Agrabah manages to steal a magic lamp from the "Cave of Wonders" and is transformed into rich young Prince Ali with the help of his friendly Genie. He is always accompanied by his faithful friend Abu, a little monkey, and he gets around on a magic carpet.

Where to find Aladdin? In **Le Passage Enchanté d'Aladdin.**

Alice, the White Rabbit, the Queen of Hearts, Tweedledee and Tweedledum

Alice

Year of birth: 1951 in the animated feature film *Alice in Wonderland*.

Origin: Tale by **Lewis Carroll**. Under this pseudonym **Charles Lutwidge Dodgson** (1832-1898) is most famous for writing *Alice's Adventures in Wonderland*, published in 1865 with illustrations by Sir John Tenniel and since translated into over 50 languages. Dodgson, born in Daresbury, Cheshire, was professor of mathematics at the University of Oxford, but he is best remembered for the books he wrote for children, which appeal tremendously to young and old alike.

Dodgson got on very well with children and loved making up stories for them. It was on a boat trip in summer 1862 with some children, including Alice Pleasance Liddell, a colleague's daughter, that he first recounted the adventures of a little girl called Alice who fell down a rabbit hole. Alice Liddell asked him to write the story down for her, and the rest is history.

Profile: Little girl with long blond hair held back by a ribbon (Alice-band).

Where to find Alice? In **Alice's Curious Labyrinth.**

Ariel

Year of birth: 1990 in the animated feature film *The Little Mermaid*.

Origin: Tale by the Danish writer **Hans Christian Andersen** (1805-1875). His work included novels, plays, travel books, and especially fairy tales (the first were published in 1865) which brought him international fame. The *Little Mermaid* is also the name of one of Copenhagen's most famous monuments, a memorial to Andersen's tale and Denmark's dependence on the sea.

Profile: Ariel wanted to become an "earth person" like Prince Eric, whom she saved from drowning and with whom she fell in love.

Bagheera

Year of birth: 1967 in the animated feature film *The Jungle Book.*

Origin: *The Jungle Book,* a novel by Rudyard Kipling *(see under Mowgli).*

Profile: The panther Bagheera is Mowgli's devoted friend and very much the English gentleman, pompous and a bit old-fashioned. He is extremely wise.

Baloo

Year of birth: 1967 in the animated feature film *The Jungle Book.*

Origin: *The Jungle Book,* a novel by Rudyard Kipling *(see under Mowgli).*

Profile: Another of Mowgli's friends and protectors, Baloo the bear is a lazy, happy-go-lucky but affable fellow. He also turns out to have hidden talents as a dancer.

Bambi

In all languages: Bambi.

Year of birth: 1942 in the cartoon of the same name.

Origin: Book, *The History of Bambi,* written in 1923 by Siegmund Salzmann (known as Felix Salten), an Austrian writer born in Budapest in 1869, who died in Zurich in 1945.

Profile: Bambi incarnates freedom from care, childlike innocence, and grace.
Who could forget this moving story? Two of the most memorable scenes are Bambi gambolling happily in the forest with his friends Thumper the mischievous rabbit and Flower the skunk, and the hunters chasing down Bambi's mother.

Bashful

In French: Timide; *in German:* Seppl; *in Spanish:* Romántico; *in Italian:* Mammolo; *in Dutch:* Bashful; *in Portuguese:* Dengoso.

Year of birth: 1937 in the film *Snow White and the Seven Dwarfs.*

Profile: He is incurably romantic and almost pathologically shy.

Where to find Bashful? In **Blanche-Neige et les Sept Nains** (Snow White and the Seven Dwarfs).

Bernard and Bianca

Year of birth: 1977 in the animated feature film entitled *The Rescuers.*

Profile: Intrepid mice. With the help of their friend Orville, who is an albatross and also an air cargo carrier, Bernard and Bianca from the International Rescue Aid Society save a young orphan, Penny, held prisoner by the horrible shrew Madame Medusa and her bodyguards, two terrible alligators.

The Big Bad Wolf

In French: Le Grand Méchant Loup; *in German:* Grosse Böse Wolf; *in Spanish:* El Lobo Feroz; *in Italian:* Ezechiele Lupo; *in Dutch:* Grote Boze Wolf; *in Portuguese:* Lobo Mau.

Year of birth: 1933 in the cartoon *Three Little Pigs.*

Profile: This wolf has big sharp teeth.
The eternal enemy of the three little pigs dresses himself in various disguises to try and catch them.

How about breakfast with a real, live Disney character,
as soon as the park has opened?

Hurry along to **Plaza Gardens Restaurant** *in Main Street, USA, where Minnie Mouse, Alice, the Queen of Hearts, Captain Hook, Mr Smee, Pluto and many others are waiting to see you…*

Captain Hook

In French: Capitaine Crochet; *in German:* Kapitän Huk; *in Spanish:* Capitán Garfio; *in Italian:* Capitan Uncino; *in Dutch:* Kapitein Haak; *in Portuguese:* Capitão Gancho.

Year of birth: 1953 in the animated feature film *Peter Pan.*

Origin: *See Peter Pan.*

Profile: A wicked pirate chief with a hook in place of his left hand, which was cut off by Peter Pan.
Captain Hook is no stranger to misadventure! The crocodile that ate his severed left hand has no intention of leaving it at that! It tracks him without mercy, while at the same time Peter Pan makes more trouble for him.

Where to find him? In **Peter Pan's Flight.**

Cheshire Cat

In French: Le Chat de Chester.

Year of birth: 1951 in the animated feature film *Alice in Wonderland.*

Profile: A large stripy marmelade cat with an even larger, enigmatic grin – often the only part of him you can see, as he likes to keep fading in and out of sight. Not really a cat you can trust...

Where to find the Cheshire Cat? In **Alice's Curious Labyrinth.**

Chip'n'Dale

In French: Tic et Tac; *in German:* A- und B-Hörnchen; *in Spanish:* Chip y Chop; *in Italian:* Cip e Ciop; *in Dutch:* Knabbel en Babbel; *in Portuguese:* Tico e Teco.

Year of birth: 1943 in the cartoon *Private Pluto.*

Profile: Black-nosed Chip and red-nosed Dale are smart, resourceful and crazy about hazel-nuts. These lovable chip-munks just love to play tricks, and the good-natured Pluto and Donald Duck are often the unfortunate victims.

© Disney

Chip'n'Dale

Cinderella

In French: Cendrillon; *in German:* Aschenputtel; *in Spanish:* La Ceni-cienta; *in Italian:* Cenerentola; *in Dutch:* Assepoester; *in Portuguese:* Cinderela.

Year of birth: 1950 in the animated feature film *Cinderella.*

Origin: Tale by the French storyteller Charles Perrault (1628-1703).
This rags-to-riches tale has all the ingredients of a good story: the evil Stepmother, two ugly Stepsisters, the Fairy Godmother, the glass slipper, the ball, Prince Charming, the pumpkin drawn by mice.

Profile: Sweet young girl in rags, until her Fairy Godmother takes her in hand.

Cleo

Year of birth: 1940 in the animated feature film *Pinocchio.*

Profile: Cleo, faithful friend of Geppetto, lives in her fish bowl and is on excellent terms with Figaro the cat. Thus, she is not worried when Figaro delicately dines on a couple of ...fish!

Where to find Cleo? In **Les Voyages de Pinocchio** (Pinocchio's Travels).

The Crocodile

Year of birth: 1953 in the animated feature film *Peter Pan*.

Profile: Short-legged, scaly character with lots of teeth. The "tick tock" of an alarm clock he once swallowed announces his presence. Luckily for Captain Hook!

Where to the find the Crocodile? In **Peter Pan's Flight.**

Daisy Duck

In French: Daisy; *in German:* Daisy Duck; *in Spanish:* Daisy; *in Italian:* Paperina; *in Dutch:* Katrien Duck; *in Portuguese:* Margarida.

Year of birth: 1937 in the cartoon *Don Donald.*

Profile: Her life is a series of ups and downs with Donald, her suitor. She can be tender, irascible, coaxing and catty.

Donald Duck and Daisy Duck

Doc

In French: Prof; *in German:* Chef; *in Spanish:* Sabio; *in Italian:* Dotto; *in Dutch:* Doc; *in Portuguese:* Mestre.

Year of birth: 1937 in the film *Snow White and the Seven Dwarfs.*

Profile: A plump little fellow in glasses, he is the acknowledged leader of the Seven Dwarfs. He is the wise one of the group, serious, and reflective.

Where to find Doc? In **Blanche-Neige et les Sept Nains** (Snow White and the Seven Dwarfs).

Donald Duck

In French: Donald; *in German:* Donald Duck; *in Spanish:* Donald; *in Italian:* Paperino; *in Dutch:* Donald Duck; *in Portuguese:* Pato Donald.

Year of birth: 1934 in the cartoon *The Wise Little Hen.*

Profile: A duck who often wears a sailor suit.

Undoubtedly the most versatile of all the characters, Donald Duck's reactions are sometimes surprising. An eternal complainer, but with a heart of gold, he is also a dreamer who makes promises he can't always keep.

Dopey

In French: Simplet; *in German:* Pimpel; *in Spanish:* Mudito; *in Italian:* Cucciolo; *in Dutch:* Dopey; *in Portuguese:* Dunga.

Year of birth: 1937 in the film *Snow White and the Seven Dwarfs.*

Profile: Ears that stick out. His clothes are so long they make him trip. The youngest of the Seven Dwarfs, Dopey is not very talkative!

Where to find Dopey? In **Blanche-Neige et les Sept Nains** (Snow White and the Seven Dwarfs).

Dumbo

In all languages: Dumbo.

Year of birth: 1941 in the cartoon of the same name.

Profile: Dumbo has enormous ears and he never speaks.

Born in a circus, this little elephant is constantly being mocked and teased because of his huge ears. Luckily Timothy, a mouse employed as a caretaker in the circus, befriends Dumbo and helps him overcome his handicap. Dumbo learns to fly with his huge ears and wins the public's adulation.

Where to find Dumbo? In **Dumbo the Flying Elephant.**

Eeyore

In French: Bourriquet.

Year of birth: 1966 in the film *Winnie the Pooh and the Honey Tree.*

Profile: A rather gloomy old grey donkey, Eeyore is well known for his pessimism and the fact that his tail often comes unattached. He is extremely partial to thistles.

Eeyore

Figaro

Same name in French, Spanish, Italian, Dutch, and Portuguese; in German: Klein Figaro.

Year of birth: 1940 in the film *Pinocchio.*

Profile: Could this adorable little black kitten be a bit jealous of Pinocchio? Devoted to Geppetto, Figaro is easily frightened.

Where to find Figaro? In **Les Voyages de Pinocchio** (Pinocchio's Travels).

The Genie

Year of birth: 1992 in the animated feature film *Aladdin.*

Origin: One of the tales of *A Thousand and One Nights.*

Profile: Colourful, wisecracking spirit who can be summoned from the magic lamp in which he lives. He grants Aladdin three wishes and gives him friendly advice.

Where to find the Genie? In **Le Passage Enchanté d'Aladdin.**

Geppetto

Year of birth: 1940 in the film *Pinocchio.*

Profile: Geppetto, who creates toys and other objects out of wood in his workshop, carves a wooden marionette in the shape of a little boy. When he sees a wishing star in the sky one night, the kind hearted wood carver wishes for a real son instead of a boy of wood. His wish brings him more excitement than he bargained for!

Where to find Geppetto? In **Les Voyages de Pinocchio** (Pinocchio's Travels).

Pinocchio and Geppetto

From dreams to reality

Imagineers are the chief magicians of Disney Theme Parks.

With their own brand of "pixie dust" they make dreams into reality by creating the enchanted world of Disney.

Gideon

In French: Gédéon; *in German:* Giddy; *in Spanish:* Gedeon; *in Italian:* Il gatto; *in Dutch:* Gideon; *in Portuguese:* Gedeao.

Year of birth: 1940 in the film *Pinocchio*.

Profile: This good-for-nothing imitates his friend Honest John by abducting children. A somewhat amusing character with his wrinkled trousers and his little hat, Gideon often finds himself in ludicrous situations.

Where to find Gideon? In **Les Voyages de Pinocchio** (Pinocchio's Travels).

Goofy

In French: Dingo; *in German:* Goofy; *in Spanish:* Goofy; *in Italian:* Pippo; *in Dutch:* Goofy; *in Portuguese:* Pateta.

Year of birth: 1932 in the cartoon *Mickey's Revue*.

At first a minor character, Goofy has had increasingly important roles in films such as *Goofy and Wilbur*, *How to Ride a Horse* and *Motor Mania*. He has more recently made a career move into the world of sport, where he promotes the idea that taking part enthusiastically is just as important as winning, or perhaps even more so.

Goofy

Profile: Goofy is a gangling beanpole of a dog, with buck teeth and a faintly silly hat.

He is a lovable bumbler who, despite thinking long and hard before he does things, almost invariably then goes on to do them wrong. Despite the chaos that surrounds his every enterprise, he remains cheerfully optimistic, and ever ready to lend a hand. The secret of his popularity is doubtless the fact that we are all prone to goofs once in a while...

Grumpy

In French: Grincheux; *in German:* Brummbär, *in Spanish:* Cascarrabias; *in Italian:* Brontolo; *in Dutch:* Grumpy; *in Portuguese:* Zangado.

Year of birth: 1937 in the film *Snow White and the Seven Dwarfs*.

Profile: A sceptic, eternal pessimist and grumbler with a heart of gold.

Where to find Grumpy? In **Blanche-Neige et les Sept Nains** (Snow White and the Seven Dwarfs).

Doc, Grumpy and Bashful

Happy

In French: Joyeux; *in German:* Happy; *in Spanish:* Bonachon; *in Italian:* Gongolo: *in Dutch:* Happy; *in Portuguese:* Feliz.

Year of birth: 1937 in the film *Snow White and the Seven Dwarfs.*

Profile: Happy is jovial and an eternal optimist.

Where to find Happy? In **Blanche-Neige et les Sept Nains** (Snow White and the Seven Dwarfs).

Honest John (J. Worthington Foulfellow)

In French: Grand Coquin; *in German:* Fuchs Tunichtgut; *in Spanish:* Honrado Juan; *in Italian:* La volpe; *in Dutch:* Meneer Fatsoen; *in Portuguese:* Joäo Honesto.

Year of birth: 1940 in the film *Pinocchio.*

Profile: This good-for-nothing fox likes to think himself tremendously elegant in his worn top hat and large blue cape over a green outfit with patched trousers. He has more than one trick up his sleeve and uses them all to trap unsuspecting little boys and sell them to the "great puppeteer" Stromboli and his fat coach driver who take them to Pleasure Island and turn them into donkeys to pull carts in the mines.

Where to find Honest John? In **Les Voyages de Pinocchio** (Pinocchio's Travels).

Huey, Dewey and Louie

In French: Riri, Fifi, Loulou; *in German:* Tick, Trick, Track; *in Spanish:* Juanito, Jorgito, Jaimito; *in Italian:* Quo, Qui, Qua; *in Dutch:* Kwik, Kwek, Kwak; *in Portuguese:* Huguinho, Zezinho, Luizinho.

Year of birth: 1938 in the cartoon *Donald's Nephews.*

Profile: The adventures never stop with Donald's nephews! They are undisciplined and dizzy, but clever and so lovable! As Junior Woodchucks they are well-behaved and obedient beyond recognition!

Jafar

Year of birth: 1992 in the animated feature film *Aladdin.*

Origin: Tale from *A Thousand and One Nights.*

Profile: The Sultan's vizier is a slippery customer who is greedy for power. He has a sceptre in the shape of a cobra, which he uses to hypnotise his followers, and a parrot of dubious character, Iago. His evil plot is to seize the magic lamp for himself and marry Princess Jasmine, so that he can become Sultan.

Where to find Jafar? In **Le Passage Enchanté d'Aladdin.**

Jiminy Cricket

In French: Jiminy Criquet; *in German:* Jiminy Grille; *in Spanish:* Pepito Grillo; *in Italian:* Il Grillo Parlante; *in Dutch:* Japie Krekel; *in Portuguese:* Grilo Falante.

Year of birth: 1940 in the film *Pinocchio.*

Profile: The Blue Fairy made Jiminy Cricket Pinocchio's conscience to help the puppet distinguish between right and wrong and so earn the right to become a real boy. This elegant cricket, who was once clothed in rags, now wears a top hat and tails, white gloves and carries an umbrella.

Where to find Jiminy? In **Les Voyages de Pinocchio** (Pinocchio's Travels).

John

In French: Jean; *in German:* Hans; *in Spanish:* Juan; *in Italian:* Gianni; *in Dutch:* Jan; *in Portuguese:* Joao.

Year of birth: 1953 in the animated feature film *Peter Pan.*

Profile: Brother of Wendy and Michael Darling; wears glasses, a top hat, and carries an umbrella.

Where to find John? In **Peter Pan's Flight.**

King Louie

In French: le Roi Louis.

Year of birth: 1967 in the animated feature film *The Jungle Book*.

Profile: King of the Monkeys. He holds Mowgli prisoner and would like to become a man himself. Occasionally he also sings jazz, accompanied by his wild, swinging band of monkey musicians.

Little Wolf

In French: P'tit Loup.

Year of birth: 1936 in the cartoon *Three Little Wolves*.

Profile: The son of the Big Bad Wolf is the three little pigs' friend, luckily for them!

Mad Hatter

In French: le Chapelier Fou.

Year of birth: 1951 in the animated feature film *Alice in Wonderland*.

Profile: This small gentleman in a huge top hat loves tea parties, especially with his friends the March Hare and the Dormouse. Likes celebrating "unbirthdays" and being rude.

Where to find the Mad Hatter? In the Mad Hatter's Tea Cups.

March Hare

In French: Lièvre de Mars; *in German:* Der Märzhare; *in Italian:* il Leprotto Bisestile.

Year of birth: 1951 in the animated feature film *Alice in Wonderland*.

Profile: Lives with the Mad Hatter and is also a practical joker, especially where the long-suffering dormouse is concerned.

Mary Poppins

© Disney

Mary Poppins

Year of birth: 1964 in the musical comedy of the same name. The starring role was played by Julie Andrews, while Dick Van Dyke played Bert the pavement artist, whose drawings lead into a magical adventure world. The film contains live action mixed with animation, and some "supercalifragilisticexpialidocious" songs by the Sherman brothers.

Origin: Series of books by P L Travers (*Mary Poppins*, published in 1934, was the first).

Profile: Magical powers include being able to fly with her umbrella.
This governess, who comes down from the sky, causes a commotion in the London home of the Banks family, by taking the children on wild adventures.

Michael

In French: Michel; *in German:* Michael; *in Spanish and Portuguese:* Miguel; *in Italian:* Michele; *in Dutch:* Chieltje.

Year of birth: 1953 in the animated feature film *Peter Pan*.

Profile: Baby brother of Wendy and John Darling; always carries his teddy.

Where to find Michael? In Peter Pan's flight.

Mickey Mouse

In French: Mickey; *in German:* Micky Maus; *in Spanish:* Raton Mickey; *in Italian:* Topolino; *in Dutch:* Mickey Mouse; *in Portuguese:* Mickey.

Year of birth: 1928.

Profile: Without a doubt the most famous of the Walt Disney characters. The beloved little mouse, drawn by Ub Iwerks, was supposed to have been called Mortimer but was baptised Mickey instead through the influence of Lillian, Walt's wife. Mickey was first animated in a film called *Plane Crazy*, inspired by the exploits of aviator Charles Lindbergh's nonstop solo flight across the Atlantic the year before.

Minnie Mouse and Mickey Mouse

On 18 November Mickey made his screen début in the cartoon *Steamboat Willie*, then became a comic strip hero in 1930.

In 1940, Walt Disney turned him into the Sorcerer's Apprentice for the film *Fantasia:* Mickey in his famous pointed hat performed magical tricks accompanied by the frenzied music of Paul Dukas.

Mickey's success grew and grew. Television shows and clubs were formed in honour of the little mouse who will forever be associated with the name Disney.

Mickey is everyone's friend, symbol of courage, honesty, loyalty and intelligence.

He is very elegant in his red trousers and black frock coat.

Minnie Mouse

In French: Minnie; *in German:* Minnie Maus; *in Spanish:* Minnie; *in Italian:* Minni; *in Dutch:* Minnie Mouse; *in Portuguese:* Minie.

Year of birth: 1928 in the cartoon *Steamboat Willie*.

Profile: Singer, dancer, actress, Mickey's sweetheart participates in many of his adventures and gives him valuable advice.

Mr. Smee

In French: Monsieur Mouche; *in German:* Der Dicke Koch; *in Spanish:* Sr. Smee; *in Italian:* Zibbibo; *in Dutch:* Vetje; *in Portuguese:* Bonifácio.

Year of birth: 1953 in the animated feature film *Peter Pan*.

Profile: This pudgy little pirate cook with glasses is the sinister Captain Hook's bumbling confidence man. His devotion is endless.

Where to find Mr. Smee? In **Peter Pan's Flight.**

Monstro the Whale

In French: Monstro la Baleine; *in German:* Monstro; *in Spanish:* Monstruo; *in Italian:* La balena; *in Dutch:* Monsterdier; *in Portuguese:* Monstro.

Year of birth: 1940 in the film *Pinocchio*.

Profile: Dreadful animal with an enormous appetite. Will Pinocchio and his friends manage to escape from him?

Where to find Monstro? In **Les Voyages de Pinocchio** (Pinocchio's Travels).

Don't forget that many of your favourite Disney characters are waiting to greet you at Disneyland Paris, where they will be happy to sign your autograph book or have their photo taken with you!

Mowgli

Year of birth: 1967 in the animated feature film *The Jungle Book.*

Origin: A novel, *The Jungle Book,* published in 1894 by the British author **Rudyard Kipling** (1865-1936). The writer was born in Bombay, India, where he spent his early years. Throughout his career as a journalist, poet, traveller and author Kipling remained greatly attached to India.

Profile: Mowgli, a "man-child" discovered in the jungle and raised by wolves, has two faithful friends and protectors in Bagheera the panther and Baloo the bear. But Mowgli should beware of Shere Khan, the man-eating tiger, and of Kaa, the python with the hypnotic stare.

Peter Pan

Same name in French, German, Spanish, Italian, Dutch, and Portuguese.

Year of birth: 1953 in the animated feature film of the same name.

Captain Hook and Peter Pan

© Disney

Origin: British literature. We owe our hero to the Scottish author **James Matthew Barrie** (1860-1937). Barrie was born in Kirriemuir, a small village north of Dundee, and studied at the University of Edinburgh before becoming a journalist in Nottingham and London. It was for the Llewellyn Davies boys that Barrie invented the Peter Pan stories. Peter first appeared in a play in 1904 and then in a novel published in 1911. An immortal character, Peter Pan has a statue in Kensington Gardens, which is well known to small Londoners. Every Christmas season the story is revived as part of London's festive entertainment and even today all royalties on Barrie's book go to the Great Ormond Street Hospital for Sick Children in London.

Profile: A little boy who refused to grow up.

Peter and Tinker Bell take the Darling children to the Never Never Land where they encounter the Lost Boys, the Redskins and the Pirates.

Where to find Peter Pan? In **Peter Pan's Flight.**

Pinocchio

In Spanish: Pinocho; *in Portuguese:* Pinóquio.

Year of birth: 1940 in a cartoon of the same name.

Origin: Italian tale. Born in Florence in 1826, Carlo Lorenzini wrote Pinocchio under the name of **Carlo Collodi.** He took the pen name around 1859 to protect himself as he was involved in the movement for Italian unity.

Profile: A wooden puppet brought to life by the Blue Fairy, with a pointed nose which grows when he tells a lie.

To become a real boy Pinocchio has to prove himself brave, truthful and unselfish and to help him, Jiminy Cricket acts as his conscience. But Pinocchio is not always obedient and likes to court danger.

Where to find Pinocchio? In **Les Voyages de Pinocchio** (Pinocchio's Travels).

Pluto

Same name in French, German, Spanish, Italian, Dutch, and Portuguese.

Year of birth: 1930 in the cartoon *The Chain Gang.*

Profile: This good-natured hound has drooping ears that can shoot straight up on occasions – a way of communicating, since he does not speak. Naïve, fearful, shy, sentimental and eager-to-please, Pluto is Mickey's loyal friend.

Practical Pig, Fifer Pig, and Fiddler Pig

In French: Naf-Naf, Nif-Nif, Nouf-Nouf; *in German:* Schweinchen Schlau, Pfeifer, Fiedler; *in Spanish:* Práctico, Flautista, Violinista; *in Italian:* Gimmi, Timmi, Tommi; *in Dutch:* Knor, Knir, Knar; *in Portuguese:* Porquinho Prático, Cícero, Heitor.

Year of birth: 1933 in the Silly Symphony *Three Little Pigs*, which earned Walt Disney his third Academy Award. Frank Churchill's refrain is still famous.

Profile: Fiddler Pig and Fifer Pig rely on the common sense of Practical Pig to help them be on constant guard against the Big Bad Wolf whose sole aim is to devour them.

Prince John

In French: Prince Jean.

Year of birth: 1973 in the animated feature film *Robin Hood*.

Profile: A somewhat dubious character, Prince John usurps the throne of his brother, King Richard the Lionheart, while he is away on a Crusade. The vain Prince John wears a crown and a coat with ermine trimmings. He burdens King Richard's subjects with taxes.

© Disney

Prince John, Robin Hood, Little John, Friar Tuck and the Sheriff of Nottingham

Princess Jasmine

Year of birth: 1992 in the animated feature film *Aladdin*.

Origin: Tale from *A Thousand and One Nights*.

Profile: Only daughter of the Sultan, who must find herself a husband before her next birthday... in only three days time. Will she find her handsome prince? She must beware of Jafar, the Sultan's sinister vizier. Luckily, her faithful friend, Rajah the tiger, is there to look after her.

Where to find Princess Jasmine? In **Le Passage Enchanté d'Aladdin**.

Queen of Hearts

In French: la Reine de Cœur.

Year of birth: 1951 in the animated feature film *Alice in Wonderland*.

Profile: A stout woman (her husband looks tiny at her side) and not at all nice, the Queen of Hearts lives in a bizarre palace and plays croquet with pink flamingos instead of mallets and hedgehogs instead of balls. She has a personal guard of playing cards who watch over her.

Robin Hood

In French: Robin des Bois.

Year of birth: 1973 in the animated feature film *Robin Hood*.

Origin: Middle English folk legend. While King Richard the Lionheart is off fighting in the Crusades, his brother Prince John seizes the throne. His subjects suffer tyranny during the reign of this grasping usurper.

Profile: Fox dressed in green, with a yellow hat with a red feather. Robin Hood, hero of Sherwood Forest, defends the poor and downtrodden and is a master of disguise.

Roger Rabbit

Year of birth: 1988 in the film *Who Framed Roger Rabbit*.

Profile: Accused of murder and plagued with problems of the heart on account of his wife Jessica, a *femme fatale*, this zany and energetic rabbit is a handful for Valiant, the private detective who takes him under his wing.

© Disney/Amblin Entertainment

Roger Rabbit

Scrooge McDuck

In French: Oncle Picsou; *in German:* Onkel Dagobert; *in Spanish:* Tío Gilito; *in Italian:* Paperon de' Paperoni; *in Dutch:* Dagobert Duck; *in Portuguese:* Tio Patinhas.

Year of birth: 1947 in a comic book. Appeared on screen for the first time in 1967 in *Scrooge McDuck and Money*.

Profile: Very much the businessman, he wears a pince-nez, top hat, red topcoat, spats and flourishes a cane.
This brilliant duck, rich as Croesus, accumulates mountains of coins and bills. Careful with money (some might go so far as to call him stingy), Scrooge McDuck counts and recounts his stash.

The Seven Dwarfs

See also under individual names.

Year of birth: 1937 in the film *Snow White and the Seven Dwarfs*.

Profiles: Their names are Sneezy, Sleepy, Grumpy, Happy, Doc, Dopey, and Bashful. Snow White finds shelter in the Dwarfs' cottage when the huntsman abandons her in the forest instead of obeying the orders of the Wicked Queen to kill her. The Dwarfs are best known for their joyful chorus of "Hi ho, hi ho, it's off to work we go!" which they sing on their way to the diamond mine.

Sleeping Beauty

In French: La Belle au Bois Dormant; *in German:* Dornröschen; *in Spanish:* La Bella Durmiente; *in Italian:* La Bella Addormentata nel Bosco; *in Dutch:* Doornroosje; *in Portuguese:* A Bela Adormecida.

Year of birth: 1959 in the animated feature film *Sleeping Beauty*.

Origin: Tale by the French author **Charles Perrault** (1628-1703), who was elected to the French Academy in 1674 and best known for his book of children's fairy-tales *(Contes de ma Mère l'Oye)* published in 1697. Sleeping Beauty inspired a ballet with music by Tchaikovsky and choreography by Marius Petipa, first performed in the Mariensky Theatre of St Petersburg in 1890.
Following a spell cast on her by the Wicked Fairy, Princess Aurora pricks her finger on a spinning needle and falls into a deep sleep. Only a kiss from her handsome prince can awaken her...

Sneezy, Happy and Sleepy

Sleepy

In French: Dormeur; *in German:* Schlafmütz; *in Spanish:* Dormilón; *in Italian:* Pisolo; *in Dutch:* Sleepy; *in Portuguese:* Soneca.

Year of birth: 1937 in the film *Snow White and the Seven Dwarfs.*

Profile: This virtuoso yawner snoozes anywhere, anytime and in any position.

Where to find Sleepy? In **Blanche-Neige et les Sept Nains**.

Sneezy

In French: Atchoum; *in German:* Hatschi; *in Spanish:* Mocoso; *in Italian:* Eolo; *in Dutch:* Sneezy; *in Portuguese:* Teimoso.

Year of birth: 1937 in the film *Snow White and the Seven Dwarfs.*

Profile: His sneezes rattle the very walls!

Where to find Sneezy? In **Blanche-Neige et les Sept Nains**.

Snow White

In French: Blanche-Neige; *in German:* Schneewittchen; *in Spanish:* Blancanieves; *in Italian:* Biancaneve; *in Dutch:* Sneeuwwitje; *in Portuguese:* Branca de Neve.

Dopey and Snow White

Year of birth: 1937 in the first full-length animated feature film *Snow White and the Seven Dwarfs.*

Origin: The internationally famous story of Snow White and the Seven Dwarfs comes from the fairy tales of the brothers **Jakob** (1785-1863) and **Wilhelm** (1786-1859) **Grimm**. Born in Hesse, Germany, the brothers studied philology at the University of Göttingen before turning to German folk tales. Their tales were published in three volumes (1812, 1815, and 1818).

Profile: Snow White is a beautiful young princess with lips as red as blood, skin as white as snow and hair as black as ebony. She embodies beauty, sweetness and grace. Snow White is condemned to death by her jealous Stepmother, the Queen. But the huntsman charged with carrying out the order abandons the princess in the forest. Snow White finds shelter with the Seven Dwarfs, but falls prey to the Wicked Queen who, disguised as an ugly old Witch, tempts her with a poisoned apple.

Where to find Snow White? In **Blanche-Neige et les Sept Nains** (Snow White and the Seven Dwarfs).

Stromboli

Year of birth: 1940 in the film *Pinocchio.*

Profile: This boorish puppeteer with his black beard drives his caravan from town to town. But the poor puppets who have brought him fame are pitilessly condemned to be burned as soon as they become old and, according to Stromboli, useless. Can Pinocchio escape him?

Where to find Stromboli? In **Les Voyages de Pinocchio** (Pinocchio's Travels).

Tigger

In French: Tigrou.

Year of birth: 1968 in the film *Winnie the Pooh and the Blustery Day.*

Profile: Tigger is a good sort, although he is always bouncing into people. He is Pooh's good friend, but doesn't get on quite so well with Eeyore...

Tinker Bell

In French: Clochette; *in German:* Glöckchen; *in Spanish:* Campanilla; *in Italian:* Campanellino; *in Dutch:* Rinkerbel; *in Portuguese:* Fada Sininho.

Year of birth: 1953 in the film *Peter Pan.*

Profile: Without this tiny blond fairy and "pixie dust", Peter Pan never could have flown, for it is she who accompanies him wherever he goes (but she is extremely jealous of Wendy)!

Where to find Tinker Bell? In **Peter Pan's Flight.**

Tod and Copper

In French: Rox et Rouky.

Year of birth: 1981 in the animated feature film *The Fox and the Hound.*

Origin: A book (1967) by Daniel P. Mannix, a Roman Catholic prelate of Irish origin who lived in Australia. The story tells of the unusual friendship between a fox cub, Tod, and a hunting hound, Copper.

Tweedledum and Tweedledee

Year of birth: 1951 in the film *Alice in Wonderland.*

Profile: Identical clothing. To tell them apart: they wear their names embroidered on their collars; also, Tweedledum lisps. Not particularly agreeable, these two cronies think they are the only ones with good manners.

The Walrus

In French: Le Morse.

Year of birth: 1951 in the animated feature film, *Alice in Wonderland.*

Profile: Whiskered and tuskered gentleman. The dubious pair, Tweedledum and Tweedledee, introduce Alice to the cigar-smoking Walrus who, in the company of the Carpenter, makes a meal of the unsuspecting oysters.

Where to find the Walrus? In **Alice's Curious Labyrinth.**

Wendy

In Portuguese: Maninha.

Year of birth: 1953 in the film *Peter Pan.*

Profile: Wendy Darling is the picture of goodness and sweetness and watches over her brothers John and Michael like a mother. At bedtime she tells them stories of Peter Pan and the Never Never Land.

Where to find Wendy? In **Peter Pan's Flight.**

The White Rabbit

In French: Lapin Blanc; *in German:* Das Weiße Kaninchen.

Year of birth: 1951 in the animated feature film *Alice in Wonderland.*

Profile: He always carries a large pocket-watch and scurries past muttering "I'm late, I'm late, for a very important date!".

Where to find the White Rabbit? In **Alice's Curious Labyrinth.**

Wicked Queen *(see also The Witch)*

In French: la Reine.

Year of birth: 1937 in the film Snow White and the Seven Dwarfs.

Profile: Consults her magic mirror daily to see who is the fairest in the land. Jealous of all rivals she wickedly plots to kill her beautiful stepdaughter, Snow White.

Where to find the Wicked Queen? In **Blanche-Neige et les Sept Nains** (Snow White and the Seven Dwarfs).

Winnie the Pooh

In French: Winnie l'Ourson; *in German:* Winnie Puuh; *in Spanish:* El Osito Winnie; *in Italian:* Winny Puh; *in Dutch:* Winnie the Pooh; *in Portuguese:* O Ursinho Puff.

Year of birth: 1966 in the cartoon *Winnie the Pooh and the Honey Tree.*

Origin: A. A. Milne's classics (the first of which dates from 1923), illustrated by E.H. Shepard's pencil sketches, which recount the misadventures of that nursery favourite Winnie the Pooh or just plain Pooh. This "bear of very little brain" has a great weakness for honey.

Profile: Pooh's love of honey is often the cause of his downfall.

The Witch *(see also Wicked Queen)*

In French: la Sorcière.

Year of birth: 1937 in the film *Snow White and the Seven Dwarfs.*

Profile: The Wicked Queen transformed herself into the Witch by means of a magic potion.
She is a bent-over old woman dressed in black with bulging eyes, toothless gums, and hooked nose with a wart. Will Snow White be moved by this poor old woman who wants to give her an apple?

Where to find the Witch? In **Blanche-Neige et les Sept Nains** (Snow White and the Seven Dwarfs).

Winnie the Pooh   Tigger

Sightseeing
in the area

This guide is not intended
to give readers
a detailed description of the sights of Paris.
Nonetheless,
it will allow them to form
an idea of the city through brief descriptions
of the main attractions
for which Paris is famous *(in alphabetical order)*.

For further information,
consult the Michelin Green Guide to Paris in English.

Likewise,
the section entitled Trips in the Vicinity
covers a selection of sights within easy reach
of Disneyland Paris
for tourists with only a limited
amount of time available.
It gives some idea
of the wealth of sights in the area.

For further information,
consult the Michelin Green Guides Flanders, Picardy
and the Paris Region in English
and Ile-de-France and Champagne Ardennes in French.

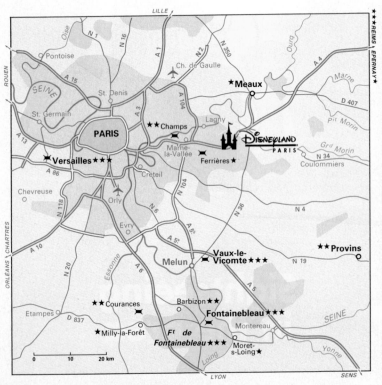

▲ PARIS ▲

HOW TO GET THERE FROM DISNEYLAND PARIS

By car – The A4 motorway.

RER and the métro – Journey time from Marne-la-Vallée-Chessy station to Paris is about 35min. Price of a Rtn ticket: 74F (includes travel on the métro). First train leaves for Paris at 05.14. Trains run every 10-30mins depending on the time of day. Last train leaves Paris (Charles-de-Gaulle-Étoile station) at 00.30 (arrives at Marne-la-Vallée-Chessy at 01.20). For information, call ☎ 43 46 14 14.

SPECIAL RATES

Transport

Within Paris you need only one ticket for any métro trip, no matter what the distance (7F). For journeys outside the Paris city limits (roughly defined as the Boulevard Périphérique) you must pay a supplement before you begin the trip (there is no "excess fare" facility at the end of your journey).
Paris-Visite Ticket: 2 types, 3 consecutive days 200F or 5 consecutive days 275F. These tickets permit unlimited travel on all Parisian public transport: métro, bus and RER, and on SNCF trains in Paris and the Ile-de-France zones 1-5 (Disneyland Paris is in zone 5). Tickets may be purchased at RER and métro stations.

Museums and Monuments Pass

3 types: 1 day: 60F; 3 consecutive days: 120F; 5 consecutive days: 170F.
These tickets give access without queuing at 65 museums and monuments in Paris and the Paris region. In the following pages, the museums and monuments accessible with this ticket are marked with the symbol 🐾.
Tickets may be purchased at museums and monuments, larger métro stations and at the tourist office.

ORGANIZED TOURS

Bus tours – Time: approximately 2 hours.
Paris Vision, 214 Rue de Rivoli (1st). *Métro Tuileries.* ☎ 42 60 31 25.
Cityrama, 147 Rue St-Honoré (1st). *Métro St-Philippe-du-Roule.* ☎ 44 55 61 00.

Boat trips on the Seine – Interesting and unusual views of the city.

- **Bateaux-Mouches:** embarkation Pont de l'Alma, right bank. *Métro Alma-Marceau.* ☎ 42 25 96 10. Cruises from 10.00 to 23.00 on the half hour; time: 1 hour 15 min; 40F, children under 14: 20F. Restaurant on board.

- **Bateaux Parisiens Tour Eiffel:** Port de la Bourdonnais, left bank (16th). *Métro Trocadéro, RER Champ de Mars.* ☎ 47 05 50 00. Guided cruises, departures on the hour, from 10.00 to 21.00; time 1 hour; 45F, children 20F. Lunch cruise: departure 12.15; adult price: 300F, children: 200F. Dinner cruise: departure 20.30; adult price: 550F.

- **Bateaux Parisiens Notre-Dame:** Quai de Montebello. *Métro and RER Saint-Michel.* ☎ 43 26 92 55. Guided cruises, Easter to 11 November, departures on the hour: 10.00 to 22.00; time: 1 hour.

- **Bateaux Vedettes du Pont Neuf:** Square du Vert Galant (4th). *Métro Pont Neuf.* ☎ 46 33 98 38. Guided cruises, departures:10.30, 11.15, 12.00. Sunday departures: 10.30, 11.15, 12.00, and 14.00 to 17.00 on the half hour; time: 1 hour; 40F, children under 10: 20F.

- **Bateaux Vedettes de Paris-Ile-de-France:** Port de Suffren, left bank (15th). *Métro Bir-Hakeim, RER Champ de Mars.* ☎ 47 05 71 29 and 45 50 23 79. Cruise departures from 10.00 to 19.00; 40F, children: 20F.

Paris en Images – An audiovisual show on a panoramic screen (headsets available for soundtrack in languages other than French) which traces the history of the city and its monuments from the days of Lutetia to contemporary Paris.

Paristoric: Espace Hébertot, 78bis Boulevard des Batignolles (17th). *Métro Rome.* Hourly from 09.00 to 18.00 (21.00 on Fridays and Saturdays); 70F, children: 40F; ☎ 42 93 93 46.

TOURIST EVENTS AND SHOWS

Consult the calendar published every year by the Tourist Office, Accueil de France (127 Avenue des Champs-Elysées, ☎ 49 52 53 54) and *l'Officiel des Spectacles* (2F) or *Pariscope* (3F) published Wednesdays.

From the Arc de Triomphe

to reach the Champs-Elysées, take bus 73, or métro line 1 direction Château de Vincennes (Franklin D. Roosevelt station).

From the Champs-Elysées

to reach Concorde, take bus 73, or métro line 1 direction Château de Vincennes (Concorde station).

From Concorde

to reach the Louvre, take bus 72, or métro line 1 direction Château de Vincennes (Palais Royal-Musée du Louvre station).
to reach the Musée d'Orsay, take bus 94, or métro line 12 direction Mairie d'Issy (Solferino station).

From Les Halles-Beaubourg

to reach Notre-Dame, take métro line 4 direction Porte d'Orléans (Cité station).

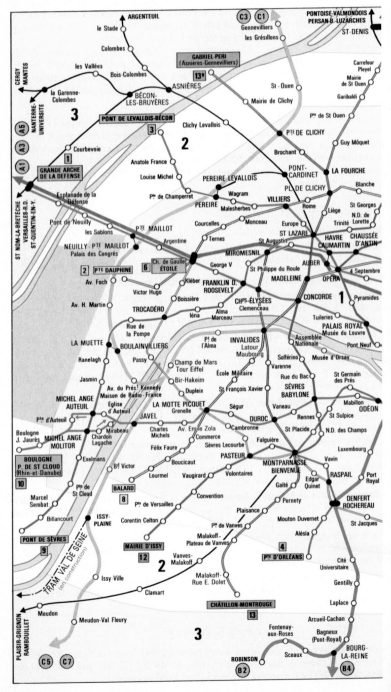

From the Invalides

to get to the Eiffel tower, take RER line C direction Versailles Saint-Quentin (Champ-de-Mars Tour Eiffel station).

From the Louvre

to reach the Beaubourg quarter and the Marais, take bus 76, or métro line 1 direction Château de Vincennes (Châtelet, Hôtel de Ville or Saint-Paul stations).

From the Opéra

to reach the Louvre, take bus 27, or métro line 7 direction Mairie d'Ivry (Palais Royal-Musée du Louvre station).

From the Musée d'Orsay

to reach the Invalides, take bus 63, or RER line C direction Versailles Saint-Quentin (Invalides station).

From the Eiffel tower

to reach the Trocadéro, take bus 82 as far as Iéna then bus 32 or 63, or métro line 6 direction Charles-de-Gaulle-Étoile (Trocadéro station).

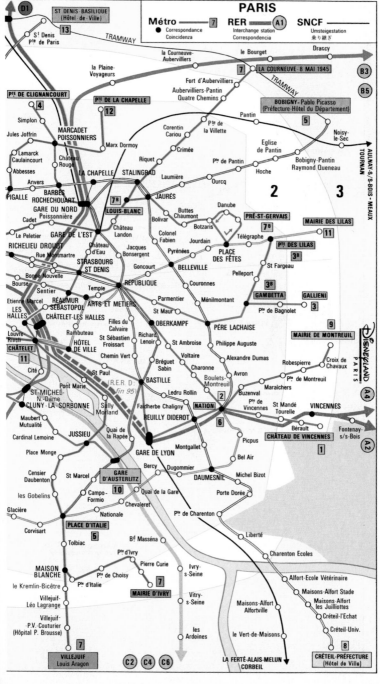

Families visiting the capital city, take your children:

– to the **Eiffel tower**★★★ *(p 135)*;

– to the **Musée Grévin**★ (waxworks, historical scenes): 10 Boulevard Montmartre (9th), *métro Rue Montmartre; open daily 13.00 to 19.00 (opens 10.00 on holidays and school holidays); 48F; children 6 to 14: 34F;* ☎ *42 46 13 26*;

– to the **Espace Grévin**★ at the **Forum des Halles** (1st) (waxworks, historical scenes): level-1, *métro Les Halles; open weekdays 10.30 to 18.45, Sundays and holidays 13.00 to 18.30; 42F, children 6 to 14: 32F;* ☎ *40 26 28 50*;

– to the **Palais de la Découverte**★★ (popular science, planetarium): Avenue Franklin D. Roosevelt (8th), *métro Franklin D. Roosevelt; open 09.30 to 18.00 (10.00 to 19.00 on Sundays and holidays); closed Mondays; 22F; reduced rate 11F;* ☎ *40 74 80 00*;

– on the **bateaux-mouches** *(p 119)*.

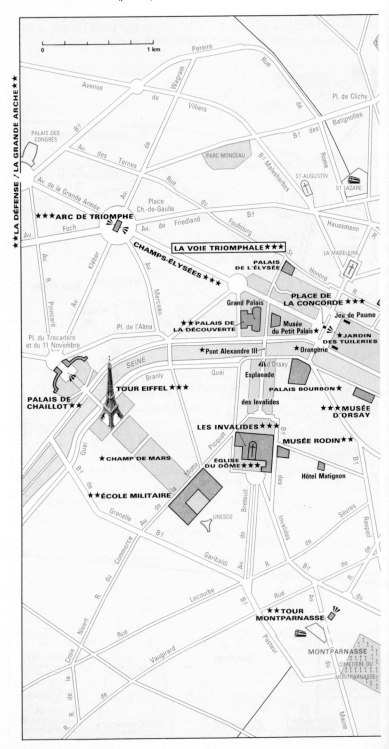

Useful bus routes

Bus 72 (Pont de Saint-Cloud - Hôtel de Ville). Along the right bank: Alma-Marceau, Grand Palais, Concorde, Palais Royal, Louvre, Châtelet and Hôtel de Ville.

Bus 73 (La Défense – Musée d'Orsay). Route includes: Charles-de-Gaulle-Étoile, Champs-Elysées, Concorde and Musée d'Orsay.

Balabus: discover Paris by bus, 3 April to 25 September, on Sundays and public holidays 12.30 to 20.00. Bus stops at: Gare de Lyon, Saint-Michel, Louvre, Musée d'Orsay, Concorde, Champs-Élysées, Charles-de-Gaulle-Étoile, Porte Maillot, Pont de Neuilly and La Défense (only bus stops marked "**Bb**").

Parisbus: a red double-decker bus which stops at Trocadéro, Tour Eiffel, Champ-de-Mars, Musée du Louvre, Notre-Dame, Musée d'Orsay, Opéra, Champs-Élysées-Étoile and Grand Palais. Ticket valid for 2 days.

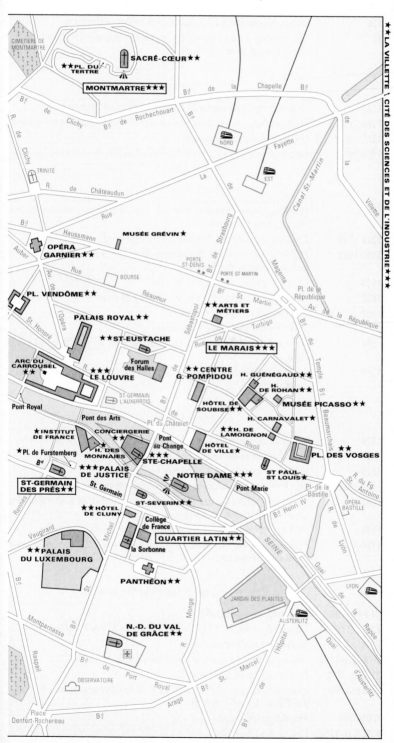

HISTORICAL FACTS

Gallo-Roman period and Early Middle Ages

3C BC	The Parisii settle on the Ile de la Cité.
52 BC	Labienus, Caesar's lieutenant, defeats the Gauls under Camulogenes; the Gauls set the Ile de la Cité on fire and abandon it.
1C AD	The Gallo-Romans build the city of Lutetia.
280	Barbarians destroy Lutetia.
360	Lutetia becomes Paris.
451	St Geneviève turns Attila away from Paris.
508	Clovis makes Paris his capital and settles in the Cité.
8C	Charlemagne sets himself up in Aix-la-Chapelle (Aachen). Paris, abandoned, declines.

The Capetians

1163	Maurice de Sully undertakes construction of Notre-Dame.
1180-1223	Philippe Auguste erects a wall around Paris and builds the Louvre.
1215	University of Paris founded.
1226-1270	Reign of St Louis. Pierre de Montreuil builds the Sainte-Chapelle.

The Valois

1358	Uprising under Étienne Marcel. The monarchy moves to the Marais and the Louvre.
1364-1380	Charles V builds the Bastille and a new wall around Paris.
1408-1420	Fighting between the Armagnacs and the Burgundians. Paris is handed over to the English.
1429	Charles VII besieges Paris in vain.
1430	Henry VI of England is crowned King of France in Notre-Dame.
1437	Charles VII recaptures Paris.
1572	St Bartholomew's Day Massacre.
1588	The Catholic League turns against Henri III who is forced to flee Paris.
1589	Paris is invested by Henri of Navarre and Henri III, who is assassinated.

The Bourbons

1594	Henri IV converts to Catholicism: Paris opens her gates to him.
1622	Paris becomes an episcopal see.
1635	Richelieu founds the Académie Française.
1648-1653	The Fronde, a revolution against absolutism, stirs Paris.
1667	Colbert establishes the Observatoire and the Manufacture des Gobelins (tapestry factory).
1722	First fire brigade, the Compagnie de Pompiers, created.
1784-1791	Erection of the farmers general city wall, the Enceinte des Fermiers Généraux.

The Revolution and the First Empire

14 July 1789	Storming of the Bastille.
17 July 1789	Louis XVI at the Hôtel de Ville: adoption of the tricolour.
14 July 1790	Festival of the Fédération.
10 August 1792	Taking of the Tuileries and the fall of the monarchy.
21 Sept. 1792	Proclamation of the Republic.
21 Jan. 1793	Execution of Louis XVI on the Place de la Révolution, which is now the Place de la Concorde.
1793-1794	The Reign of Terror.
9-10 Nov. 1799	Fall of the Directoire.

1800	Bonaparte creates the offices of the Prefect of the Seine and of the Police.
2 Dec. 1804	Napoleon's coronation at Notre-Dame.
1806-1814	Napoleon continues construction of the Louvre and erects the Arc de Triomphe and the Colonne Vendôme.
31 March 1814	The Allies occupy Paris.

The Restoration

2 May 1814	Louis XVIII signs the Charter of St-Ouen.
1830	The Three Glorious Days (27, 28 and 29 July) overthrow Charles X.
1832	A cholera epidemic kills 19 000 Parisians.
1837	The first French railway line opens, Paris-St-Germain.
1840	Return of Napoleon's remains.
Feb. 1848	Fall of Louis-Philippe. Proclamation of the Second Republic.

From 1848 to 1870

June 1848	Suppression of the national workshops causes riots in the Faubourg St-Antoine. End of the 1848 Revolution.
1852-1870	Major restructuring of the city under the supervision of Baron Haussmann.
1855, 1867	World Exhibitions.
4 Sept. 1870	Proclamation of the Third Republic at the Hôtel de Ville.

The Third Republic

Winter 1870-1871	Paris, besieged by the Prussians, capitulates.
March-May 1871	The Paris Commune is repressed.
1889	The World Exhibition around the Eiffel tower.
1900	First métro line opens : Maillot-Vincennes. The Sacré-Coeur basilica is erected on the Butte Montmartre.
June 1940	Paris is bombed, then occupied by the Germans.
19-26 Aug. 1944	Liberation of Paris.

Since 1945

1964	Reorganization of the Paris region : Nanterre, Créteil and Bobigny become *préfectures*.
May 1968	Demonstrations (Nanterre, Quartier Latin, the Boulevards and Champs-Élysées).
25 March 1977	Election of the 12th mayor of Paris (Jacques Chirac), the first mayor elected by the Parisians themselves since 1871. Eleven appointees bore the title between 1789 and 1871.
1989	Commemoration of the French Revolution Bicentenary along with the inauguration of the Grande Arche de la Defense and the new Opéra-Bastille.
1992	The quays along the Seine and the famous views of the Concorde, the Madeleine, the Assemblée Nationale, the Pont Alexandre-III, the Invalides, the Champ-de-Mars and the Palais de Chaillot are acknowledged by the World Heritage scheme.

A capital at the forefront of contemporary art and architecture

Paris has a wealth of striking examples of

Buildings: *Forum des Halles, Centre Georges-Pompidou, the Cité des Sciences et de l'Industrie at La Villette, the Institut du Monde Arabe, Opéra-Bastille, the Louvre pyramid and the Grande Arche at La Défense.*

Sculptures: *Jacques Monestier's animated clock, Le Défenseur du Temps, in the Horloge quarter north of the Centre Georges-Pompidou; César's Centaure at the intersection of Rue du Cherche-Midi and Rue du Four; as well as the open-air sculpture museums at Quai St-Bernard near the Institut du Monde Arabe and on the podium at La Défense.*

Fountains: *Canyone australe by Singer near the Palais Omnisports de Bercy-Paris; the inclined circular Creuset du Temps on Place de Catalogne overlooked by Ricardo Bofill's neo-classical façades; and the entertaining, perpetual motion of the colourful Stravinsky fountain on Place Igor Stravinsky near the Centre Georges-Pompidou.*

PICTURESQUE PARIS

PARIS VIEWED FROM ABOVE

Montparnasse tower - 33 Avenue du Maine (15th). *Métro Montparnasse-Bienvenüe.* ☎ *45 38 52 56. 59th floor: the highest terrace in Paris; 56th floor: covered look-out; open 1 April to 30 September 09.30 to 23.30; 1 October to 31 March 09.30 to 22.30 (23.00 on Fridays, Saturdays, and the eve of public holidays); last ascent half an hour before closing; 40F; children 24F* .

Eiffel tower – *Description p 135.*

The Arc de Triomphe viewing platform – *Description p 130.*

Notre-Dame towers – *Description p 149.*

Sacré-Cœur dome – *Description p 147.*

Cafés and restaurants with panoramic views:

– **Centre Georges-Pompidou Restaurant**, Rue Rambuteau (4th). *Métro Rambuteau, RER Châtelet-Les Halles.* ☎ *44 78 12 33. Open 12.00 to 22.00; closed Tuesdays.* 5th floor fast-food terrace restaurant.

– **Galeries Lafayette Restaurants**, 40 Boulevard Haussmann (9th). *Métro Chaussée-d'Antin, RER Auber. Store open Mondays to Saturdays 09.30 to 19.00 (late-night shopping Thursdays, until 21.00);* ☎ *42 82 34 56.* 8th floor: panoramic terrace restaurant.

The Palais de Chaillot seen from the Eiffel tower

VIEWS

Champs-Élysées – *Métro Charles-de-Gaulle-Étoile, George V, Franklin D. Roosevelt and Champs-Élysées-Clemenceau.* Stretching from the Arc de Triomphe to Concorde, the Triumphal Way is one of the most magnificent vistas of the capital.

Place de la Concorde – *Métro Concorde.* The obelisk platform in the centre of the square affords a view in two directions and gives an astonishing sense of space in the heart of Paris.
The east-west view is of the Jardin des Tuileries and the Champs-Élysées up to the Arc de Triomphe. The north-south view looks towards the façades of the Madeleine church and the Palais Bourbon.

Palais de Chaillot – *Métro Trocadéro.* From the terrace of the Palais de Chaillot, the view extends across the Seine and past the Eiffel tower to the gardens of the Champ-de-Mars and the École Militaire.

Pont Alexandre-III – *Métro Invalides.* To the south the view is of the Invalides esplanade which stretches up to the elegant façade of the hôtel of the same name.

PARIS VIEWED FROM THE BRIDGES

Certain bridges over the Seine provide unusual and picturesque views of Paris.

Pont des Arts – *Métro Louvre-Rivoli or Cité.* View of the Ile de la Cité.

Pont au Change – *Métro Cité.* View of the Conciergerie.

Pont Marie – *Métro Pont Marie.* View of the Ile St-Louis.

Pont Royal – *RER Musée d'Orsay.* View of the Louvre, the Musée d'Orsay and Quai Voltaire.

On the terrace of the Café de Flore

FAMOUS CAFÉS

With their historic settings, these cafés boast true Parisian atmosphere.

Le Flore – 172 Boulevard St-Germain (6th). *Métro St-Germain des Prés*. The Flore is favoured by artists and intellectuals.

Café de la Paix – 12 Boulevard des Capucines (9th). *Métro Opéra*. The terraces of this well-known café are an international meeting place.

Le Procope – 13 Rue de l'Ancienne Comédie (6th). *Métro Odéon*. Since its foundation in 1686 the Procope has always been the haunt of writers, poets, revolutionaries and philosophers.

La Coupole – 102 Boulevard du Montparnasse (14th). *Métro Vavin*. One of the Montparnasse cafés where talk went on for hours and Russian political exiles, musicians, artists and poets met.

UNIQUELY PARISIAN

Arcades – Mostly built at the end of the 18C or beginning of the 19C, these covered passages shelter boutiques, some of which are falling into disrepair.

- **Passage des Panoramas:** 11 Boulevard Montmartre (2nd). *Métro Rue Montmartre*.
- **Passage Choiseul:** 23 Rue St-Augustin (2nd). *Métro 4-Septembre*.
- **Passage des Princes:** 97 Rue de Richelieu (2nd). *Métro Palais Royal-Musée du Louvre*.
- **Galerie Vivienne:** 4 Rue des Petits-Champs (2nd). *Métro Bourse*.

Book stalls – Along the quays, from the Pont du Carrousel to the Pont Sully. Old books, engravings and reproductions.

Markets – Among the most picturesque and original:

- **the market at Place d'Aligre** *(daily; métro Ledru Rollin)*,
- **flea markets:** Porte de Vanves *(weekends; métro Porte de Vanves)*, Porte de Clignancourt *(Saturdays, Sundays and Mondays; métro Porte de Clignancourt)*; Porte de Montreuil *(Saturdays, Sundays and Mondays; métro Porte de Montreuil)*,
- **the stamp market:** corner of Avenues Marigny and Gabriel *(Thursdays, Saturdays, Sundays, and holidays; métro Champs-Élysées-Clemenceau)*,
- **the flower markets:** Place Louis-Lépine *(daily except Sundays; métro Cité)*, Place de la Madeleine *(daily except Mondays; métro Madeleine)* and Place des Ternes *(daily except Mondays; métro Ternes)*,
- **the bird market:** place Louis-Lépine *(Sundays; métro Cité)*,
- **the Carreau du Temple:** *(09.00 to 12.00, or 12.30 at weekends; closed Mondays; métro Temple)*.

Remember! The price of a drink in a French café may vary depending on whether you are standing "au bar" (cheapest), sitting inside "en salle", or sitting outside "à la terrasse" (most expensive).

SHOPPING IN PARIS

LUXURY BOUTIQUES

These are concentrated in a few quarters whose very names evoke the luxury of Paris.

Champs-Élysées

Access: métro George V (exit near the Arc de Triomphe end of the Champs-Élysées); métro Franklin D. Roosevelt (exit midway) and métro Champs-Élysées Clemenceau (exit near Concorde end). The Champs-Élysées is very long; therefore, it is advisable that you get out at Franklin D. Roosevelt station to walk up the Champs-Élysées to the Arc de Triomphe (this is the stretch where the shops are).
All along the avenue, as well as along the neighbouring streets (notably Avenue Montaigne where grand couturiers such as *Céline, Chanel, Dior* and *Nina Ricci* have set up shop), luxury boutiques compete with each other through their sumptuous windows displaying fashion, perfumes, and leather goods. But there are also stores offering more moderately priced articles.

Opéra/Madeleine/Place Vendôme

Grand couturiers and ready-to-wear boutiques – Rue du Faubourg-St-Honoré *(Courrèges, Hermès, Lagerfeld and Lanvin)*.
Jewellery – Place Vendôme *(Chanel, Van Cleef & Arpels, Boucheron and Chaumet)*, Rue de la Paix *(Cartier)*.
Leather goods – Place de l'Opéra *(Lancel)*, Rue du Faubourg-St-Honoré *(Hermès)*.
Tableware – Rue Royale *(Bernardaud, Cristalleries St-Louis and Lalique, and Christofle)*, Place de la Madeleine *(Baccarat)*.
Perfume – 24 Rue du Faubourg-St-Honoré *(Hermès)*, Rue Tronchet *(Guerlain)*.

MAJOR DEPARTMENT STORES

These are undoubtedly the ideal solution for a tourist with little time. The most famous names in fashion, perfume and leather goods are found under one roof.
Tax refunds:
– If you live outside the European Union and spend 2000F or more, you are entitled to a refund of 13%.
Printemps – 64 Boulevard Haussmann (9th). *Métro Havre-Caumartin.* ☎ 42 82 50 00. *Open Mondays to Saturdays 09.30 to 19.00 (late night shopping on Thursdays until 22.00).* 6th floor: restaurant, bar, salon de thé.
Galeries Lafayette – 40 Boulevard Haussmann (9th). *Métro Chaussée d'Antin.* ☎ 42 82 34 56. Information in English. ☎ 42 82 36 40. *Open Mondays to Saturdays 09.30 to 19.00. 6th floor: self-service restaurant and tea room; 8th floor: panoramic terrace restaurant.*
Samaritaine – 19 Rue de la Monnaie (1st). ☎ 40 41 20 20. *Métro Pont-Neuf. Open Mondays to Saturdays 09.30 to 19.00 (22.00 on Thursdays).*
Bazar de l'Hôtel de Ville – 52 Rue de Rivoli (4th). ☎ 42 74 90 00. *Métro Hôtel-de-Ville. Open Mondays to Saturdays 09.30 to 19.00 (22.00 on Wednesdays).*
Au Bon Marché – 22 Rue de Sèvres (7th). ☎ 44 39 80 00. *Métro Sèvres-Babylone. Open Mondays to Saturdays 09.30 to 19.00.*

For more everyday items:
Prisunic – *(one of a chain)* 109 Rue de la Boétie (8th). ☎ 42 25 27 46. *Métro Franklin D. Roosevelt. Open Mondays to Saturdays 09.00 to 24.00.*

And for homesick Brits…
Marks and Spencer – 35 Boulevard Haussman (9th). ☎ 47 42 42 91. *Métro Havre-Caumartin. Open Mondays to Saturdays from 09.30 (10.00 Tuesdays) to 19.00 (20.00 Thursdays).* 88 Rue de Rivoli (4th). ☎ 44 61 08 00. *Métro Châtelet. Open Mondays to Saturdays from 09.30 to 19.30 (22.00 on Wednesdays).*

SHOPPING CENTRES AND MALLS

Arcades on the Champs-Élysées – On the north side of the Champs-Élysées between Rond-Point des Champs-Élysées and Rue de Berri. *Métro George V or Franklin D Roosevelt.*
Carrousel du Louvre – Luxury boutiques beneath the Louvre. *Métro Palais Royal - Musée du Louvre.*
Forum des Halles – *Métro Les Halles, RER Châtelet-Les Halles.*
Maine-Montparnasse – *Métro Montparnasse-Bienvenüe.*

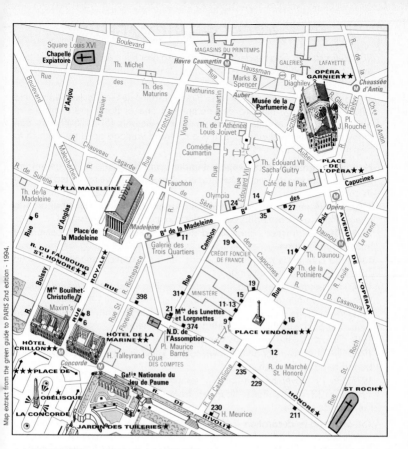

ANTIQUES - ART GALLERIES

Remember: art galleries and antique dealers are generally not open before 10.30 and close for lunch (12.00 to 14.00). Works of art are not eligible for tax refunds.

Le Louvre des Antiquaires – 2 Place du Palais Royal (1st). *Métro Palais Royal-Musée du Louvre.*

Carré Rive Gauche – Rues du Bac, de Beaune, de Lille, de l'Université, des St-Pères and Quai Voltaire (7th).

Le Village Suisse – 54 Avenue de la Motte Picquet (15th). *Métro La Motte-Picquet-Grenelle.*

Art Galleries – Rue du Faubourg-St-Honoré and Avenue Matignon (8th).

GOURMET SHOPS

Traiteurs (gourmet grocers) – Fauchon: 26 Place de la Madeleine (8th) ☏ 47 42 60 11, and Hédiard: 21 Place de la Madeleine (8th) ☏ 42 66 00 64. *Métro Madeleine.* Comtesse du Barry: 13 Rue Taitbout (9th) ☏ 47 70 21 01. *Métro Chaussée d'Antin.*

Wine – Legrand: 1 Rue de la Banque (2nd) ☏ 42 61 25 51. *Métro Bourse*

Cheese – La Ferme St-Hubert: 21 Rue Vignon (8th) ☏ 47 42 79 20. *Métro Madeleine.*

Bread – Poilâne: 8 Rue du Cherche-Midi (6th) ☏ 45 48 42 59. *Métro St-Sulpice.*

Pâtisserie – Lenôtre: 3-5 Rue du Havre (8th) ☏ 45 22 22 59. *Métro St-Lazare.*

Ice cream – Berthillon: 31 Rue St Louis-en-l'Ile (4th). ☏ 43 54 31 61. *Métro Pont-Marie.*

E. Baret

The ARC DE TRIOMPHE★★★

RER-métro station Charles-de-Gaulle-Étoile. To reach the Arc de Triomphe take the underground passage which starts from the north pavement of the Champs-Élysées.

Rising from the centre of the vast Place Charles-de-Gaulle (known as the "Étoile", or "star"), the Arc de Triomphe is one of Paris' most impressive examples of 19C architecture. From its lofty heights (50m-164ft) you can enjoy an excellent view of Paris; it is a splendid vantage point from which to begin a tour of Paris.

Napoleon's great project completed under Louis-Philippe – At the end of the 18C the square was already star-shaped although only five roads led out from its centre.

1806: Napoleon commissioned the construction of a giant triumphal arch to honour the French armed forces. Chalgrin was selected to design it.

1832-1836: Construction, abandoned during the Restoration, was completed under Louis-Philippe.

1840: The chariot bearing the Emperor's remains passed beneath the Arc de Triomphe in a moving ceremony.

1854: Haussmann redesigned the square, creating seven new avenues. Hittorff designed the uniform façades of the buildings surrounding the arch.

1885: Victor Hugo's body lay in state for one night beneath the crêpe-draped arch. The poet was then transported to the Panthéon.

1919: On 14 July the victorious troops paraded through the arch.

1920: On 11 November an unknown soldier killed in the First World War was buried beneath the arch.

1923: On 11 November the flame of remembrance was lit for the first time.

1944: On 23 August Paris, liberated from German occupation, acclaimed General de Gaulle.

The arch and its decoration – Although the arch was inspired by Antiquity, it is colossal compared with its Antique forebears (twice as high as the Arch of Constantine in Rome). It is designed with reliefs relating the major military events of the Revolution and the Empire, of which Rude's sculpture group on the right leg of the arch facing the Champs-Elysées, *The Departure of the Volunteers in 1792*, is the most famous. Beneath the monument, the Tomb of the Unknown Soldier pays homage to anonymous victims of the War. Each evening at 18.30 the flame of remembrance is rekindled.

The Viewing Platform ▧ – *Open daily 09.30 to 18.30 (10.00 to 17.00 1 October to 31 March); closed 1 January, 1 and 8 May, 14 July, 1 and 11 November, 25 December; 31F, 7 to 17 year-olds: 7F; lift. ☎ 43 80 31 31.* From the platform there is an excellent **view★★★** of the capital city with the twelve avenues radiating from the square in the foreground. The arch stands on the highest point of the Triumphal Way and away to the west there is a lovely view of La Défense with its own huge arch. A small museum houses a variety of documents and mementoes relating to the construction of the arch.

To reach the Champs-Élysées from the Arc de Triomphe take bus 73, or métro line 1 direction Château de Vincennes (get out at Franklin D. Roosevelt station).

The Champs-Elysées and the Arc de Triomphe

The CHAMPS-ÉLYSÉES★★★

RER station Charles-de-Gaulle-Étoile (Arc de Triomphe level); métro line 1: stations George V, Franklin D. Roosevelt (halfway down the avenue), Champs-Élysées Clemenceau (Rond-Point des Champs-Élysées level).

The Champs-Élysées is known for its spectacular view, for being an ideal place for strolling and sightseeing, and for its luxury shops.

Beginnings – Under Henri IV the area was nothing but fields and swamps. In 1616 Marie de Medici created the Cours la Reine, a long avenue lined with trees which began at the Tuileries and followed the Seine to the present day Place de l'Alma. It became a fashionable place for carriage rides.

In 1667 Le Nôtre lengthened the Tuileries' vista; the entire expanse called the Great Way (grand cours) was planted with rows of trees. In 1709 this calm and shady area became known as the Champs-Élysées (Elysian Fields). In 1724 the duc d'Antin, Director of the Royal Gardens, extended the avenue all the way to the Chaillot Mound (today the star-shaped Place Charles-de-Gaulle-Étoile). His successor, the marquis de Marigny, continued the avenue to Neuilly Bridge (1772). Two years later, Soufflot, to reduce the slope of the avenue, lowered the Chaillot butte by more than 5m - 16ft.

In fashion – At the end of the 18C the Champs-Élysées was still a deserted wilderness with only six private mansions. The Allies, occupying France in 1814, divided up the city's green areas with the Prussians and English camping in the Tuileries and on the Place de la Concorde, while the Cossacks bivouacked under the trees of the Champs-Élysées. It took two years to repair the damage.

The avenue, under the care of the City by 1828, was beautified with fountains, paths, gas lights, and by the presence of the rich, especially during the Second Empire. Under the eyes of the curious cavaliers, their escorts riding side-saddle, tilburies and broughams circulated in a cloud of dust. Café orchestras (among them the Alcazar rebuilt in 1840 by Hittorff), the restaurants, the views, and the circuses attracted an elegant crowd, all the more numerous when there were meetings at Longchamp or during the World Exhibitions of 1855, 1867 and 1900. In the gallant Widows Alley (now Avenue Montaigne), the Mabille ball attracted Parisian high society until 1870. Under 3000 gas lights, Olivier Metra conducted polkas and mazurkas with gay abandon. Nearby in the Winter Garden, the musician Sax played his new instrument, the saxophone.

The Rond-Point to Concorde – This is the green section of the Champs-Élysées. Bordered by English gardens, it still retains today its avenues lined with handsome chestnut trees and the occasional pavilion. Overlooking Place de la Concorde are two marble groups, the **Marly Horses** (1745), by Guillaume Coustou (1745) (originals in the Louvre).

Heart of the nation – Today little of the aristocratic remains, but the avenue has lost neither its sparkle nor its attraction. The military parade of 14 July attracts an immense crowd every year. At times of great national emotion the people of Paris assemble spontaneously on the Triumphal Way. Some examples were the procession of the Liberation of 26 August 1944, the demonstration of 30 May 1968, and the silent march in honour of General de Gaulle of 12 November 1970.

THE QUARTER

This residential area is among the most luxurious of the city. Many headquarters of national and international firms are located here, as well as embassies and ministries.

Petit Palais and Grand Palais – Built for the World Exhibition of 1900 (like the Pont Alexandre-III), they now play a cultural role.

Today the **Petit Palais** houses the **Museum of the Petit Palais★** ▥ (Avenue W. Churchill, *métro Champs-Élysées-Clemenceau. Open 10.00 to 17.40; closed Mondays and holidays; 27F; free on Sundays;* ☎ *42 65 12 73)* containing among other things a large collection of 19C works, rich in sculpture and official decorations.

Opposite the Petit Palais, the **Grand Palais** houses temporary exhibits.
☎ *42 89 23 13.*

Palais de l'Élysée – Since 1873 the Palais de l'Élysée has been the residence of France's presidents.

To reach Concorde from the Champs-Élysées take bus 73, or métro line 1 direction Château de Vincennes (get out at Concorde station).

★★★PLACE DE LA CONCORDE

Métro : Concorde

Place de la Concorde is renowned for its impressive size, elegance and its location as the transition point between the Champs-Élysées and the Tuileries.

The square passes from Royalty to the nation – The aldermen of Paris, hoping to curry favour with Louis XV, commissioned Bouchardon to sculpt an equestrian statue of the Well Beloved and organized a competition to find an architect for the square. Servandoni, Soufflot and Gabriel submitted plans; Gabriel won. The octagonal area covering 84 000m^2 - 21 acres was bordered by a dry moat and balustrades. Eight massive pedestals intended to support statues were placed in the corners. Twin edifices with beautiful colonnades flanked the Rue Royale. Work continued from 1755 to 1775.

In 1770 during a fireworks display celebrating the marriage of the Dauphin and Marie-Antoinette, the crowd panicked, and 133 people were crushed to death in the moats. In 1792, the royal statue was toppled and the Place Louis XV became the Place de la Révolution.

Place de la Concorde and the Palais Bourbon

On 21 January 1793 a guillotine was erected near where the statue of the city of Brest now stands for the execution of Louis XVI. From 13 May onwards, the "nation's razor", which had been moved to near the entrance gate of the Tuileries, gave 1 343 victims the chop, among them Marie-Antoinette, Mme du Barry, Charlotte Corday, the Girondins, Danton and his friends, Mme Roland who before she died cried out : "Liberty, what crimes we commit in your name!", and Robespierre and his supporters.

The last heads rolled in 1795. The Directory, motivated by hope for the future, renamed the bloody spot Place de la Concorde. The Concorde bridge opened in 1790. The architect Hittorff completed the square's decoration under Louis-Philippe. Because the central statue might arouse contention when a regime changed, the King replaced it with a non-political monument, an obelisk. Two foun-

tains, inspired by those in St Peter's Square in Rome, were installed. Eight statues of French cities top the pedestals set out by Gabriel. Cortot sculpted Brest and Rouen. Pradier sculpted Lille and Strasbourg. Juliette Drouet modelled for this last statue at whose foot Deroulede gathered patriots when Strasbourg fell to the Germans. Lyon and Marseille are by Petitot and Bordeaux and Nantes by Caillouette.

*Obelisk (Obélisque) – The obelisk comes from the ruins of the temple at Luxor. Mohammed Ali, Viceroy of Egypt, seeking support from France, offered it in 1829 to Charles X although it did not arrive in Paris until 1833 under Louis-Philippe.
This pink granite monument, 33 centuries old, is covered in hieroglyphics. The pedestal of the 23m-75ft tall 220-ton monolith depicts how it was transported and erected.

***Views – Views of the Champs-Élysées, the Madeleine church and the Palais Bourbon, seat of France's house of representatives, the Assemblée Nationale.

**The two mansions – Imposing but not overbearing, they stand on either side of the entrance to Rue Royale. Inspired by Perrault's colonnades at the Louvre, Gabriel created these still more elegant colonnades which are fine examples of early Louis XVI style.
To the right, the Hôtel de la Marine served as the royal store, becoming the Admiralty Office in 1792. It is now the Navy Headquarters.

The mansion across the street was at first occupied by four noblemen. Today it houses the French Automobile Club and the internationally acclaimed Hôtel Crillon.

The two buildings are flanked by the United States Embassy on the left and the Hôtel Talleyrand, designed in the 18C by Chalgrin for the duc de la Vrillière on the right. Talleyrand died there in 1838.

*THE JARDIN DES TUILERIES

Métro Tuileries

Magnificently situated on the banks of the Seine, the Tuileries gardens epitomise the French style of garden design. From the terrace you have a sweeping view of the gardens, the Seine and part of the Louvre.

The first garden – In the 15C the area was used as a public dump by butchers and tawers of the Châtelet district. The clay soil was used for making tiles (*tuiles*), hence the name Tuileries.

In 1563, when the Queen Mother Catherine de' Medici decided to build a residence next to the Louvre, she had an Italian-style garden laid out. It included fountains, a maze, a grotto decorated with terracotta figures by Bernard Palissy, and a menagerie. Under Henri IV the park became a fashionable place to be seen.

Le Nôtre French Garden – Colbert entrusted the embellishment of the park to Le Nôtre in 1664. To level the sloping land, the King's gardener raised two terraces of unequal height lengthways across the garden. He created the magnificent central alley view, dug basins and laid out flower beds, the quincunxes and the slopes.

Colbert was so pleased with the result that he wanted the gardens reserved for the royal family, but his adviser in matters of art and letters, Charles Perrault – the writer of popular tales – persuaded him that the park should also be enjoyed by the public.

The Revolution – When rioters invaded on 10 August 1792, Louis XVI and his family fled the Palais des Tuileries, crossed the garden, and climbed the stairs (facing Rue Castiglione) to seek refuge with the National Assembly, then in session in the Manège (Riding School). The Swiss Guards who had been ordered by the king to cease fire also tried to escape through the Park but two-thirds of them were massacred.

The Festival of the Supreme Being organized by the painter David took place in the park on 8 June 1794. A monument representing atheism was raised on the Round Basin. After his speech, Robespierre lit the fire in a symbolic gesture. The enormous procession then moved on to the Champ-de-Mars.

The Tuileries today – Although Le Nôtre's original design has not been altered, a number of monuments have been erected. Since 1965, the sculptures of Maillol have been exhibited on the lawn of the Carrousel.

Orangerie and the Jeu de Paume – These two buildings standing opposite one another near the Place de la Concorde were built under the Second Empire.

*Musée de l'Orangerie ⬛ – *Open daily 09.45 to 17.15 except Tuesdays; closed 1 January, 1 May, 25 December; 27F; 18F on Sundays; ☎ 42 97 48 16.*
The horseshoe staircase with wrought ironwork by Raymond Subes leads to the first floor galleries, where the Walter-Guillaume collection (144 works from Impressionism to 1930) is on display. There are good examples of canvases by several artists: Soutine's (1894-1943) portraits and still-lifes *(Young Pastrycook)* reflect a tortured mind; like Picasso *(Nude with a red backdrop)* and Modigliani *(Antonia)* he belonged to a group of foreign artists working in Paris; Cézanne (1839-1906) concentrated on still-lifes *(Apples and Biscuits)*; Renoir (1841-1919) showed special interest in portraiture *(Bather with long hair, Woman with a letter)*; Derain (1880-1954) used brown tones in his severe compositions *(A blond model)*; Matisse (1869-1954) experimented with colour *(Three sisters)*; Henri Rousseau (Le Douanier, 1844-1910) achieved special light effects in his naive compositions *(Old Junier's Cart)*.

The two oval rooms on the ground floor are the setting for the series of paintings made by Monet in the garden of his house at Giverny in Normandy (where he lived 1883-1926) of water-lilies and known as the **Nymphéas★**.

Galerie Nationale du Jeu de Paume – *Open Tuesdays 12.00 to 21.30; Wednesdays to Fridays 12.00 to 19.00; Saturdays and Sundays 10.00 to 19.00; 35F; under 13 free. ☎ 47 03 12 50.*
Like its twin on the other side, the Jeu de Paume was intended to be an orangery but Napoleon III converted it into a real tennis court. By 1909 it had become an art gallery and soon became very popular for its collection of Impressionist art. The gallery has recently been refurbished to stage temporary exhibitions of contemporary art.

To reach the Louvre from Concorde take bus 72 or 73, or métro line 1 direction Château de Vincennes (get out at Palais Royal-Musée du Louvre station).
To reach the Musée d'Orsay take bus 94, or métro line 12 direction Mairie d'Issy (get out at Solferino station).

The EIFFEL TOWER★★★

Métro Bir-Hakeim, RER Champ-de-Mars (line C).

The Eiffel tower's futuristic metal framework has become the symbol of Paris throughout the world.

A. Ell

A technological masterpiece – Built between 1887 and 1889 according to the plans of engineer **Gustave Eiffel**, the tower was the tallest edifice in the world at the time (300m-984ft). Three hundred skyjacks assembled 2 1/2 million rivets, and more than 5 000 preliminary drawings were needed. Many artists and writers, among them Charles Garnier and Maupassant, were outraged by the strange new addition to the Parisian skyline and signed a protest called "The Protest of the 300." But the tower fascinated such artists and poets as Apollinaire, Cocteau and Dufy. Additions to the television broadcasting control room have extended its height to 320.75m-1 051ft today. It weighs 7 000 tons.

Ascent: *09.30 to 23.00 from 19 September to 18 March; 09.00 to 23.00 from 19 March to 18 September (until 24.00 in July and August); for the lift: 1st floor 20F; 2nd floor 36F; 3rd floor 53F; for the stairs (south leg): 1st and 2nd floors 12F; ☏ 45 55 91 11.*

The panoramic **view**★★★ from the 2nd floor (115m-377ft) is actually better than that from the summit (276m-899ft). From here you can see the monuments clearly and explanatory panels detail the city's landmarks. On this floor there is also a cafe, restaurant, boutique and post office (*open 10.00 to 19.30; the mail bears the special "Tour Eiffel" postmark*).

On the 1st floor (57m-187ft) there is a small museum with an audio-visual show (*about 20 minutes*) retracing the tower's history (*entrance free*).

THE QUARTER

The famous Eiffel tower is not the only monument in the neighbourhood.

★★Palais de Chaillot – *Métro Trocadéro.*
This vast monumental ensemble was built in 1937 on the site of Trocadéro by architects Carlu, Boileau and Azéma. From the terrace the **view**★★★ extends all the way to the Champ-de-Mars.
The Palais de Chaillot contains a film library and several **museums**, the Musée de la Marine, the Musée des Monuments Français, the Musée de l'Homme, and the Musée du Cinéma Henri-Langlois.

★Champ-de-Mars – Lying between the Eiffel tower and the École Militaire, this former parade ground was transformed into a garden by J.C. Formigé at the beginning of the 20C.

★★École Militaire – The École Militaire completes the view from the Champ-de-Mars. Constructed in the middle of the 18C by Jacques-Ange Gabriel, and under the protection of Mme de Pompadour, the school was intended to train young gentlemen without private means to become officers. Bonaparte was admitted in 1784. The school was closed by the Revolution but the buildings, which were enlarged in the 18C, retained their military function, serving both as barracks and training centres.

To reach Trocadéro from the Eiffel tower take bus 82, or métro line 6 direction Charles-de-Gaulle Étoile (get out at Trocadéro station).

Les HALLES-BEAUBOURG★★

Métro Rambuteau or Châtelet, RER Châtelet-Les Halles (lines A, B and D).

The plateau of Beaubourg (named after a village enclosed within Paris by Philippe Auguste's curtain wall) was chosen in 1977 for the construction of a cultural centre dedicated to contemporary art on the initiative of President Georges Pompidou (1911-1974).

With 24 000 visitors each day and more than 90 million since it opened its doors, the Centre Georges-Pompidou at Beaubourg has introduced the general public to modern art.

Centre Pompidou

★★CENTRE GEORGES-POMPIDOU

Open 12.00 to 22.00 (10.00 to 22.00 Saturdays, Sundays, and public holidays); closed Tuesdays and 1 and 8 May; 28F for the Musée d'Art Moderne; 57F for a day pass; ☎ 42 77 12 33.

Architecture – Completed in 1977, this futuristic building was designed by the architects Richard Rogers and Renzo Piano. It provoked (and still provokes) lively and mixed reactions. The gigantic parallelepiped, 166m - 545ft long, 60m - 197ft wide, and 42m - 138ft high, flaunts its steel frame, glass walls and bright colours. Devoid of decoration, it looks more like a pile of steelwork; a surrealistic sculpture, confronting traditional sensibilities. The rigging of pipes latticed across the façade gives an impression of both stability and suppleness. Escalators rise through clear tubes supported by rings. The relegation of all utilities to the exterior – escalators, elevators, stairs, corridors, ventilation shafts, water and gas conduits – leaves an open space of 75 000m² – 80 722sq ft on each floor inside.

The gently sloping square in front of the Centre is the museum's outdoor reception area and theatre for a variety of street performers from troubadour, fire-eater, poet and mimer to juggler. Through the window on the right you can see the children's workshop.

Inside on the ground floor, a large open area forming a balcony and surrounded with galleries, you will see the portrait of Georges Pompidou by Vasarely, a hexagonal assembly of white strips, and the Volume Virtuel in yellow and white by de Soto.

Activities – The Centre seeks to draw artistic activity and daily life closer together. It has four departments, the public library (Bibliothèque Publique d'Information, entrance 2nd floor), the industrial design centre (Centre de Création Industrielle, entrance ground floor), the national museum of modern art (entrance 3rd floor), and the institute for acoustic and musical research (Institut de Recherche et de Coordination Acoustique/Musique, entrance underground). The Centre also includes a film library (Salle Garance, level 0, 3 films a day shown), facilities for discussion groups, and the Grande Galerie on the 5th floor for temporary exhibitions.

On the 5th floor are a restaurant and a terrace with a panoramic view.

***Musée National d'Art Moderne ◼

This is one of the most important modern art museums in the world. Picking up where the Musée d'Orsay leaves off, it follows the evolution of art from the beginning of the century through to strictly contemporary art.

It includes over 30 000 works, including 16 000 sketches, although only a small percentage are on display at any one time.

4th floor – From 1900 to 1965.

Espace Sud – The tour begins to the right of the entrance with paintings and sculpture by **Matisse** (1869-1954) and a room dedicated to **Fauvism** (Derain, Dufy, Vlaminck). Then, moving chronologically, we find rooms devoted to **Cubism** (Braque, Picasso, Juan Gris, Fernand Léger).

Espace Nord – Here is **Dadaism** (Marcel Duchamp), born during the Great War out of a violent rebellion against a society which seemed to be hastening its own destruction. Other important trends from after the First World War through to the 1960s on display are: abstraction, Surrealism and those waves of representational art of the 1950s, the New Realism and Pop Art. Renouncing all traces of representation, **abstract painters** expressed themselves through simple series of lines and colours. This art form, which began in 1910 with Kandinsky and his *Improvisations*, found new expression in Kupka and Mondrian. Klee's poetic compositions do not completely lose touch with reality.

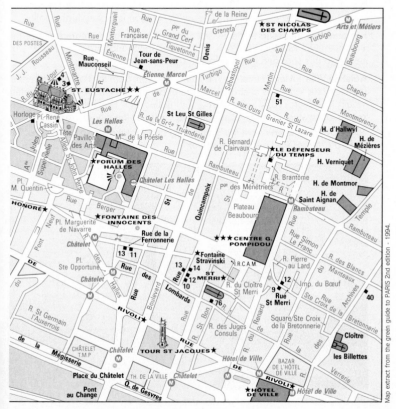

Robert and Sonia Delaunay mark the midpoint between geometric cubism and colour experimentation. Constructivism appears in Pevsner's spiral sculptures. From 1910 to 1930 Montparnasse was the centre of the foreign artists who formed the Paris School. They wanted to translate their spiritual state into art: the tormented expressionism of Soutine, the bewitching universe of Chagall, the decorative arabesques of Modigliani.

Surrealism, represented by Salvador Dalí, Magritte and especially by Miró and Masson, regards painting as a means of expressing the subconscious.

During the 1950s abstraction attracted numerous artists from France as well as from abroad. Some emphasized line (Hartung), others divided the surface into large blocks of colour (Poliakoff, De Stael) or tried to add a third dimension to painting: tar and sand (Dubuffet), and interlocking sculptures (Kemeny).

3rd floor – Contemporary Art from 1960-1990.

Access: from the 4th floor, go back towards the museum entrance and take the escalator down.

A reflection of urban civilization, the New Realism of the 1960s used materials borrowed from daily life; Arman piled up everyday objects, Cesar compressed them and Christo wrapped them. In the United States, the Pop Art of Rauschenberg and Andy Warhol was popular.

A special area is devoted to works representing the most up-to-the-minute artistic creation, including French, American and German contemporary movements (Joseph Beuys) and Italian Arte Povera. The exhibits are renewed regularly.

THE QUARTER

The Beaubourg quarter is popular and animated, a place where groups of young people, some of whom might be considered slightly marginal, like to gather. In the Rue Bernard-de-Clairvaux an unusual brass and steel clock, **Le Défenseur du Temps★**, sounds the hour with an electronically-operated Jack which fights one of three animals, representing the elements, surrounding it.

But this quarter, so dedicated to modernity, also retains its ties with the past.

Forum des Halles – Standing on the spot of the old central market Les Halles (which was moved to Rungis in 1969), the forum's underground concourse extends over 7 hectares - more than 17 acres. The vast structure is above all filled with boutiques although it is also a cultural centre, housing the Maison de la Poésie and the Pavillon des Arts, and decorated with sculptures and frescoes by modern artists like Moretti.

★★St-Eustache – Begun during the Renaissance in 1532 and consecrated in 1637, this church continues the Gothic tradition of architecture while the façade, added in 1754, is classical. The interior decoration is of very high quality.

★Fontaine des Innocents – Pierre Lescot and Jean Goujon created one of the most beautiful fountains in Paris. This Renaissance masterpiece (1550) was moved to this spot and given a fourth façade in the 18C.

★Hôtel de Ville – *Métro Hôtel-de-Ville, 5-minute walk from the Pompidou Centre.* The Hôtel de Ville was destroyed by fire under the Commune and completely rebuilt between 1874 and 1882 by Ballu and Deperthes in the neo-Renaissance style. It is the administrative centre of the city of Paris.

To reach Notre-Dame from the Beaubourg quarter take métro line 4 direction Porte d'Orléans (get out at Cité station).

Church of St-Eustache

The INVALIDES★★★

Métro Invalides.

Situated at the heart of the 7th *arrondissement*, the Invalides is one of the most beautiful monumental groups in Paris.

Louis XIV's great project – In 1670 Louis XIV commissioned Libéral Bruant to construct a vast edifice where war victims could be cared for. Jules Hardouin-Mansart, architect of the royal chapel at Versailles, completed the ensemble with the erection of the church of Saint-Louis (or Église des Soldats), then, in 1715, with the **Église du Dôme.** The latter was inspired by Italian baroque architecture although the church was constructed in a style tempered by classicism, more in keeping with French tradition and taste. The façade consists

The Invalides

M. Guillot/MICHELIN

of a projecting central section flanked by two lateral wings in the Jesuit style. All are the same height as the nave, avoiding the need for heavy buttresses. On the ground floor between the Doric columns are statues of St Louis (by Nicolas Coustou) and Charlemagne (by Coysevox). Above a projecting entablature, the Corinthian columns and statues of the Four Virtues are topped by a pediment carved by Coysevox. Inside, the cupola is decorated with Biblical and historical themes by Charles de la Fosse and Jouvenet.

Prestigious surroundings – A large **esplanade,** designed between 1704 and 1720 by Robert de Cotte, affords a spectacular vista of the Invalides.

★★★Tombeau de Napoléon – *Église du Dôme crypt; open 10.00 to 18.00 (17.00 October to March, 19.00 June to August); joint ticket with Musée de l'Armée.* To integrate the tomb of Napoleon with the architecture of the church, the architect Visconti had to restructure the interior of the crypt. Completed in 1861, the low-reliefs are by Simart and the twelve allegorical statues by Pradier represent the military campaigns of Napoleon. In the centre, the red porphyry sarcophagus houses six coffins one inside the other.

The Invalides today – The Invalides have once again assumed their vocation as a hospital and also house administrative offices and the army museum.

★★★Musée de l'Armée 🖼 – *Open 10.00 to 18.00 (17.00 October to March); closed 1 January, 1 May, 1 November, 25 December and holidays; 34F, 6-18 years olds: 24F; ticket valid for two days for museum, exhibition of models, and Dôme church.* ☎ *44 42 30 11.* This museum focuses on military art, technology and history from the Palaeolithic era to the Second World War. On the ground floor *(east side):* documentary films on the two world wars; **Galerie des Plans-Reliefs** on the 4th floor *(west side):* history of French fortifications over the last three centuries.

THE QUARTER

This is primarily a residential area. Not far from the Invalides at no 57 Rue de Varenne is the **Hôtel Matignon,** prime minister's residence since 1958.

★★Musée Rodin 🖼 – *Hôtel de Biron, 77 Rue de Varenne. Open April to September 09.30 to 17.45 (last admission 17.15); the rest of the year 09.30 to 16.45 (last admission 16.15); closed Mondays, 1 January, 1 May, 25 December; 27F, Sundays 18F; 5F garden only;* ☎ *44 18 61 10.* Rodin's sculptures (bequeathed to the French State by the artist).

Eiffel tower from the Invalides: RER line C direction Versailles-Saint-Quentin.

The LOUVRE★★★

Métro: Palais Royal-Musée du Louvre or Louvre-Rivoli
The Louvre is Paris' largest royal palace and one of the most famous art museums in the world.

From royal keep to museum – Shortly after 1190 Philippe Auguste had a fortress built for military and defensive purposes. Charles V converted it into a royal residence, setting up his famous and erudite library. Although it was neglected for years afterwards, the Louvre profited from the architectural innovation of the Renaissance, first under François I, then under Henri IV. Marie de Medici had the Palais des Tuileries (no longer standing) built. Louis XIV preferred Versailles to the Louvre; during his reign Le Vau nevertheless built part of the Cour Carrée. With the fall of the monarchy came a new vocation for the Louvre: the revolutionaries decided to turn it into a museum for the edification of artists and the populace. Napoleon furthered this goal while at the same time restoring the Louvre's residential function. He lived at the Tuileries, where he was later followed by Louis XVIII, Charles X and Louis-Philippe. Under Napoleon III the last of the ambitious construction projects was undertaken under the direction of the architects Visconti and Lefuel.

Tour of the exterior

★★**Colonnade** – Designed by Le Brun, Le Vau and Perrault in 1667, this is an example of French classicism: respect for Antiquity and concern for symmetry. The central pediment dates from the 19C.

★★**Arc de Triomphe du Carrousel** – The Carrousel, a pastiche of the Roman Arch of Septimius Severus, was built between 1806 and 1808 and designed by Percier and Fontaine to celebrate Napoleon's victories of 1805. The eight rose marble columns came from the old Château in Meudon. Six low-reliefs illustrate the Emperor's great victories: Austerlitz, Ulm... The quadriga on the platform was sculpted by Bosio.

From beneath the arch, there is a marvellous **view★★★** all the way along the Triumphal Way to the Grande Arche in La Défense.

Cour Napoléon – The Louvre's majestic façades frame a strictly geometrical **pyramid★★** 21m - 69ft high and 33m - 108ft wide at its base. The pyramid, designed by Ieoh Ming Pei, is constructed of a fine network of stainless steel and cables draped in glass that relies on innovative techniques and materials. Surrounded by pools, fountains and three small pyramids built according to the same model, it is the main entrance to the museum. The equestrian statue of Louis XIV (replica of a statue by Bernini) faces up the Champs-Élysees, off-centre with respect to the Old Louvre.

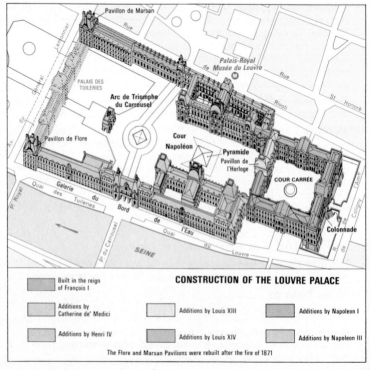

CONSTRUCTION OF THE LOUVRE PALACE

Built in the reign of François I

Additions by Catherine de' Medici

Additions by Louis XIII

Additions by Napoleon I

Additions by Henri IV

Additions by Louis XIV

Additions by Napoleon III

The Flore and Marsan Pavilions were rebuilt after the fire of 1871

The Louvre pyramid by night, with the Arc du Carrousel in the background

★★★MUSÉE DU LOUVRE 🚇

Open daily from 09.00 to 18.00; late night opening on Mondays (Richelieu wing only) and Wednesdays (whole museum) until 22.00; closed on Tuesdays; galleries start closing up to half an hour before closing time; the Medieval Louvre and the galleries on the History of the Louvre are open from 09.00 to 22.00; the bookshop, restaurants and cafés are open from 09.30 to 22.00; 40F, or 20F after 15.00, under-18s free; last tickets sold 45 min before closing time; for general information ☎ 40 20 51 51; audioguides available (30F) in 5 languages from the mezzanine level at the entrance to the Denon, Sully and Richelieu wings.

Video screens beneath the Pyramid, at the entrance to the Galerie du Carrousel, give details of museum activities each day.

Hall Napoléon – *Under the pyramid. Reception, cafeteria, restaurant, bookshop, card shop, gift shop and post office.*

To help you plan your visit – *It is recommended that you pick up a museum map (available free at the reception). Audio guides may be rented (30F).*

The museum is divided into sections with Sully, Denon, and Richelieu accessible from the Hall Napoléon. Collections may be moved for redisplay; therefore, the following descriptions are accordingly subject to change.

History of the Louvre – *Access Sully.*

Two **galleries★** hold paintings, engravings and other documents relating to the various historical stages of the Louvre.

★★Medieval Louvre

Visitors can admire at close quarters the impressive **fortress** built by Philippe Auguste in the early 13C, which was uncovered by the excavations carried out in 1983. The wooden walkway follows the line of the north and east moats. On the left is the counterscarp wall, a simple façade showing visible signs of repair work; on the right is the 2.6m – 7ft thick curtain wall.

★★★Egyptian Antiquities

The backbone of the collection was assembled by **Jean-François Champollion** in 1826, after he had finally unravelled the mysteries of hieroglyphics (drawing on the work of English physicist Thomas Young). The exhibits were discovered in tombs, as Egyptian art is essentially funerary. The galleries on the ground and first floors contain works of art dating from prehistory, through the early pharaonic dynasties and the art of the Old and Middle Empires, to the Graeco-Roman Period. Particularly notable works of art include: the **Mastaba of Akhout-Hetep** (civil tomb) from the Fifth Dynasty; the **Seated Scribe**, with strikingly lifelike features in painted limestone; the **tomb of Chancellor Nakhti**; the **jewels of Rameses II** (great breast plate, ring with horses); inlaid bronze **statuette of Queen Karomama**, the divine consort of Amon.

Rameses II's breast-plate (Sakkara, c1290 - 1220 BC)

Denon

★★★Greek Antiquities *Ground and 1st floors*

In addition to the remarkable collection of Greek vases (in the **Galerie Campana★★**), this section of the Louvre contains two world-famous works: the **Venus of Milo** (or Aphrodite, 2C BC), swathed in a graceful spiral swirl of drapery; and the **Winged Victory of Samothrace** (early 2C BC), the stone figurehead from a ship's prow, with beautifully sculpted draperies moulding the winged woman's body as if streaming against it in a strong wind.

★★Etruscan Antiquities *Ground floor*

The Etruscans appeared in central Italy in the 7C BC and migrated to Campania and northern Italy, where their civilization reached its apogee in the 6C BC. It declined steadily from the following century until 265 BC, when Etruria finally succumbed to Rome.

The famous terracotta **sarcophagus of the Reclining Couple** (6C BC) from the Cerveteri necropolis is to be found in gallery 18.

★★Roman and Palaeo-Christian Antiquities *Ground floor*

This section contains numerous sculpted portraits in the **Ancien appartement d'été d'Anne d'Autriche★★** *(galleries 22-26)*: *Marcellus*; four effigies of *Augustus* at different stages of his life; bust in basalt of *Livia Drusilla*, wife of Augustus.

The jewellery collection on the first floor includes the **Boscoreale treasure★★**, which was found in the ruins of an ancient Roman villa destroyed by the eruption of Vesuvius (79 AD) – coins, jewellery, silver tableware.

★★★Galerie d'Apollon *1st floor*

This gallery provides a sumptuous Grand Siècle setting for what remains of the fabulous treasure of the Kings of France. The **Regent diamond★★★**, which weights 140 carats, is the prize of the collection. Other marvellous precious stones include the **Côte de Bretagne** ruby (107 carats), the pink diamond known as *Hortensia* (hydrangea) and Queen Amélie's **sapphire jewellery set**.

★★Sculpture: Italy and the Northern Schools *Entresol and ground floor*

Michelangelo's **Slaves** are generally acknowledged to be the masterpieces of the Louvre's collection of Renaissance Italian sculpture. They were executed between 1513 and 1520 for the tomb of Pope Julius II.

The intricate and deeply folded drapery of the **Virgin of Isenheim**, near Colmar, is typical of sculpture of the German School of the late Middle Ages, much of which was executed in polychrome wood.

The Fortune-Teller by Caravaggio

★★★Italian Painting *1st floor*

This collection is one of the glories of the Louvre. The works of the Italian Primitives (13-15C) are exhibited in the Grande Galerie (Florentine School: **Saint Francis of Assisi receiving the stigmata** by Giotto; Sienese School: panel of Christ bearing the Cross on the *Way to Calvary* by Simone Martini). The Quattrocento is represented by works by most notably Fra Angelico, Giovanni Bellini and Botticelli.

Three of the marvellous works of the Italian High Renaissance have won particular acclaim world-wide: the **Mona Lisa** *(La Joconde)* by Leonardo da Vinci; **The Man with the Glove** by Titian; and **Wedding at Cana** by Veronese.

★★★Large Format 19C French Painting *1st floor*

Works painted during the Revolution, the Empire and the first half of the 19C, including **The Oath of the Horatii** by David, **The Raft of the Medusa** by Géricault and **Liberty leading the People** (the street barricades of the 1830 Revolution) and **The Massacres at Chios** by Delacroix.

★★Spanish Painting *1st floor*

Religious paintings: **Christ on the Cross** by **El Greco** and **Funeral Ceremonies of Saint Bonaventura** by Zurbaran; humane realism and social comment: **Club-footed Boy** by José de Ribera and *The Young Beggar* by Murillo; portraits: *Portraits of the Infantas* by Velasquez and the **Marquesa de la Solana** *(Beistegui Collection, 2nd floor, Sully wing)* by Goya.

Richelieu

★★★Northern Schools Painting *2nd floor*

Marvellous collection of paintings by the German, Flemish and Dutch schools from the 14C to 17C. **Flemish Primitives** represented by Jan van Eyck (**Madonna with Chancellor Rolin**), Rogier van der Weyden and Hans Memling; **German School** by Hans Holbein the Younger (**Portrait of Erasmus**), Lucas Cranach the Elder and Albrecht Dürer; **Flemish Renaissance** art (16-17C) by Quentin Metsys (**The Moneylender and his Wife**), Brueghel the Elder, Velvet Brueghel, Rubens (gallery devoted to his series of 21 canvases on the **Life of Queen Marie de Medici**) and Jacob Jordaens; **17C Dutch School** by Frans Hals, Van Goyen, Jacob van Ruisdael and **Rembrandt** (poignant **Self-Portrait before an Easel**).

★★★French Painting *2nd floor*

73 galleries display works illustrating the main currents in and, more interestingly, the strong individual talents which marked French painting from the 14-19C in chronological order (French Primitives, Renaissance art, Fontainebleau Schools, Caravaggisti, 17C religious paintings etc.). Particularly outstanding collections include those of works by **Nicolas Poussin** (*Inspiration of the Poet, Shepherds of Arcadia*), **Claude Lorrain** (land- and seascapes with beautiful light effects), **Chardin** (still-life studies), **Fragonard** (*The Bathers*) and **Corot** (landscapes).

★★★Objets d'art *1st floor*

One of the high points of the visit is the collection of **medieval treasure of the Louvre★★★** in which the most famous exhibits come from the royal abbey of Saint-Denis (*north of Paris*) – gold- and silverwork and ivories.

★★★French Sculpture *Ground floor*

The sculpture groups which once adorned the great royal parks in the 17 and 18C can now be admired from all angles beneath the splendid glazed roofs of the Marly and Puget courtyards.

Note in particular the sculptures by Goujon, Coysevox, Puget, Bouchardon, Pigalle, Houdon, Rude and Barye.

★★★Oriental Antiquities *Ground floor*

Impressive collection of Assyrian artefacts: steles, friezes of bas-reliefs, statuettes etc.

★★Islamic art *Entresol level*

Small but rich department illustrating the breathtaking degree of sophistication and stylisation in Muslim art and craftsmanship (gold- and silverwork, marquetry, ceramics).

THE QUARTER

It owes its renown to its architectural richness. Facing the Louvre on the **left bank** of the Seine stands a row of famous monuments.

★Institut de France– *Métro Louvre-Rivoli or Odéon. Open to cultural associations by appointment.*

It began as the College of Four Nations founded by Mazarin. The palace which houses the institute was raised on the site of the old Nesle tower and is the work of Le Vau (1662). Its cupola and semi-circular wings make it one of the most baroque monuments of Louis XIV's century. The Institut de France is composed of five academies: the Académie Française (founded 1635 by Richelieu), the Académie des Inscriptions et Belles Lettres (founded 1663 by Colbert), the Académie des Sciences (founded 1666 also by Colbert), the Académie des Sciences morales et politiques (founded 1795) and the Académie des Beaux Arts (founded 1816).

The Institut de France

★Hôtel des Monnaies ▨ – *Open 13.00 to 18.00 (21.00 on Wednesday evenings); closed Mondays and public holidays except 8 May, 1 and 11 November; 20F; ☎ 40 46 55 35.*

The building was originally the Hôtel de Nevers and then the Hôtel de Conti, before Louis XV decided to transfer the mint to this spot. From 1768 to 1775 the architect Antoine constructed the new workrooms in the obligatory neo-classical style of that period. Inside is a suite of rooms and a coin museum.

Near the Louvre on the **right bank** of the Seine are two more monuments particularly worthy of note.

★★Palais-Royal – *Métro Palais Royal-Musée du Louvre; not open to the public.*

Here are the offices of the Council of State. Constructed in 1632 by Jacques Le Mercier for Richelieu, the Palais-Cardinal became the Palais-Royal in 1642, then the property of the House of Orléans. The gardens are framed with façades by Victor Louis, also architect of the theatre of the Comédie Française (no 2 Rue de Richelieu).

★★Musée des Arts Décoratifs ▨ – *Métro Palais Royal-Musée du Louvre, 107 Rue de Rivoli; open 12.30 (12.00 Sundays) to 18.00; closed Mondays and Tuesdays; 25F; ☎ 42 60 32 14.*

The exhibits present the evolution in form and taste in furniture, tapestries, gold and silverware, porcelain, painting and sculpture.

To reach the Beaubourg Quarter and the Marais from the Louvre take bus 76, or métro line 1 direction Château de Vincennes (get out at Châtelet, Hôtel-de-Ville or Saint-Paul stations).

The MARAIS★★★

The Marais Quarter is without parallel. In contrast to Paris' grand boulevards, the narrow streets lined with private mansions create a friendlier atmosphere.

★★PLACE DES VOSGES

Métro Saint-Paul or Chemin-Vert.

This is the oldest monumental square in Paris.

Hôtel des Tournelles – After the assassination of the Duke of Orléans in 1407 the Crown acquired the Hôtel des Tournelles. Charles VII settled himself there, and it was in this hôtel that Louis XII ended his days. After Henri II was killed in a tournament, Catherine de' Medici took an intense dislike to the hôtel and had it torn down.

Place Royale – After first planning to establish a silk factory here, Henri IV decided in 1605 to transform the abandoned area into a district of style. Borrowing an idea of Catherine de' Medici, he envisaged a vast square whose pavilions would all be symmetrical. When the work – probably by Métezeau – was finished in 1612, the Royal Square became the centre of elegant life, tourneying and merry-making, and the meeting place of duelists who ignored Richelieu's ban. In 1627, Montmorency-Bouteville and des Chapelles who duelled beneath the Cardinal's windows were beheaded in the Place de Grève.
During the Revolution the square was christened Place de l'Indivisibilité and the statue of Louis XIII was taken down (it was put back in 1818). The name Place des Vosges appeared in 1800 to honour the Vosges *département* which was the first to pay its taxes.

The square today – Despite years of renovation, the 36 houses retain their original symmetry with alternating stone and brick facing, ground level arcades, two storeys topped by steeply sloping slate roofs pierced with dormer windows, back courts and hidden gardens.
The largest is the **Pavillon du Roi** at the centre of the southern side, echoed by the **Pavillon de la Reine** on the northern side. Their decoration is very sober.

★HÔTEL CARNAVALET

From Place des Vosges take Rue des Francs-Bourgeois. The address is no 23 Rue de Sévigné.

Begun in 1548 by Jacques des Ligneris, President of the Parliament, the hôtel passed to the widow of sire de Kernevenoy, a member of Queen Margot's famous Flying Squadron (Escadron Volant). The name, deformed, became Carnavalet. In 1660 François Mansart gave the Renaissance building its present appearance. Marie de Rabutin, Marquise de Sévigné, rented the hotel from 1677 to 1696. Then Carnavalet became home to various financiers and magistrates before housing the School of Civil Engineering under the Restoration. The buildings surrounding the three gardens date from the 19C. At the centre of the court stands a 17C **statue★** of Louis XIV by Coysevox.
In 1989 the Hôtel Carnavalet was linked to the neighbouring hôtel, Le Peletier de Saint-Fargeau, built in 1690 according to the design of Pierre Bullet. The Musée Carnavalet now occupies these two hôtels.

★★**Musée Carnavalet** ◪ – *23 Rue de Sévigné; open 10.00 to 17.40 except Mondays and public holidays; 27F; 7-17 year olds: 14.50F.* ☏ *42 72 21 13.* The museum is dedicated to Paris history. It is organized chronologically with displays ranging from archaeological finds to views of Paris. *A bookshop to the right of the entrance specialises in books on Paris.*

★HÔTEL SALÉ

This mansion was constructed between 1656 and 1659 by Pierre Aubert, salt tax collector, hence the name given to the Hotel Salé by Parisian wits. Occupied until the 18C by the Juigné family, the Hôtel housed the École Central (1829-1884) then the École des Métiers d'Art from 1944 to 1969. It was restored by the architect Simounet to house the Musée Picasso.

Inside is a beautiful **stairway★** with splendid wrought-ironwork and a sculpted ceiling.

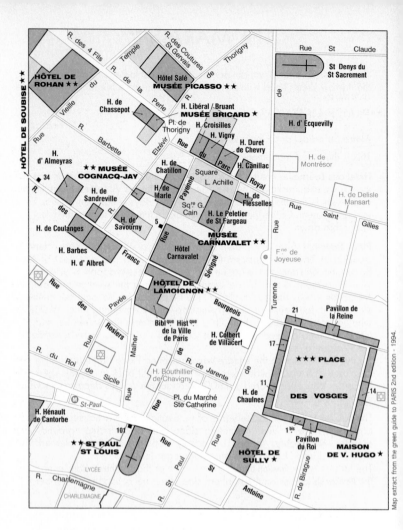

★★Musée Picasso 🏛 – *5 Rue de Thorigny; coming from the Hôtel Carnavalet take Rue Payenne; open daily 09.30 to 17.30; closed Tuesdays; 27F; Sundays 18F;* ☎ *42 71 25 21. Museum bookshop and cafeteria on the ground floor.*

The museum owes its richness to an early donor, whose gift was added to by a donation from Jacqueline Picasso in 1990.

Born in Malaga on 25 October 1881, Pablo Ruiz Picasso studied at the School for Fine Arts in Barcelona, then in Madrid. In 1904 he moved to France which he never left thereafter except for brief trips abroad. He died in Mougins on 8 April 1973.

The visit begins on the first floor with *Self Portrait in Blue* and follows his life which is closely tied to his work (there are explanatory notices). All the stages in his development and all his techniques are represented, with studies for *Les Demoiselles d'Avignon, Still life with a Cane Chair,* and *Pipes of Pan.* Also included is Picasso's personal collection of about fifty works by artists he admired such as Braque, Cézanne and Rousseau; it is called the Donation Picasso.

There are films on the painter shown on the third floor.

If you have time

★★Hôtel de Soubise – *60 Rue des Francs-Bourgeois.*

Delamair was commissioned to remodel the Guise residence for the Prince of Rohan-Soubise. The 18C interior decoration is characteristic of French rococo.

★★Hôtel de Rohan – *87 Rue Vieille-du-Temple.*

Delamair also built this 18C hôtel for the Rohan family and it was occupied successively by four prince-bishops of Strasbourg (note architecture and interior décor).

★Church of St-Paul-St-Louis – *99bis Rue Saint-Antoine.*

Baroque architecture of the 17C inspired by the Gesù Church in Rome.

To reach the left bank from the Marais take bus 96, which crosses the Seine.

MONTMARTRE***

Take the métro to Anvers station, then go up the Rue de Steinkerque and either take the funicular, or go up the steps, to the parvis of the basilica of Sacré-Cœur.

The **"Montmartrobus"** follows a circular route around the Montmartre hill, between the town hall of the 18th *arrondissement*, Place Pigalle and Sacré-Cœur.

The "Butte", as it is known locally, still retains the atmosphere of the independent village it once was. It is a part of Paris which is full of contrasts – anonymous boulevards run close to delightful village streets and courtyards, steep flights of stone steps lead up to shady squares or terraces which open onto marvellous views over the rest of Paris.

Bohemian Life – Throughout the 19C, artists and writers were drawn to the free and easy, picturesque life that was seen to be led on the hill of Montmartre. The composer Berlioz and the writers and poets Nerval, Murger and Heine were here, the precursors of the great 1871-1914 generation; young painters sought inspiration in the Place Pigalle; artists' models and seamstresses led a Bohemian existence. The early poets' circles transformed themselves into café societies from which flowed songs (Aristide Bruant), poems, humour, drawings (Caran d'Ache, André Gill, Toulouse-Lautrec). Everyone flocked to the newly opened Moulin-Rouge (1889) to see the singers, clowns and dancers – Yvette Guilbert, Valentin le Désossé, Jane Avril and La Goulue. The Butte remained the capital's literary and artistic centre – thanks to the Lapin Agile café and the Bateau-Lavoir studios – until 1914, when inspiration moved to Montparnasse, and Montmartre abandoned itself to night life.

★★Basilica of Sacré-Cœur – The gleaming white shape of the basilica towering on its hill is an important element in the Parisian landscape. Abadie drew on Romano-Byzantine inspiration for his design. The many cupolas are dwarfed by the dome and the 80m – 262ft high campanile. Inside, the basilica is decorated with mosaics.

The parvis of Sacré-Cœur overlooks the Square Willette, laid out in 1929 100m – 320ft above the Seine, from which there is a wonderful **view** of Paris. From the dome (*access via the steps down into the moat to the left of the church, open from 09.00 to 19.00, or 18.00 1 October to 31 March; 15F, combined ticket with the crypt: 25F; ☎ 42 51 17 02*) there is a bird's eye view of the interior and, from the gallery outside, on a clear day, a **panorama★★★** extending for 30km – 19 miles.

In the belfry hangs the Savoyarde, one of the heaviest bells in the world (19 tons).

★★Place du Tertre – This long-standing meeting place still retains its village atmosphere early in the morning, but is transformed before long into one of the busiest tourist centres in Paris, as crowds wander between the trees watching unknown artists at work, or pause in front of the many restaurants or bars. No 21 (the old 19bis) is the seat of the Free Commune founded in 1920 by Jules Dépaquit to preserve the imaginative and humorous traditions of the Butte; it now houses the tourist information centre. No 3, once the local town hall, is now Poulbot House, commemorating the local children (P'tits Poulbots) immortalised in the artist's delightful drawings early this century.

R. Mazin/TOP

The Lapin Agile café in Montmartre

Around the vineyards – *Take Rue du Mont Cenis, then turn left into Rue Cortot.* The house at no 12 has had as its tenants over the years Renoir, Othon Friesz, Utter, Dufy, Émile Bernard, Suzanne Valadon and her son Utrillo. It now houses the **Musée du Vieux Montmartre** *(open from 11.00 to 18.00; closed Mondays, 1 January, 1 May, 15 August, 1 November and 25 December; 25 F; ☎ 46 06 61 11)* with plenty of memorabilia from Montmartre's Bohemian days with its nightclubs and artists.

In Rue de Saules *(turn right)* is the famous Montmartre **vineyard** (great festivities on the first Saturday in October every year in honour of the start of the grape harvest). The **crossroads★** with the Rue St-Vincent is one of the prettiest parts of Montmartre; small flights of steps lead off mysteriously, the road climbs steeply up alongside the cemetery, the leaves around the vista of Sacré-Cœur add a rustic charm to the scene, further enhanced by the sight of the **Lapin Agile** café, half hidden by an acacia.

Turn left into Rue St-Vincent, then left up some steps at Place C-Pecqueur to Rue de l'Abreuvoir. Turn right to walk round the Château des Brouillards (18C folly) via Square S-Buisson. Turn right into Avenue Junot.

Moulin de la Galette – *(Good view of mill from outside no 10 Avenue Junot.)* The old mill was once a dance hall and all the rage at the beginning of the century; Renoir, Van Gogh and many other painters came here for inspiration. The windmill, which has topped the Montmartre hill for more than six centuries, is the old Blute-fin defended against the Cossacks in 1814 by the heroic mill-owner Debray, who ended up being crucified on its sails.

Take the stepped street to the right of the mill, then turn right into Rue Lepic. Follow this downhill, as it curves left to join Rue des Abbesses. Stroll along here until Rue Ravignan on the left.

★Picturesque old streets – Rue Ravignan leads up to the bottom of Place Jean-Baptiste Clément (after the writer of the famous song *Le Temps des Cerises*), which you cross to take Rue Norvins on the right. The **crossroads★**, so typical of Montmartre, formed by Rue Norvins with Rue des Saules and Rue St-Rustique was immortalised in Utrillo's canvases. The Bonne-Franquette cabaret was extremely popular around 1890.

The narrow Rue St-Rustique marks the highest point of the Butte and of Paris (129.37m - 427ft). There is an exceptional view of Paris from the tiny Place du Calvaire.

★Cimetière de Montmartre – *Access from the Rue Caulaincourt (by the steel bridge spanning the cemetery).*
A wonderful, tranquil place to stroll around, admiring the elaborate and often slightly crumbling tombs of the famous and the unknown side by side (Zola, Berlioz, Heine, Degas, Offenbach and Nijinsky are just some of the names you might recognise).

NOTRE-DAME***

Métro Cité, RER Saint-Michel (line B).

The cathedral of Notre-Dame, a supreme masterpiece of Gothic art, presents a fascinating visual resumé of the most brilliant artistic skills of the Middle Ages.

History of Notre-Dame – The cathedral was founded by Maurice de Sully, Bishop of Paris. With the basilica of St-Denis *(north of Paris)* it is one of the first buttressed structures in Europe. The galleries inside, however, demonstrate this Gothic cathedral's debt to Romanesque architecture. Construction began in 1163 with the chancel; thirty years later in about 1210 the west façade with its ornate sculptures was finally completed. Notre-Dame was altered in the 13C and again in the 14C with the construction of chapels at the east end, the lengthening of the transept, and construction of the Portal to the Virgin on the north and to St Stephen (St Étienne) on the south. Work was completed in about 1345. Seriously damaged by the revolutionaries for whom the cathedral symbolized the power of the monarchy and the religious orders, Notre-Dame was restored in the 19C by Viollet-le-Duc.

Ceremonial occasions – From its construction to the present, Notre-Dame has furnished the setting for important political and religious ceremonies like Napoleon's coronation by Pope Pious VII on 2 December 1804, and more recently, the Te Deum on 26 August 1944, the Requiem Masses for Presidents de Gaulle (November 1970) and Pompidou (April 1974) and the celebration Mass held by Pope John Paul II in May 1980.

The Notre-Dame façade

Overlooking the Place du Parvis where mystery plays were performed during the Middle Ages, the façade has three levels, separated by the Gallery of Kings which rises above the portals, and the Great Gallery at the base of the towers.

The Portals – The three portals owe their names to the Biblical scenes illustrated in their tympana: on the left the Coronation of the Virgin, in the centre the Last Judgment, and on the right St Anne.

The Rose Window Level – The rose window measures 10m-30ft across. The glass work dates from the 19C.

Towers – The towers overlook Paris from a height of 69m-226ft. The south tower houses Emmanuel, the famous bell weighing 13 tons.

Ascent ▨ – *Access to the north tower: 386 steps (allow 5 to 10 minutes); 09.30 to 18.30 (10.00 to 17.00 1 October to 31 March); last admission*

The east end of Notre-Dame seen from the left bank of the Seine

30 min before closing time; closed 1 January, 1 May, 1 and 11 November, 25 December; 31F, 7-17 year olds; 7F; ☏ 43 29 50 40.

The **view**★★★ includes the steeple and the outer architecture of Notre-Dame (close-up view of some of the gargoyles!) as well as all of Paris. Video-museum in the south tower.

The Cathedral interior

Notre-Dame is 130m-427ft long, 48m-158ft wide and 35m-115ft high. Its layout includes a nave with double aisles, a transept, and a double ambulatory. The interior pillars (1) supporting the towers are 5m-16ft in diameter. The stained glass, produced using medieval methods and colours, was installed in 1965.

Chapels – These are decorated with the "Mays", gifts offered by the goldsmiths of Paris – according to an old tradition these gifts are given every May. Some were commissioned from great painters like Le Brun (2-3) or Le Sueur (4).
On the left are tombstones of a 15C canon (5) and Cardinal Amette (6).

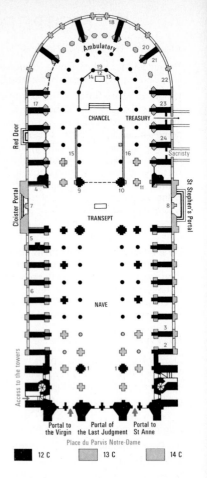

Transept – Thanks to the buttresses supporting the construction, daylight floods the cathedral through the exceptionally large windows (13m-42 1/2ft in diameter). The north rose (7), which has remained nearly intact since the 13C, shows characters from the Old Testament surrounding the Virgin. The restored south rose (8) shows Christ seated among the angels and saints.
The statue of St Denis (9) by Nicolas Coustou makes a pair, against the transept pillars at the entrance to the chancel, with the beautiful 14C **Virgin and Child** (10) – Our Lady of Paris, previously in St-Aignan. A pavement inscription recalls the conversion of the 20C poet Paul Claudel (11).

Chancel – Still without an heir after 23 years of marriage, Louis XIII consecrated France to the Virgin (1638), a vow symbolised by a refurbishment of the chancel undertaken by Robert de Cotte. It consisted of the stalls and a Pietà (12) by Coysevox flanked by Louis XIII (13) by Guillaume Coustou and Louis XIV (14) by Coysevox. The stone chancel screen was cut back at this time, and of the 14C low-reliefs later restored by Viollet-le-Duc only the **Life of Christ** (15) and **His Visions** (16) remain.
Bishops and Archbishops of Paris are buried in the crypt under the chancel. The funerary monuments in the ambulatory are:
17) Monsignor de Juigné, archbishop of Paris during the Revolution. Pierre Lescot is buried in this chapel.
18) Monsignor Pierre de Gondi, ancestor of Cardinal de Retz.
19) The recumbent effigy of a 14C bishop.
20) Monsignor Darboy, taken as hostage and shot during the Commune.
21) The mausoleum of the Duc d'Harcourt by Pigalle.
22) Praying figure of Jean Juvénal of the Ursins and his wife.
23) Monsignor Sibour, assassinated in 1857.
24) Monsignor Affre, killed during the riots of 1848.

Treasury – *Open 09.30 to 18.00; closed Sundays and certain religious holidays; 15F.*
The former sacristy built by Viollet-le-Duc contains illuminated manuscripts, ornaments and 19C church plate. The Crown of Thorns, the Holy Nail and a fragment of the True Cross are displayed on Fridays during Lent and on Good Friday in the main area of the cathedral.

The Ile de la Cité as well the entire Notre-Dame quarter has played an important historical role, as is illustrated by the various monuments.

★★★**Palais de Justice** – *Métro Cité; open 08.00 to 18.00 except Sundays and public holidays ☎ 44 32 67 19.*

The law courts or "Palais", secular seat of civil and judicial authority, were the residence of Roman governors, Merovingian kings, the children of Clovis, the mint of Dagobert, and the fortress of Count Eudes standing on the right bank of the Seine upstream from the invasion route. Later the building became the royal palace of the Middle Ages, residence of the first Capetians (their chapel and their keep). St Louis had his apartment in the present Civil Chamber. Philip the Fair commissioned Enguerrand de Marigny to build the Conciergerie and enlarge and embellish the palace – the Gothic chambers inaugurated in 1313 won it widespread fame.

Later Charles V erected the Tour de l'Horloge which bore the first public clock in Paris. It was here that he set up the Parliament, the Supreme Court of Justice of the Realm, to which Charles VII later gave the building. To this period belong the hall of the men-at-arms with its beautiful capitals, the guard room with its magnificent pillars and the kitchens.

The Great Hall on the first floor was restored by Salomon Brosse after the fire of 1618, again in 1840, and once more after the fire of 1871.

In the first Civil Courtroom the Parliament used to hold session, including the session when the 16-year-old Louis XIV came to give his orders to the Parliament, and the session of 1788 when the parliament demanded the convocation of the Estates General. The revolutionary tribunal sat here.

The twin towers in the centre of the northern façade (the oldest part of the palace although the façade is neo-Gothic, renovated in the 19C), once guarded the entrance to the royal palace.

★★★**Sainte-Chapelle** 🎫 – *Métro Cité; open 1 April to 30 September 09.30 to 18.30; 1 October to 31 March 10.00 to 16.30; closed 1 January, 1 May, 1 and 11 November, 25 December; 26F, 7-17 years olds: 7F; combined ticket for the Sainte-Chapelle and the Conciergerie 40F; ☎ 43 54 30 09.*

With its delicate stonework and tall, slender stained glass windows, which let daylight flood in, the Sainte-Chapelle is the masterpiece of High Gothic, both aesthetically and technically. The architect pushed the logic of the Gothic style to its limits, and, aided by the limited dimensions of the building's site, succeeded in creating a perfect balance with the simple buttresses.

The chapel was erected by Pierre de Montreuil in less than three years at Saint Louis' request to build in his palace a place to shelter the distinguished Passion relics he had recently acquired. The chapel was consecrated 25 April 1248. Like previous palatine chapels (Laon, Meaux), it has two storeys, one for the monarch, and one for the palace staff.

Windows – The upper chapel seems like a shrine in which an astonishing display of stained glass takes the place of walls, dazzling visitors from between the slender buttresses. The windows contain 1134 scenes, of which 720 are original, and rise to a height of 15m - 49ft. When the windows of Chartres were completed in 1240, the King appealed to the master glassworkers to decorate the windows of his own chapel. This explains the similarity between the two works: scenes decorating the medallions and the luminous colours which eclipse the essential simplicity of the design and composition. The theme is the Passion, from the great prophets to John the Baptist and the Biblical scenes prefiguring it. We only know of the original radiant rose from a miniature in the *Très Riches Heures du Duc de Berry*, a book of hours. The present rose, commissioned by Charles VII during the Flamboyant period, illustrates the Apocalypse of St John. It is easy to identify the period from which it dates from the design of the lancet and the shading of the painting on the glass which replaces the older process of juxtaposing tiny coloured squares.

Ste-Chapelle: stained-glass window

★★Conciergerie  – *Access, admission times and charges are the same as for the Sainte-Chapelle.*
Under the Terror the Conciergerie became the antechamber of the guillotine, sheltering up to 1 200 prisoners at one time. The most moving rooms are the Prisoners' Gallery, Marie-Antoinette's Prison, and the Girondins' Chapel.

To the south of the Seine – the Left Bank

Latin Quarter – This is Paris' intellectual quarter. The Sorbonne and the Collège de France are among the most illustrious buildings.

St-Séverin Quarter – This old quarter on the left bank is known for its beautiful **church★**, its narrow streets and its multiplicity of cabarets, cellar night-clubs, art galleries, and experimental cinemas, as well as for its active nightlife.

Boulevard St-Germain – To the right of Place St-Germain-des-Prés are the Café des Deux-Magots and the Café de Flore which owe their fame to men of letters and left bank artists. Opposite them, the Brasserie Lipp (**no 151**) is frequented by writers, politicians and current celebrities. On the same side of the boulevard stand some old 18C hôtels, most notably at **nos 159** and **173**.

★★St-Germain-des-Prés – This 11C Romanesque abbatial church was extensively altered up until the 18C without losing its splendour.

★Place de Furstemberg – The square was created by the cardinal of this name in 1699. This small, paulownia-shaded, harmoniously designed square with its old-fashioned charm and white-globed lamp-posts is one of the best preserved squares in Paris.
Go to the end of the small Rue de Furstemberg to the corner of Rue Jacob where you will find a charming **view** of the square with the imposing mass of the ancient **abbatial palace** (16C-17C) in the background.

Detail of the fountain, Place St-Michel

The OPÉRA ★★★

Métro Opéra, RER Auber (line A)

★★OPÉRA GARNIER

At the heart of Haussmann's Paris, the Opéra remains a symbol of the Second Empire's love of pomp and ceremony. With the Opéra-Bastille now the centre of the French musical scene, the Opéra Garnier continues as the home of the prestigious ballet company.

Construction and design – In 1860 the young architect Charles Garnier, still unknown even though he had won the Rome Prize, won a competition organized to select an architect for the new opera house. He supplanted the Empress's favourite, Viollet-le-Duc. Master of the architectural project, Garnier also supervised all decoration, interior and exterior, where the rule was luxuriousness, profusion and colour. The greatest painters, sculptors and decorators participated. On the façade, the La Danse group, sculpted by Carpeaux (reproduction, original in the Musée d'Orsay), which is one of the most admired sculpture groups today, caused a scandal when it was put in place. Long, costly, and interrupted by the war of 1870, the work was finally completed in 1875. Garnier had dreamed of creating a "Napoleon III style" in opposition to

Ballet by Roland Petit

the pastiches of ancient works common during that period. But his monument failed to create a new school of architecture. It is, nonetheless, one of the most beautiful achievements of the Second Empire.

The surface area of this immense theatre is 11 000m²-118 404sq ft and its stage can hold 450 actors.

Interior – *Main entrance: Place de l'Opéra. Open 10.00 to 17.00; closed when there is a matinée performance, during all of August and on 1 January and 1 May; 30F;* ☎ *47 42 07 02.*

In 1995 and early 1996, the auditorium will be closed to visitors during renovation work. Amidst opulent paintings and sculptures, the **great staircase** stuns with its immensity. When there are no rehearsals going on, you can see the **auditorium** in which the ceiling, painted by Chagall, dates from 1964.

★★★THE QUARTER

Place de l'Opéra – Haussmann envisioned the Place de l'Opéra as something more than the location of the National Academy of Music. He turned the square into a circus from which avenues radiated.

Public opinion accused the Prefect of excessively grand vision, for at the time the square seemed immense. Today it is hardly large enough to handle modern traffic, which is very busy in this area. Beside the square, on the Rue Scribe, is the **Café de la Paix**, an ideal spot for a break.

★★Place Vendôme – *About a 15-min walk from the Opéra.*

A vast royal square conceived by Louvois around 1680, Place Vendôme today retains all the majesty of its origins. The plan is by Jules Hardouin-Mansart, the architect who worked on Versailles. At the centre of the square is an equestrian statue of Louis XIV by Girardon. It was destroyed during the Revolution. The surrounding buildings date from the 18C.

In 1810 Napoleon had the **Colonne Vendôme** erected, a copy of the Trajan column in Rome. Its entwining bronze spiral was cast with 1 250 cannon captured at Austerlitz.

One of Paris' most prestigious squares – Nowadays the square is known essentially as a prestige area offering luxury goods, especially jewellery.

To reach the Louvre from the Opéra take bus 27, or métro line 7 direction Mairie d'Ivry (get out at Palais Royal-Musée du Louvre station).

Musée d'ORSAY★★★

Métro Solferino, RER Musée d'Orsay (line C).

From train station to museum

Constructed in 1900 by the architect Victor Laloux, the old Orsay station was chosen in 1977 to house a museum devoted to art of the second half of the 19C (1848-1914). While adapting the station for its new function, the architects P. Colboc, R. Bardou, and M.P. Philippon respected the original architecture.

The interior design and decoration are the work of Gae Aulenti.

The museum was inaugurated in 1986.

TOUR

Main entrance: *1 Rue de Bellechasse. Entrance to the exhibitions on the Quay Anatole-France. Restaurant entrance after museum closes: 62bis Rue de Lille. Open daily 10.00 (09.00 on Sundays and on weekdays between 20 June and 20 September) to 18.00 (21.45 on Thursdays); last admission 30min before closing time; closed Mondays, 1 January, 1 May, 25 December. 36F, 24F on Sundays. Further information on a recorded message:* ☎ *45 49 11 11.*

To help you plan your visit: *it is advisable that you equip yourself with a map of the museum, available at the reception; audio guides 28F.*

Ground floor

Sculpture 1850-1870 *Central Aisle*

The influence of the beautiful ideal inspired by Antiquity strongly marks the sculptors' work.

The works exhibited in the Central Aisle show the supremacy of academic taste (*Sapho* by Pradier). Little by little subjects and style evolved through Romanticism and then Realism. The art of Carpeaux *(assembled at the end of the central aisle in the room on the right)* bears witness to the evolution towards naturalism and expressiveness *(Ugolin)*.

Painting 1830-1870

At points along the central aisle, rooms are devoted to certain painters or certain themes (realism, orientalism).

On the right. Ingres and his students represent the classical trend in opposition to the Romanticism of painters like Delacroix and Chassériau. Further on are the canvases by Puvis de Chavannes, Gustave Moreau and Edgar Degas, precursors of Symbolism.

On the left. The Chauchard collection (indivisible bequest) possesses numerous landscapes of the Barbizon school by Corot, Millet and Daubigny. The other rooms are devoted to the realism of Courbet, to the early works of the Impressionists (Monet, really the founder of the movement, Fantin-Latour and Manet).

The great clock above the central aisle, with Antonin Mercie's (1845-1916) David

The decorative arts 1850-1880

Middle of the central aisle, to the right behind the Thomas Couture painting.
This section of the museum includes furniture, objets d'art, and gold work which draw on and sometimes pastiche the Renaissance or Classicism. These works represent the triumph of eclecticism.

New technical processes like galvanoplastics and the rise of industry laid the foundation for these productions. The house of Christofle owed considerable growth in business to the process of galvanisation which opened up the possibility of silver-plating production lines whilst enabling the firm to continue its tradition of producing luxury silver ware.

Cabinet-maker Diehl produced numerous distinctive cabinets in a variety of styles and materials as well as other small items of furniture.

Architecture of the Second Empire (1852-1870)

At the end of the central aisle, note the scale model of Garnier's opera house.

The tour continues on the upper level (chronological arrangement). Access via the escalator at the end of the aisle.

Dance at the Moulin de la Galette by Auguste Renoir

Musée d'Orsay, Paris/R.M.N.

Upper level

Impressionism after 1870

In the 1870s Impressionism was an avant-garde movement, despised by those in power. The painters themselves organized exhibits in 1874 and 1886 to make themselves known and to try and sell a few works, often unsuccessfully. The novelty of their work lay in the attention they gave to style as well as subject, in this case the impressionist "touch" which rendered the flickering of light on matter. The title Monet gave to one of his works, *Impression: Sunrise*, earned the group of painters in this style the name Impressionists. The works are organized by artist, except when they come from a collection donated as an indivisible bequest (the Moreau-Néloton and Gachet collections). Canvases by Monet, Pissarro, Sisley, Degas, Manet, Renoir, Cézanne and Van Gogh.

Neo-impressionism

Pont-Aven School – Inspired by primitive art, the Pont-Aven artists (Émile Bernard, Sérusier, Lacombe) proceeded with large areas of frequently pure colour. Gauguin began his work among these painters caught up by the charm of this pretty Breton village.

Divisionism – Pushing their impressionist exploration of colour to the limit, painters like Seurat *(The Circus)* or Signac *(Women at the Well)* covered the canvas with tiny dots of pure colour.

The Nabis – The movement was started in 1880 at Pont-Aven. Serusier painted *The Talisman* which fired his friends' enthusiasm and they formed the Nabis group (the name comes from a Hebrew word meaning prophet).

Go back down to the middle level for the last part of the tour.

This is partially housed in the former hotel of the train station which retains its splendid décor of 1900.

Decoration and official commissions of the Third Republic – *Go left from the escalator.*

Academism in painting – Often very large, the canvases exhibited here reflect the Administration's commissions for public buildings. Here, in contrast with contemporary Impressionism we see the triumph of mythology like *The Birth of Venus* by Bouguereau Hall or historical subjects such as *Cain* by Cormon.

Monumental Sculpture – As a result of a period of "statuemania" under the Third Republic, public places were filled with memorials, often allegorical in nature. Projects, models and sculptures of Dalou and Barrias exemplify this trend.

Art Nouveau in France and Belgium – A desire to free oneself from the past and express oneself in a new style lies at the origin of an important movement which developed in Europe around 1890, especially in architecture and applied arts: Art Nouveau or Modern Style. This movement, which was tied to industrial progress, was characterized by a profusion of sinuous forms and plant motifs.

The fundamental concept of total art encouraged artists to group together. A movement of artists brought together under Émile Gallé, the Nancy school, was the point of departure for the French Art Nouveau.

The glass-ware of Lalique and Gallé and the furniture of Carabin, Guimard and Van de Velde are representative of this school.

Towards the 20C – The right wing is dedicated to the last artistic trends of the 19C, and a prelude of art in the 20C. In sculpture there is a "return to style" characterized by Bourdelle and Maillol in their simple shapes and purified forms.

After 1900 the style of the Nabis group evolved into softer colours and more complex designs as in the works of Maurice Denis, Valloton, Vuillard and Bonnard.

Birth of cinematography – Work of the Lumière brothers.

To reach the Invalides from the Musée d'Orsay take bus 63, or RER line C direction Versailles-St-Quentin (get out at Invalides station). To reach Notre-Dame take bus 24, or RER line C direction Massy-Palaiseau (get out at St-Michel station).

Church at Auvers, by Van Gogh

▲ TRIPS IN THE VICINITY ▲

Château de CHAMPS★

Michelin map 101 south of fold 19
About 24km – 15 miles west of Disneyland Paris

The Château de Champs, built towards the end of Louis XIV's reign, is a model of 18C architecture and decoration.

★★**Park**  – *Open daily 09.30 to sundown; closed Tuesdays, 1 January, 1 May, 1 and 11 November and 25 December.* A masterpiece of French gardening with a sweeping perspective, patterned boxwoods, fountains, and groves.

★**Château**  – *Guided tours (time: 45min) daily 10.00 to 12.00 and 13.30 to 17.30 (16.30 from 1 October to 30 March); closed Tuesdays, 1 January, 1 May, 1 and 11 November, and 25 December; 27F;* ☎ *60 05 24 43.* Completed in 1716, the château is remarkable for the obvious attention to comfort in its construction. The rooms do not open into each other, the corridors are carefully arranged, and each room possesses a dressing room and closet. On the first floor notice the corner room's magnificent rococo **wainscoting**★ and on the ground floor the **Salon Chinois**★★ with its rich **Chinoiserie decoration** by Huet.

Château de FERRIÈRES★

Michelin map 106 south of folds 21 and 22
About 11km – 7 miles southwest of Disneyland Paris

Property of the Rothschild family, the Château de Ferrières was famous under the Second Empire for its sumptuousness and the elaborate receptions held here.

A place devoted to hunting and the arts – In 1829 James de Rothschild, founder of the French line of the family, acquired the 3 000 hectare - 7 413 acre estate, formerly belonging to Fouché, minister under Napoleon. His intent was to erect a splendid home, worthy of his art collections – scattered today – and his love of ostentation. The English garden designer cum architect, **Joseph Paxton**, already famed for London's Crystal Palace, built the château between 1855 and 1859. The decoration is the work of the French specialist, Eugène Lami, whom the baroness sent to Venice for inspiration.

The château has seen numerous illustrious guests, among them Napoleon III on 16 December 1862. Enchanted, the emperor planted a commemorative sequoia which still stands in the park. On 19 September 1870, after the disaster of Sedan, Jules Favre tried in vain to negotiate an armistice with Bismarck in the "Interview of Ferrières". In 1977 after restoring the château, Baron Guy and Baroness Marie-Hélène de Rothschild donated it along with part of the estate to the Chancellery of the Universities of Paris.

Guided tours (time: 30min) 1 May to 30 September 14.00 to 19.00; the rest of the year on Wednesdays and at weekends 14.00 to 17.00; closed Mondays and Tuesdays; château and park: 19F; park only: 12F (same admission times); ☎ *64 66 31 25.*

The rectangular château is set on a raised foundation, flanked by square towers. Architecturally it is a Renaissance blend, mixing balusters, colonnades and galleries in the eclectic style fashionable under the Second Empire.

Interior – The main entrance porch with the monogram (J R) of the Baron James and the family coat of arms (the five Rothschild arrows) leads to a pavilion with a large clock. The central hall is bathed in light from a glass roof. Above the main door, a musicians' gallery rests upon bronze and black marble telamones and caryatids, favourite decorative features under the Second Empire.

In the Salon Bleu, which opens onto the park, the busts of the Empress Eugénie and Betty (Bettina) Rothschild, first mistress of the château, are noteworthy. In the Salon Louis XVI, E. Lami recreated the charm of the 18C with white and pink wainscoting and the Boucher-style ceiling.

Musée de l'Imaginaire – *2nd floor.* The unusual works by several painters – Pierre Lacombe, Judson Huss, Christian Lepère, Wojtek Suidmak, Marc Halingre and André Martins de Barros – and a sculptor – Jean-Jacques Lamenthe – are exhibited in rotation, reflecting the variety and fertility of the artistic imagination.

★**Park** – The park, designed by Paxton, is laid out in the English style. Special varieties include ornamental conifers, cedars of Lebanon, Atlas cedars, sequoias (introduced to France around 1850) and swamp cypress.

FONTAINEBLEAU***

Michelin map 106 folds 45 and 46
About 64km – 40 miles south of Disneyland Paris

The origin of its name is shrouded in mystery. It has been said to derive from Bliaut, a hound of the royal pack who is said to have discovered a pure spring on this site, or from "fontaine-belle-eau," the fountain of beautiful water... Today it is believed the name refers to Blaut or Bliaut, owner of the fountain, who gave his name to this site.

Fontainebleau, its past linked with royalty from the 12C to the 19C, has also been home to various military and equestrian organizations in an unbroken tradition lasting to the present.

***THE PALACE

Like many royal residences, the palace originated in the 12C as a hunting lodge. During his exile in France in 1169 Thomas Becket consecrated the chapel for Louis XII. Philip the Fair was born at Fontainebleau in 1268 and died here in 1314. Gradually transformed into a sumptuous residence, the palace was favoured by royal rulers up to Napoleon III.

The Spirit of the Renaissance – On his return from captivity in Madrid in 1525, François I turned his attention from the Loire Valley to his residences in Ile-de-France. In 1528 he had the medieval buildings, except for the old dungeon, demolished to make way for Gilles Le Breton's additions: on the east side an oval-shaped pavilion which was linked to the west block by a long gallery. Influenced by his travels in Italy, François I introduced innovations of the Italian Renaissance to his court.

In 1532 François Ier called on the Florentine Rosso, one of Michelangelo's pupils, to decorate the interior. At his death in 1540, the Bolognese Primaticcio took over the work. The frescoes and stucco-work from this period, called the **First Fontainebleau School**, are characteristic of the international Mannerist movement. Inspired by humanist thought, the allegorical decorations, many of which have been destroyed, represent mythology and ancient and modern history, as well as the glories of the king. In 1539, François I received his rival Emperor Charles V, who was enthralled with the palace, rapidly becoming famous in European courts. A great collector, François I gathered gems, sculptures, and paintings at Fontainebleau, including a number of masterpieces like Leonardo da Vinci's *Mona Lisa*, now in the Louvre. Henri II continued his father's work with the construction of the ballroom. There are many monograms of the royal H and the two intertwined C's of Catherine de' Medici. The C's flanking the H form a double D, initials of Diane de Poitiers, the king's mistress. Artists such as Niccolo dell'Abbate, who used brighter colours, worked here.

Henri IV and the Second Fontainebleau School – The religious wars halted construction at Fontainebleau. With the realm restabilized, Henri IV had the Cour des Offices (Kitchen Court) and the Jeu de Paume (real tennis court) constructed and altered the Cour Ovale (Oval Court). The decoration is mainly the work of three painters who defined the Second School of Fontainebleau: Toussaint Dubreuil, Ambroise Dubois and Martin Fréminet. Influenced by their Italian predecessors and Flemish art, they followed the Bellifontain tradition and foreshadowed classicism.

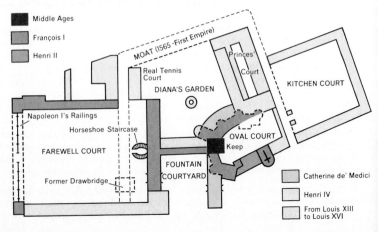

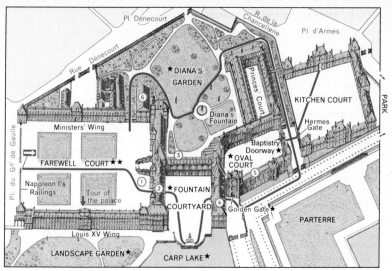

① Horseshoe Staircse ③ François I Gallery ⑤ Ballroom
② Queen Mothers' Wing ④ Fine Fireplace Wing ⑥ Real Tennis Court

The House of Eternity – Louis XIV, Louis XV and Louis XVI carried out extensive renovations, especially in the decoration of the apartments. During the Revolution the palace was spared although emptied of furniture. First as Consul, then as Emperor, Napoleon loved to visit Fontainebleau. He preferred this palace to Versailles where he felt haunted by his rival in glory, Louis XIV. He called the palace the "House of Eternity" and left his mark in many restorations. The palace was turned into a museum under the Republic.

Exterior

The palace's stages of construction are visible in the disparity of architectural styles, which lends the palace a certain charm and originality.

★★Cour des Adieux or Cour du Cheval-Blanc (Farewell Court or White Horse Court) – Once the service courtyard, this is now the main entrance to the palace. The courtyard remains architecturally unified despite centuries of renovation. Of the three walls with stone courses built under François I, only the Ministers' Wing on the left remains. The right wing was constructed by Gabriel for Louis XV. The main façade was transformed several times between 1545 and the 18C, which accounts for its assymmetry. The Fer-à-Cheval (Horseshoe) Staircase ① by the architect Jean Androuet du Cerceau was added between 1632 and 1634. The farewell ceremony for Napoleon I on the occasion of his departure for Elba was held in this courtyard on 20 April 1814. Officers and veterans listened, deeply moved by his address, "Continue to serve France; my only thought was for her happiness...."

Cross the **Cour de la Fontaine★** (Fountain Courtyard) where the remarkably fresh water issuing from this fountain was reserved for the king. On the other side of the **Aile de la Belle cheminée** (Fine Fireplace Wing) ④ (1570) by Primaticcio are the Oval Court and the Golden Gate.

★Porte Dorée (Golden Gate) – Constructed by Gilles Le Breton starting in 1528, this was the main entrance to the palace until the Baptistry Door was built under Henri IV. It was in fact the entrance to the fortress castle, but the pilasters and two upper levels of loggias show Italian influence. The frescoes are by Primaticcio.

★Cour Ovale (Oval Court) – Built by Gilles Le Breton, this is the oldest courtyard in the palace. It stands on the site of the courtyard of the original fortress of which François I saved only the keep. Henri IV had the irregular shape straightened out. He lengthened the ballroom and built an enormous domed gateway called the **Porte du Baptistère★** (Baptistry Door) for the baptismal ceremony of the future Louis XIII and his sisters in the courtyard on 14 September 1606.

Cross the **Cour des Offices** (Kitchen Court). At the entrance are sandstone heads of Hermes by the sculptor Gilles Guérin (1640).

Gardens – These include: the **Jardin de Diane★** (Diana's Garden), designed for Catherine de' Medici then re-landscaped in the 19C; the present **Jardin Anglais★** (Landscape Garden) created in 1812; the **Parterre** or formal garden, redesigned by Le Nôtre in the 17C; and finally Henri IV's park.

★★★Grands Appartements (Grand Apartments)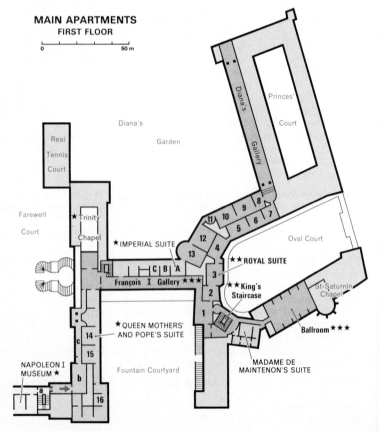

Guided tours daily 09.30 to 12.30 and 14.00 to 17.00; closed Tuesdays, 1 January, 25 December, and certain other holidays; 31F (Musée Napoleon Ier included), 14F on Sundays ☎ 60 71 50 70.

You reach the Grand (State) Apartments by the stucco staircase (**a**), the Galerie des Fastes (Hall of Splendour) (**b**), and the Galerie des Assiettes (Gallery of Plates) (**c**) created under Louis-Philippe.

★**Chapelle de la Trinité (Trinity Chapel)** – It owes its name to the ancient church of the Trinitarians erected by St Louis on this site. Henri IV had the sanctuary vaulted and decorated. The painter Martin Fréminet (1567-1619) painted scenes of the Redemption and characters from the Old Testament on this vault in a Mannerist style marked by bold foreshortening.

Louis XV married Maria Leczczynska in this chapel in 1725.

Louis Napoleon, the future Napoleon III, was christened here in 1810.

★★★**Galerie de François Ier (François I Gallery)** – Built between 1528 and 1530, it was originally open on both sides, forming a covered bridge. Louis XVI, who enlarged the gallery in 1786, blocked the view of Diana's Garden. False French windows were installed for symmetry. The decoration, supervised by Rosso, mixes fresco and stucco-work, and the wood panelling was executed by an Italian woodworker, Scibec of Carpi. The F of François I and his mascot the salamander appear everywhere. The scenes contain several layers of meaning, referring to ancient history, the life of the king, and mythology. The main themes are religion, filial piety and war.

★★**Escalier du Roi (King's Staircase)** – Under François I, this was the chamber of the Duchesse d'Étampes, the king's favourite. To facilitate access to his state apartment, Louis XV had J.A. Gabriel transform the room into a staircase in 1749. The 16C frescoes by Primaticcio and Niccolo dell'Abbate illustrate the story of Alexander the Great.

★★★**Salle de Bal (Ballroom)** – 30m -100ft long and 10m - 33ft wide, this was the hall of banquets and celebrations. It was begun under François I and finished under Henri II by Philibert Delorme. A recent restoration revived frescoes painted by Niccolo dell'Abbate over drawings by Primaticcio. The marquetry of the parquet floor executed under Louis-Philippe reproduces the coffered ceiling, richly decorated with gold and silver. The two telamones supporting the chimneypiece are cast after ancient statues *(photograph opposite)*.

Appartements royaux (Royal Suite)

Appartements royaux (Royal Suite) – The palace of François I consisted of a single suite of apartments overlooking the Oval Court. About 1565, the regent Catherine de' Medici enlarged the palace between the Oval Court and Diana's Garden. Gradually the sovereigns set up their bedchambers, offices and private salons on the side of Diana's Garden; the former apartments then became antechambers, guardrooms and salons for the courtiers. The "Great Dinners" were also held here.

Ch. Sappa/CEDRI

Chimneypiece in the Salle de Bal

Salle des Gardes (Guardroom) (1) – First room of the King's Suite. The ceiling and frieze are in the Louis XIII style.

Salle du Donjon (Keep) – From the Salle du Buffet (2), a large arcade leads to the "fat old tower" room, the oldest in the palace. Until Henri IV this sombre room, also known as St Louis' room, was the king's bedroom (3).

The equestrian low-relief on the chimney representing Henri IV by Mathieu Jacquet (c1600) is one of the ornaments of the Belle Cheminée ("Fine Fireplace").

Salon Louis XIII (4) – Louis XIII was born in this room on 27 September 1601, an event recalled by the coffered ceiling (Cupid riding a dolphin). Over the painted panelling are eleven pictures by Ambroise Dubois illustrating the loves of Theagenes and Chariclea.

Salon François Ier (5) – Of Primaticcio's work only the fireplace remains.

Salon des Tapisseries (6) – Successively the Queen's Room, the Queen's Guardroom, and first antechamber of the Queen, this room became the first salon of the Empress in 1804, Guardroom once again in 1814, and finally the Tapestry Room in 1837. The chimney dates from 1731, the Renaissance-style northern pine ceiling is "signed by Poncet" (1835). The furniture is Second Empire. The early 17C tapestries illustrating the story of Psyche come from Paris.

Antichambre de l'Impératrice (Empress's Antechamber) (7) – Previously the Queen's Guardroom, constructed over the old Queen's staircase, the floor and woodwork of this room date from 1835. The Gobelins tapestries in the style of Le Brun evoke the seasons. The furniture is Second Empire.

Galerie de Diane (Diana's Gallery) – Gilt gallery, 80m - 263ft long, designed under the Restoration and turned into a library under the Second Empire.

Salon Blanc (White Room), Petit salon de la Reine (Queen's Parlour) (8) – Decorated in 1835 with earlier pieces (woodwork Louis XV, chimney Louis XVI, adorned with bronze). The furniture is Empire.

Grand salon de l'Impératrice, Ancien salon des Jeux de la Reine (former Gaming Room of the Queen) (9) – The ceiling by Berthélémy shows Minerva crowning the Muses. The Empire furniture includes a Sévres porcelain table painted by Georget in 1806-1807 and Louis XVI furniture.

Chambre de l'Impératrice (Empress's Bedchamber) ancienne chambre de la Reine (formerly the Queen's Bedchamber) (10) – The main part of the ceiling was made in 1644 for Anne of Austria, the woodwork, the alcove ceiling and the chimney for Maria Leczczynska in 1747 and the arabesque-style doors for Marie-Antoinette in 1787. Louis XVI furniture.

Boudoir de la Reine (11) – Made for Marie-Antoinette by the architect Rousseau.

Salle du Trône (12) – This was the king's bedroom from Henri IV to Louis XVI. Napoleon I converted it into the throne room.

Salle du Conseil (Council Chamber) (13) – Magnificent Louis XV ensemble. On the ceiling five pictures by Boucher illustrate the seasons.

★Appartement intérieur de l'Empereur (Imperial Suite) - Napoleon had this suite installed in the wing built by Louis XVI, parallel to the François I gallery. The visit takes you past two bedchambers, the **Chambre de Napoléon (A)** and the **Petite chambre à coucher (B)**, and the **Salon de l'Abdication (C)** where the imperial abdication was signed on 6 April 1814.

★Appartement des Reines Mères et du Pape (Queen Mothers' and Pope's Suites) - These rooms owe their name to the fact that Catherine de' Medici, Marie de Medici, Anne of Austria and Pope Pius VII (1804 and 1812-14) all stayed here. The ceiling of the Grand Salon **(14)** used to be that of Henri II's bedchamber. In the Chambre à coucher d'apparat (Ceremonial Bedchamber) **(15)** there is a Gobelins tapestry, *The Triumph of the Gods*. The Duchess of Orléans' bedchamber **(16)**, in which the pope stayed, contains a very sophisticated set of Louis XVI furniture, set off by a superb décor of deep crimson damask.

Ask at the reception to see the Empress Joséphine's apartments and the Galerie des Cerfs (Deer Gallery).

★Musée Napoléon Ier

Dedicated to the Emperor Napoleon I and his family, the museum is housed in fifteen rooms on the ground level and first floors of the Louis XV wing of the palace. It contains portraits (paintings and sculpture), gold ware, weapons, ceramics (the Emperor's services), coronation clothing and uniforms, and personal mementoes.

Once the Princes' apartments, these rooms retain a sumptuous, palatial character thanks to the many pieces of furniture and objets d'art which adorn them.

★★★THE FOREST

The magnificent forest of Fontainebleau covers 25 000 hectares – 62 000 acres; of these 20 000 hectares – 50 000 acres, including the forest of Trois-Pignons, are national. The ancient forest of Bière – whose name still exists in Chailly or Fleury-en-Bière – has always been a magnificent hunting ground, especially with hounds. There are numerous paths for walking and hiking.

In the surrounding area you can visit **Milly-la-Forêt★** where medicinal plants are grown and in which the chapel **St-Blaise-des-Simples** (*simples* is French for medicinal herbs) belonged to a leper-house. In 1959 Cocteau decorated the chapel *(open from Easter to 1 November 10.00 to 12.00 and 14.30 to 18.00; the rest of the year Saturdays, Sundays and public holidays 10.15 to 12.00 and 14.30 to 17.00; closed Tuesdays; 7.50F; ☎ 64 98 84 94).* Also worth seeing are the **Halles** (covered market), built of oak and chestnut, and in the forest the **Cyclop**, a colossal sculpture by Jean Tinguely.

5 km - 3 miles north of Milly is the Louis XIII style **Château de Courances★★** *(25min guided tours 2 April to 18 September on Saturdays, Sundays and public holidays 14.30 to 18.30; 24 September to 1 November weekends and holidays 14.00 to 17.30; 35F; park only 20F; ☎ 45 50 34 24).*

Not far from the Gorges d'Apremont is the famous town of **Barbizon★★**, colony during the 1830s for numerous landscape artists, forerunners of the Impressionists. Breaking with the conventions of Paris studios and official art, the Barbizon painters were landscape painters working from nature after the example of the great masters Théodore Rousseau (1812-1867) and Jean-François Millet (1814-1875).

Michelin Maps, Red Guides and Green Guides are complementary publications. Use them together.

MEAUX★

Michelin map 106 folds 22 and 23
About 18km – 11 miles northeast of Disneyland Paris

In feudal times the city was the produce market for the estate of the counts of Champagne. In 1682 **Jacques-Bénigne Bossuet**, previously the dauphin's tutor, became bishop of the city. Active and diligent in his diocese and in the fight against heresy, the "Eagle of Meaux" was also a writer, and composed here five of his greatest funeral orations. He died in Paris in 1704 and was buried in accordance with his wish in the cathedral of Meaux.

The city is notable in particular for its religious architecture. During the summer a **son-et-lumière** performance brings to life 2 100 characters in the episcopal quarter, reliving Meaux's greatest hours.

★Cathédrale St-Etienne (St Stephen's Cathedral) – 12-16C. All the important steps in the evolution of Gothic architecture are visible. The mutilated 14C sculptures on the south transept and the enormous 15C Flamboyant Last Judgment scene on the central doorway of the west front are interesting. The interior is remarkable for its well-lit nave. The double side aisles appear especially high because their galleries were taken down in the 13C; their arcades, however, still exist in three bays to the right of the chancel.

Adjoining the cathedral, the **Vieux Chapitre** (Old Chapter House) was originally the chapter's tithe barn (grange aux dîmes) (13C).

Ancien Evêché (Episcopal Palace) – Open daily 10.00 to 12.00 and 14.00 to 18.00; closed Tuesdays, 1 January, 1 May, 14 July and 31 December; 15F (free on Wednesdays); ☎ 64 34 84 45.

The bishop's palace was built in the 12C; from the Gothic period there are two magnificent chambers on the ground floor and the chapel on the first floor. The rest of the building, renovated during the 17C, today houses a **Musée des Beaux-Arts** (Fine Arts Museum). The chapter house contains part of the archaeological collection. In the apartments and western rooms is a collection of paintings from the 14C to 19C (Boullogne, de Troy, Millet and Courbet), rich in works of the Italian school thanks to a donation by Annie and Jean-Pierre Changeux.

MORET-SUR-LOING★

Michelin map 106 south of fold 46
About 75km – 46 miles south of Disneyland Paris

The charming town of Moret lies on the Loing. Branch off Route de St-Mammès to reach the Pin meadow which borders the west bank of the midstream island. The **view**★ of the waters with their shaded islands, the fishermen, the church, and the keep is lovely.

On Saturday evenings in summer, from the end of June until early September, the residents of Moret bring the town to life in a son-et-lumière show, "Spectacle de l'Été."

SIGHTS

Bridge over the Loing – This is one of the oldest bridges in Ile-de-France. Certainly as old as the town fortifications, although frequently destroyed and widened, the bridge spans the river and islands. From the side of the Burgundy gate (Porte de Bourgogne) the ramparts are visible as well as the houses with their over-hangs, one of which rises from the middle of the water.

Notre-Dame – This church is reminiscent of many of the great churches of Ile-de-France. The chancel is said to have been consecrated in 1166. Only the apse and the south side of the church bear witness to the original elevation – here one can see the large arcades supported by round columns topped with an open gallery opening onto triple arches and the clerestory windows above. The arcades and bays of the north side of the church were walled in to provide better support for the bell tower, which was extremely high for the 15C. The elevation of the transept with its openwork, and the elevation of the nave with its three-point arcades are the result of a later period of construction (13C and 14C).

Ancien Hospice (Former Hospital) – The corner post on Rue de Grez displays an effigy of St James. Walk up Rue de Grez to see a modern cartouche bearing the date of the hospice's foundation (1638). The hospice was once renowned for the barley-sugar manufactured by the sisters. Local confectioners continue to produce this sweet.

Maison de Sisley – *Not open to the public.* This house is where the British Impressionist, Alfred Sisley (1839-1899), peacefully spent the last part of his often harried life. His studio was at 19 Rue Montmartre.

Maison de François Ier – *Go through the town hall porch into the courtyard.* The gallery is an example of exuberant Renaissance decoration. Notice the salamander above the door.

Porte de Samois (or de Paris) – On the inner façade of this gate there is a statue of the Virgin Mary. Also of interest is the old royal milestone from the main road between Paris and Lyon (now the N 5).

PROVINS★★

The dome of the church of St-Quiriace and the Tour de César (tower) dominate the skyline of this city whose charm inspired some of Balzac's works and Turner's watercolours.

BRIEF HISTORY

From the 11C the lower city grew up around a Benedictine priory. Under Henri the Liberal (1152-1181) Provins became one of the commercial centres of the county of Champagne.

The Fairs of Provins – During the Middle Ages city life revolved around the two fairs in May-June and September-October which attracted merchants from all over France. Highly active until the 14C these fairs were gradually eclipsed by the fairs of Lyon and Paris.

The roses – Tradition holds that Thibaud IV, Count of Champagne, brought roses from Syria when he returned from the Seventh Crusade and planted them in Provins where they flourished. Edmund of Lancaster (1245-96), the King of England's brother who married Blanche d'Artois, widow of Henri the Fat, Count of Champagne, was suzerain of Provins for several years. He introduced this very rare flower, the red rose, into his coat of arms. Nowadays, the roses are greatly admired. June is the best time to visit Provins to admire its beautiful rose bushes.

View of Provins by Jean Houel (Musée des Beaux-Arts, Rouen)

★★UPPER CITY *time: 1 hour 30min*

By car take the road leading into Avenue Général-de-Gaulle.
The upper city has interesting civil and military architecture from the medieval period.

★★Ramparts – The walls of the upper city are the oldest in Provins. Built in the 12C and 13C on a pre-existing defence line, they have been altered many times. The most interesting part stretches from the Porte St-Jean to the Porte de Jouy. The wall, which overlooks the dry moats, is reinforced by towers of diverse shapes.
Of the 12C Porte de Jouy only the door jambs and the spur-shaped tower base on the moat remain; to the right, part of the rampart has been built with battlements and merlons.
Follow the Rue de Jouy. This street is lined with picturesque low houses with long tile roofs and houses with overhanging first storeys.
Leave your car on Place du Châtel.

Place du Châtel★ is lined with medieval houses dating from the 12C to 15C. The **tithe barn★** on Rue St-Jean was rented to merchants on fair days by the canons of St-Quiriace.

★★Tour de César – *Open 1 April to 1 November 10.30 to 18.00 (17.00 on weekdays between 6 September and 1 November); the rest of the year from 10.30 to 17.00; closed at Christmas; 17F; ☎ 64 60 26 26.*

This superb 12C keep flanked by four turrets 44m - 144ft high is the emblem of the city. It used to be attached to the walls of the upper city. The pyramid-shaped roof was built in the 16C.

Go under the vault to take the stairs on the right to the reception; then pass around the tower on the left.

The mantle wall encompassing the base of the keep was added by the English during the Hundred Years War to set up their artillery; hence the nickname "English paté." On the first floor the octagonal guardroom (11m - 37ft high) has pointed vaults. The sentry path, which no longer exists, led to tiny alcoves which served as dungeons. At the foot of the stairs leading to the upper gallery is the Governor's Room. From the gallery (once covered) which surrounds the keep, the **view★** looks out over the city and the Briarde countryside: to the west, the upper city surrounded by its ramparts, to the north the old convent of the Cordelières (founded 13C). The uppermost floor can be reached by a very narrow stairway. Under the beautiful 16C woodwork are the bells of St-Quiriace.

St-Quiriace – Construction of the church began in the 12C under Henri the Liberal on the site of an 11C collegiate church. The **chancel★** and ambulatory are characteristc of early Gothic. The dome dates from the 17C.

REIMS★★★
and the Champagne cellars

Michelin map 241 fold 17
About 104km – 64 miles northeast of Disneyland Paris

The lively cultural centre of Reims is known for the cathedral of Notre-Dame – the coronation church of the kings of France – and the basilica of St-Remi. As the principal centre of the Champagne wine-growing area, along with Épernay, its wine cellars are steeped in history.

Clovis' baptism – On Christmas Day 498, **St Remigius** (bishop from the age of 22), baptised Clovis, sealing the Franks' bond with Christianity. Gregory of Tours recounted the event in his *History of the Franks*. A procession wound its way through the flag-bedecked village from the old Imperial Palace to the baptistry, located beside the cathedral. As Clovis entered for the baptism, a messenger of God called out to him in these eloquent terms: "Bow your head, proud Sicambre; adore what you have burned and burn what you have adored". According to legend a dove (symbol of the Holy Spirit) presented Remigius, who was immobilised by the immense crowd, with a holy phial containing chrism (holy oil for anointing the king).

Thus tradition legitimates the French monarchy by associating it with divine will. In remembrance of this first anointing and later of Louis the Pious' coronation, the French kings came to Reims to be consecrated from the 11C on.

The coronation ceremony – Reims hosted 25 coronations from Louis VIII to Charles X (1223 to 1825). After taking the oath the king advanced to the altar where the dignitaries fastened his sword and fixed his spurs. With a golden needle, the archbishop removed a drop of the holy chrism from the holy phial, mixing it with oils consecrated on St Remigius' paten. After being anointed the king put on the royal robe of purple velvet decorated with fleurs-de-lys then received his ring, sceptre and hand of justice before the archbishop crowned him with the assistance of the peers. Public acclamations, a musketeers' volley and a rendition of the Te Deum followed.

★★★NOTRE-DAME *time: about one hour.*

In summer expert guides give tours at 10.30 (except Sundays) and at 14.30; from mid-June to September the upper parts of the cathedral can be visited from 10.00 to 11.30 (except Sundays) and from 14.00 to 17.30; 20F.

One of the great cathedrals of the Christian world, Notre-Dame is famous for its unity of style, its statues and its long association with the kings of France.

Building – An early cathedral was built in 401 by St Nicasius. In the 9C this was replaced by a larger edifice which was destroyed by fire in 1210. The Archbishop Aubry de Humbert decided to build a Gothic cathedral like those already being built in Paris (1163), Soissons (1180), and Chartres (1194). The design was entrusted to the master builder Jean d'Orbais, and in 1211 the first stone was laid. The five succeeding architects followed the original plans closely, thus assuring the extraordinary unity of Reims cathedral. The architects inscribed their names on the marble labyrinth inlaid in the floor of the nave. Medieval labyrinths became a substitute for a pilgrimage and the faithful followed them on their knees. Unfortunately the Reims maze was destroyed in the 18C. Jean d'Orbais worked on the chancel until 1226, then Jean le Loup built the nave and the west front, while his successor Gaucher de Reims installed the statues and worked on the west end of the nave. Bernard de Soissons designed the large rose window, the gables and the nave's vaulting. In 1285 the cathedral's interior was completed.

The towers were constructed during the 15C. Four other towers and seven bell towers were planned, but in 1481 a fire ravaged the upper part of the cathedral, bringing this project to a halt.

In the 18C the cathedral underwent several alterations (the rood screen was removed along with some windows and the labyrinth), but it survived the Revolution with remarkably little damage.

In the 19C an ambitious restoration campaign was undertaken. This had barely been finished when the First World War inflicted severe damage upon the cathedral. On 19 September 1914, shelling set the frame work on fire and the enormous blaze melted the bells, the window lead, and burst the stone. The building suffered under heavy artillery fire, but the walls held up, and at the end of the war, a new restoration project was undertaken, financed in large part by the Rockefeller donation.

Architect Henri Deneux designed the cathedral's new frame work of non-inflammable cement. In 1937, the cathedral was reconsecrated.

Exterior

A multitude of statues inhabits every available niche of the cathedral's exterior. The statues number more than 2 300 although those damaged in the war or by bad weather have been taken down and are now exhibited in the Palais du Tau. Most of these have been replaced with copies created by Georges Saupique and Louis Leyguc.

West front – This is one of the most beautiful in France. It is viewed to best advantage in late afternoon when it is bathed in the soft light of the setting sun. It resembles Notre-Dame of Paris in its loftiness, but its vertical lines are magnified by the upward sweep of the tympana, the gables, the pointed pinnacles, the slender columns and the gigantic effigies of the gallery of kings. The **three doors** correspond to the three naves. They are topped with large gables supporting sculpture groups of the sort one typically finds on the tympana. Here the tympana take the form of openwork gables.

Although they were all created during the 13C, the doors' statues come from four successive workshops.

The last of the sculptors created an original Champenois style to which we owe among others the famous **Smiling Angel** statue. The productions from this workshop are particularly charming because of the freedom of their poses, their supple, flowing robes, and the vivacity of their faces, which include both mischievous and smiling demea-

nours. Above the rose window and a scene illustrating the battle between David and Goliath, the gallery of kings contains 56 statues, each measuring 4.5m-15ft and weighing 6 to 7 tons. In the centre sculptures depict the Baptism of Clovis.

Walk along the north side of the cathedral.

The buttresses – The original appearance of the nave's side-elevations with their buttresses and flying buttresses has been preserved, as no chapel was added subsequently. The buttresses are crowned with niches, each sheltering a large angel with spread wings. From these, Notre-Dame de Reims has earned its nickname of the "Cathedral of Angels."

The Smiling Angel

Façade of north transept – The statues of these three doors are older than those adorning the west front.

The statues on the right originally stood in the former Romanesque cathedral. The tympanum decorated with the Virgin in Majesty under a semicircular arch is framed with beautiful interlacing foliage. The middle door's trumeau depicts the Pope St Callistus. The left door shows in the splays six apostles flanking the "Beautiful God", sadly now missing its head. The tympanum displays scenes from the Last Judgment in picturesque detail. Among the damned of the first register a king, a bishop, a monk and a judge are recognizable. Above, the dead writhe as they leave their tombs.

Interior

The interior is astonishing for its unity, sobriety and clarity as well as for its remarkable dimensions 138m - 453ft long and 38m - 125ft high under the vaults. The impression of soaring height is accentuated by the dimensions of the nave, narrow in relation to its length, and by the lines of its ribs forming very pointed arches.

The **nave** is three storeys high. Above the arcades supported by cylindrical pillars and beneath the clerestory windows with their rose and coupled lancets runs a blind triforium (supported by the roofs of the aisles).

The capitals, with their floral designs (more or less elaborate depending on the date of the construction), encompass within their perimeters the four semi-columns making up each pillar. The oldest (moving away from the chancel) are designed with crockets representing acanthus leaves, monsters, and even two vintners carrying a basket of grapes (the sixth pillar of the nave on the south side). The most recent illustrate the local flora in sensitively and accurately executed detail.

The **chancel** has only two bays but the section reserved for the mass extends three bays into the nave – coronations required plenty of space. At one time it was enclosed by a rood screen, and the royal throne was placed there. The chancel's pillars are narrower but mark each bay, emphasizing the effect of the elevation. The radiating chapels which open off the ambulatory are connected by a passageway at the base of the openings, a typical feature of Champenois architecture.

The **west end of the nave,** (the interior façade of the west front) the work of Gaucher de Reims, is unique in the history of Gothic architecture. The large rose window (12m - 40ft in diameter) tops the triforium, the arcade of which is decorated with windows of the same form. Below, a smaller rose window is installed in the open-work tympanum.

In some places the wall contains niches into which statues have been sculpted. The various sections are decorated with luxuriant floral patterns, recalling the patterns of the nave's capitals. The carvings of the central door of the inner façade of the west front are the best preserved, depicting the lives of the Virgin Mary *(to the left)* and of St John the Baptist *(to the right).*

**Stained glass – The windows dating from the 13C have suffered much damage. Some were replaced with plain glass during the 18C while others were destroyed during the First World War. Still intact are the window of Henri de Braine, the donor, (bottom part of the right lancet) and in places the windows representing bishops subject to the Archbishop of Reims: the bishops of Soissons, Beauvais, Noyon, Laon, Tournai, Châlon, Senlis, Amiens and Thérouanne.

The façade's large rose window, masterpiece of the 13C, is dedicated to the Virgin. In the centre the Dormition is represented, surrounded by the apostles and angel-musicians. The best time for viewing the rose is late afternoon when the sun floods through the glass.

It is impossible to speak of Reims' windows without mentioning the name Simon, the family of master glassmakers who have worked on the windows for generations. Their examination of the 13C windows before the First World War allowed Jacques Simon to restore certain parts of those windows which were badly damaged and to recreate some of those which had disappeared, such as the façade's small rose and certain windows of the transept including the vintner window. His daughter Brigitte Simon-Marcq produced a series of abstract stained glass windows entitled the Waters of the Jordan to the right of the font *(south transept).*

In 1974 the apsidal chapel was decorated with the Chagall window, striking for its dominant blue hues and its luminosity. Designed by the artist, the windows were produced in the Simon workshops. In the centre window the Sacrifice of Abraham on the left matches the Sacrifice of the Cross on the right. The window to the left represents the Tree of Jesse while the one on the right evokes great moments from the cathedral's history, including Clovis' baptism and Saint Louis' coronation.

★★PALAIS DU TAU *time: 1 hour*

Open July and August 09.30 to 18.30; 16 March to 30 June and 1 September to 14 November 09.30 to 12.30 and 14.00 to 18.00; 15 November to 15 March 10.00 to 12.00 and 14.00 to 17.00 (18.00 at weekends); closed 1 January, 1 May, 1 and 11 November, 25 December; 26F; ☎ 26 47 81 79.

The palace houses the cathedral's treasure and some of its original statues as well as fifteen very fine **tapestries★★** portraying the life of the Virgin. The latter were donated to the cathedral in 1530 by Cardinal Robert de Lenoncourt. The episcopal seat has existed on this site since 1138 and bears the curious nickname tau because of its plan in the form of the Greek letter. Later the name was also given to the late 15C great hall. The present building (1690) was the work of the architects Robert de Cotte and Mansart and it still incorporates the 13C chapel and the Salle du Tau.

★★ST-REMI *time: 1 hour 30 min*

★★Basilique St-Remi – Construction of the basilica began about 1007 and on 1 and 2 October 1049, it was solemnly consecrated by Pope Leo IX.

Exterior – Two square towers, 56m - 184ft in height, dominate the west front. The right tower dates from the 11C, while the left was rebuilt in the 19C, along with the gable which separates the two towers. The lower parts date from the 12C. Framing the centre door are Gallo-Roman columns holding statues of St Remigius and St Paul. The transept dates from the 11C.
Supported by archaic-looking buttresses, the chancel is an example of 12C Early Gothic. Notice the layout of the radiating chapels, the ambulatory and the clerestory windows grouped in threes.

Interior – The dimensions of the basilica, 122m - 400ft long by a mere 25m - 82ft wide create an impression of infinity, reinforced by the shadowy nave. The nave, a sober construction of the 11C, has eleven bays with semicircular arches, supported by columns topped by capitals decorated with animals and foliage. Two Gothic bays have replaced the former Romanesque porch and form the link to the façade. Above are immense tribunes; the pointed vaulting was built at the end of the 12C. Notice the "crown of light" pierced by 96 days symbolising the 96 years of the life of St Remigius, a copy of the one destroyed during the Revolution.
The 17C parclose screen is Renaissance in style. The Gothic chancel, a harmonious and airy structure, has four storeys lit by the bays which have retained their 12C windows representing the Crucifixion, the apostles, the prophets and the archbishops of Reims. Behind the altar is the **tomb of St Remigius,** rebuilt in 1847.

★★Musée St-Remi – The museum is housed in the old abbey of St-Remi, a beautiful ensemble of buildings of the 17C and 18C, which still bear a few signs of the original 12C abbey and the Gothic chapterhouse. The art collections are from the Middle Ages with two exceptions, the arms collection and the **St-Remi tapestries★★.**

★★THE CHAMPAGNE CELLARS

Though covering only 2% (27 000 hectares - 66 700 acres) of France's total area planted with vines, this northernmost of the country's wine-growing regions is perhaps its most prestigious. Champagne existed in Roman times, when it was still wine, but it was Dom Pérignon, the cellar master of Hautvilliers Abbey, who had the idea of making it sparkle. The "wine of kings" is a blended wine using the pinot noir, pinot meunier and chardonnay grape varieties in varying proportions, and the prestige of the famous brands depends on the expertise of the master-blenders. Épernay and Reims are the two principal centres and most of the champagne houses offer guided tours of their cellars *(caves).*

Reims

The large champagne houses are located in the Champ de Mars area *(southeast of the city centre)* and on the chalky slopes of the St-Nicaise hillside, which is dotted with caves called *crayères.* Often of Gallo-Roman origin, the caves are also of historic interest. The deep and extensive tunnels make ideal wine cellars.

Pommery – *Guided tours (time: 1 hour) 15 March to 31 October from 10.00 to 17.20; the rest of the year on weekdays only from 10.00 to 12.00 and from 14.00 to 17.00; closed late December to early January;* ☎ 26 05 05 01. Staircase with 116 steps.

Shop sign depicting the various stages in the champagne-making process
(in Oger southeast of Épernay)

Founded in 1836, the concern prospered under the guidance of Louis Alexandre Pommery's widow. Today it covers 300 hectares – 740 acres and is one of the most beautiful estates in wine-growing Champagne. The tour takes you through chalk caves decorated with 19C sculptures. Each tunnel was named after the European city which was home to the latest new clients. In the entrance hall, note the 75 000 litre wine cask by the sculptor Gallé, a piece carved for the St Louis, Missouri Fair of 1904.

Taittinger – *Guided tours (time: 1 hour) Mondays to Fridays 09.30 to 12.00 and 14.00 to 16.30; weekends and holidays 09.00 to 11.00 and 14.00 to 17.00; closed weekends and public holidays from 1 December to 28 February; 15F; ☎ 26 85 45 35.*
In 1932 Pierre Taittinger became head of the concern held by the Fourneaux, merchants in sparkling wines since 1734. In addition to its 250 hectares - 617 acres of vineyards, storehouses on the hillsides, and the mansion of the Comtes de Champagne in Reims, the house of Taittinger has superb wine cellars. On the tour 15 million bottles of wines can be seen aging in the cool tranquility of the Gallo-Roman pyramid-shaped chalk caves built in the crypts of the abbey of St-Nicaise (13C), destroyed during the Revolution.

Veuve Clicquot-Ponsardin – *Guided tours (time: 1 hour 30min) 1 April to 31 October; by appointment only (made a few days in advance) Mme Danielle Brissaud ☎ 28 89 54 41.*
Philippe Clicquot founded the concern in 1772, but the business was built up by his son and especially his son's widow *(veuve)*, whose maiden name was Ponsardin. She formed the company under its present name. The remarkably enterprising "Grande Dame du Champagne" – her nickname was given to a special vintage – created remarkable new methods including, in 1816, the practice of twisting the bottles to cause the sediment to work down to the cork. Today, with 265 hectares – 655 acres of vineyards, this house exports 75% of its production and is among the best-known houses abroad. Its cellars are housed in Gallo-Roman caves.

Ruinart – *Visits on weekdays by appointment only; ☎ 26 85 40 29. Service Relations Publiques, 4 Rue des Crayères, 51053 Reims.*
Founded in 1729 by the nephew of the mayor Dom Thierry Ruinart, a close friend of Dom Pérignon, this house flourished under the Restoration. Badly affected by the World Wars, it revived again after 1949. Today, as part of the Moët-Hennessy Louis Vuitton group, Ruinart champagne is a prestige product. Its cellars occupy three levels of a remarkable group of Gallo-Roman chalk caves.

▲ Capacity of the different bottles of Champagne ▲

Bottle: *75cl*	Mathusalem: *8 bottles*
Magnum : *2 bottles*	Salmanazar : *12 bottles*
Jeroboam : *4 bottles*	Balthazar : *16 bottles*
Réhoboam : *6 bottles*	Nabuchodonosor : *20 bottles*

Épernay *Michelin map 241 fold 21*

Moët & Chandon – *Guided tours (time: 45min) 1 April to 31 October every day from 09.30 to 11.30 and 14.00 to 16.30; also 1 November to 31 March on weekdays only at these times; closed on public holidays from 1 November to 31 March; 20F; ☎ 26 54 71 11.*

Claude Moët founded the famous wine concern in 1743. His grandson, Jean Rémy, received visits on several occasions from Napoleon I. Pierre-Gabriel Chandon, son-in-law of Jean Rémy, added his name to the family business. In 1962, the family business became a corporation. Since then the Moët-Hennessy Louis Vuitton Group has controlled Moët et Chandon, Mercier and Ruinart champagnes. The cellars, with a surface area of 18 hectares – 44 acres over 28km - 17 miles, contain the equivalent of 90 million bottles. This comprehensive tour allows the visitor to see the various stages of wine production, including twisting the bottles and extracting the sediment-coated corks.

Mercier – *Guided tours (time: 45min) 09.30 to 11.30 and 14.00 to 16.30; closed on Tuesdays and Wednesdays in December, January and February; 20F; ☎ 26 54 75 26.*

In 1858 Eugène Mercier brought together several champagne houses to create the house of Mercier, today the second largest producer of champagne after Moët et Chandon. In the entrance hall is a **giant wine cask** carved by Navlet of Chalon for the 1889 World Exhibition. After a spectacular panoramic elevator ride down, a small laser-guided train takes visitors through 18 kilometres – 11 miles of tunnels decorated with sculptures hewn out of the chalk by the same artist.

Giant wine cask

De Castellane – *Guided tours (1 hour) Easter to 1 November from 10.00 to 12.00 and from 14.00 to 18.00; at same times during Easter weekend, but from 14.00 to 18.00 only during the rest of the days in April; 20F; ☎ 26 55 15 33.*

The tour includes the cellars, the museum and the tower.

The tower (60m-197ft high) has been laid out as an exhibition on the history of the De Castellane and Mérand families. Labels and bottles are also on display. There is a good **view** of Epernay and the vineyards from the top of the tower *(237steps)*.

The **museum** is mainly given over to an explanation of the various stages of production of champagne. Tableaux illustrating cooperage, work on the vines, grape harvest and pressing have been set up. Large collection of labels.

Other champagne cellars are also open to visitors. For more complete information, consult the Michelin Green Guide Champagne-Ardennes (in French).

How to enjoy champagne at its best:

– Serve cold or chilled (about 6-8 °C or 43-46 °F), but not iced.
– Cool the champagne bottle in an ice bucket half full of ice cubes and water for 20-25 min.
– Uncork the bottle by easing the cork gently out of the top, turning it slightly as you do so, once you have removed the wire muzzle.
– The best champagne glasses are flutes, which retain the aroma, rather than the "coupes" which let all the bubbles and bouquet escape too quickly.

"A votre santé !"

Château de VAUX-LE-VICOMTE★★★

Built by Fouquet, this château remains one of the greatest masterpieces of the 17C.

The rise of Nicolas Fouquet – Born of a family of magistrates, Fouquet became a member of the Parlement de Paris by the age of twenty. He was made Procureur Général of this noble assembly and was appointed Superintendent of Finances under Mazarin. Following the customs of the time and the example of Cardinal Mazarin, he acquired the dangerous habit of confusing the credit of the State with his own. He was forever surrounded by a numerous retinue of senior personalities whose services cost vast sums of money. Intoxicated with success Fouquet chose a squirrel as his emblem – in Anjou patois *fouquet* means squirrel – and decreed his motto would be *Quo non ascendam* (Just how high shall I climb ?).

In 1656, Fouquet decided to grace his own seigneury of Vaux with a château worthy of his social success. He showed excellent taste when it came to choosing his future "collaborators": the architect **Louis Le Vau**, the decorator **Charles Le Brun** and the landscape gardener **André Le Nôtre**. He was equally discerning in other matters: the famous chef Vatel was hired as his major-domo and La Fontaine as close adviser. The builders were given carte blanche. A total of 18 000 workers took part in the project, which took five years to complete. The result was a masterpiece that Louis XIV wished to surpass with the construction of Versailles.

Le Brun created a tapestry manufacture at Maincy. After the fall of Nicolas Fouquet, it was moved to Paris, where it became the Manufacture Royale des Gobelins.

Courting royal disapproval – On 17 August 1661, Fouquet organized a banquet for the king and his court, who were staying at Fontainebleau. The reception was one of dazzling splendour. The king's table featured a service in solid gold: this detail annoyed him intensely as his own silverware had been sent back to the smelting works to meet the expenses incurred by the Thirty Years War.

After a banquet dinner at which Vatel had surpassed himself, the guests could feast their eyes on the garden entertainments, enhanced by 1 200 fountains and cascades. The king was vexed by such an extravagant display of pomp and luxury, unparalleled at his own royal court. His first impulse was to have Fouquet arrested immediately but Anne of Austria succeeded in calming him down… for a while.

The fall of Nicolas Fouquet – Nineteen days later, the Superintendent of Finances was sent to jail and all his belongings sequestrated. The artists who had designed and built Vaux entered the king's service and were later to produce the palace of Versailles. At the end of a three-year trial, Fouquet was banished from court but this sentence was altered by the king to perpetual imprisonment. The château survived the Revolution without suffering too much damage and in 1875, Vaux was bought by the industrialist Monsieur Sommier, who applied himself to restoring and refurbishing the château and its grounds.

Château de Vaux-le-Vicomte

★★Château – *Open 1 April to 31 October 10.00 to 13.00 and 14.00 to 18.00 (10.00 to 18.00 on Sundays and public holidays); 56F (includes access to gardens and Museum of Carriages); ☎ 64 14 41 90.*
Candle-lit tours Saturday evenings May to September.

The château is built on a terrace raised above the gardens and surrounded by a moat. It is approached by the northern front and makes an impressive sight; note the raised level of the ground floor and the height of the first floor windows. The whole building is characteristic of the first period of Louis XIV architecture.

The glass doors in the entrance hall – now covered up by tapestries – opened onto the Grand Salon and the perspective of the formal gardens. This vestibule leads up to the first floor, occupied by the suites of Fouquet and his wife. Visitors are shown the superintendent's antechamber (large ebony desk inlaid with gilt copper), his study and his bedroom (superb ceiling decorated by Le Brun). They are then taken round Mme Fouquet's boudoir (portrait of Fouquet by Le Brun), the Louis XV study and bedroom, embellished by contemporary furniture (large canopied four-poster attributed to F. Leroy) and the Louis XVI bedchamber.

Back on the ground floor, take a look at the square salon and its traditional French-style ceiling decoration, in which the beams and rafters have been left showing, and indeed enhanced with painted decoration.

Six reception rooms giving onto the gardens are laid out on either side of the Grand Salon. The ceilings were decorated by Le Brun, who conferred a sense of unity to the whole ensemble. Admire his rendering of *The Nine Muses* in the Salon des Muses, *Hercules entering Mount Olympus* in the Salon d'Hercule. The latter houses an equestrian statue of Louis XIV, executed by François Girardon. It is a miniature bronze of the monument set up on Place Vendôme in 1699 and destroyed during the Revolution.

★Grand Salon – This room, crowned by the central cupola, was left unfinished after Fouquet's arrest and suffers from the absence of decoration (the various studies made by Le Brun are on display). The sixteen caryatids supporting the dome symbolize the twelve months and the four seasons of the year. The only original furnishings are two marble tables, as well as six statues and six paintings discovered by M. Sommier when he moved in.

★★Chambre du Roi (King's Bedroom) – It communicates with the former antechamber (now a library beautifully furnished in the Regency style).

Its decoration is characteristic of the Louis XIV style that was to leave its mark on the State Apartments of Versailles. The ceiling features stucco-work by Girardon and Legendre, and a central painting by Le Brun representing *Time taking Truth up to Heaven*. Below the cornice is a frieze of palmette motifs alternating with tiny squirrels.

The dining room probably served a similar function in Fouquet's time. It gives onto a passageway embellished with wood panelling and hung with paintings, where a long row of dressers would hold the bowls of fruit and other dishes brought from the distant kitchens.

★★★Gardens – M. Sommier has carefully reconstituted Le Nôtre's masterpiece, of which the most striking feature is its sweeping perspective. The grounds offer several "optical illusions", namely the discovery of basins that are not visible from the château. Walk to the far end of the upper terrace to get a good view of the southern façade. The central rotunda and its surmounting lantern turret, the square corner pavilions, heavier than on the north side, and the decoration of the frontispiece, crowned by statues, form an impressive, if somewhat heavy, composition. Starting from the château, one first walks past the *boulingrin* or bowling green, two oblong areas of greenery trimmed into ornamental lace motifs.

The three main water perspectives – the moat, the two rectangular canals and the Grand Canal – suddenly spring into sight in a most impressive manner.

The Grand Canal – known as the "frying pan" on account of its rounded end – is approached by a steep flight of steps level with the small cascade, located opposite the grottoes. The niches at each end house two statues of river gods which remain a telling example of 17C sculpture at Vaux.

Skirt the Grand Canal and walk up to the foot of the Farnese Hercules which ends the wondrous perspective. The very last basin aptly called the spray – La Gerbe – affords an extensive view of the château and its stately grounds.

Dépendances (Outbuildings) – The **Musée des Équipages★** (Museum of Carriages) lies in the western outbuildings, situated next to the visitor's entrance. Its presents harnessing and saddlery, an old-fashioned smithy and fully-equipped carriages.

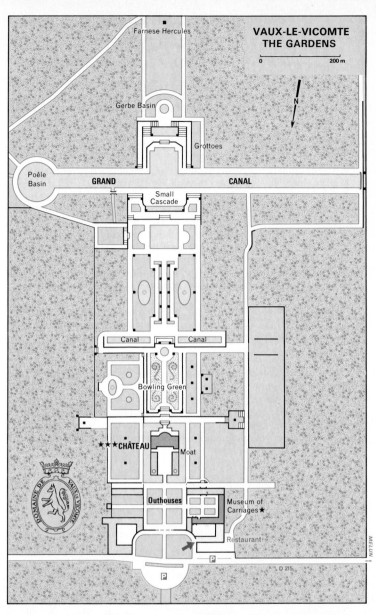

**VAUX-LE-VICOMTE
THE GARDENS**

0   200 m

N

Farnese Hercules

Gerbe Basin

Grottoes

Poêle Basin

GRAND   CANAL

Small Cascade

Canal   Canal

Bowling Green

★★ **CHÂTEAU**   Moat

Outhouses

Museum of Carriages ★

Restaurant

DOMAINE DE VAUX VICOMTE

P

P

D 215

MELUN

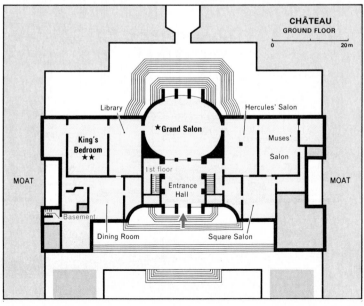

**CHÂTEAU
GROUND FLOOR**

0   20 m

Library

★ **Grand Salon**

Hercules' Salon

King's Bedroom ★★

Muses' Salon

1st floor

MOAT   MOAT

Basement

Entrance Hall

Dining Room   Square Salon

VERSAILLES★★★

Michelin map 106 folds 17 and 18
About 72km – 45 miles west of Disneyland Paris

Symbol of absolute monarchy and the apogee of the arts in France under the reign of the Sun King, Versailles became the residence of the court and seat of government on 6 May 1682 and remained so without interruption until the Revolution.

BRIEF HISTORY

In 1624 **Louis XIII** gave orders to build a small hunting lodge around the present Marble Court. Philibert le Roy reconstructed the château in brick and stone in 1631. **Louis XIV** retained his father's château; from 1661 he had the gardens embellished for his splendid festivals. In 1668 the King's architect **Louis Le Vau** constructed a stone "envelope", around the small château, building façades which concealed the old façades on the garden side of the château. **Le Nôtre** laid out the flower beds and park while Le Brun designed the sculptures for the park, notably, for the important order of 1674.

Jules Hardouin-Mansart succeeded Le Vau and modified the palace with the Galerie des Glaces (Hall of Mirrors) and two wings in the south (1682) and the north (1689).

Under Colbert and Le Brun, the Gobelins factory and the artists of the Académie Royale designed the main furniture and decoration with the remarkable stylistic unity which defines Versailles classicism.

Through a complex system of etiquette and magnificent feasts, Louis XIV managed to control the ever dangerous nobility, thwarting their political ambitions.

Under **Louis XV** changes were limited mostly to the interior which J.A. Gabriel restructured to create the "Petits Cabinets."

When the **Revolution** drove Louis XVI from Versailles, a century of royal occupation came to a close. In the 19C, **Louis-Philippe** transformed part of the palace into a museum dedicated to French history. Since 1914 the State, supported by private patronage, has carried out important restoration work and refurbished the palace.

Château de Versailles

★★★THE PALACE ◼

A complete tour of the palace, park and the Grand and Petit Trianons takes two days. If you only have one day it is recommended that you begin with the interior of the château, first floor, where the most magnificent apartments are found. The park and gardens can be enjoyed at your leisure.

EXTERIOR *time: about 1 hour*

Set back from the château on the Place d'Armes are the **Écuries Royales★** (Royal Stables) by Jules Hardouin-Mansart.

Courtyards – Beyond the palace's wrought-iron railings, created under Louis XVIII, lie three courtyards. In the centre of the forecourt, the **Cour des Ministres** (Ministers' Court), is a statue of Louis XIV commissioned by Louis-Philippe. Next is the **Cour Royale** (Royal Court) which only persons of high rank were permitted to cross in horse-drawn carriages. The two bordering wings were furnished with a colonnade under Louis XV. Finally there is the **Cour de Marbre★★** (Marble Court) with its black and white marble pavement, the heart of Louis XIII's château.

★★★**Garden Façade** – *Go through the north arcade, skirt the central part of the palace and step back for a good view.*
Designed by Le Vau in 1669, the façade is lined with pillars and Ionic columns rising from a bossaged base. The balustrade crowning the façade bears trophies and vases and conceals the flat Italian-style roof. Le Vau created a terrace in the space in front of the building, but in 1678, Jules Hardouin-Mansart covered the space, and it became the Hall of Mirrors. This he extended with two wings.
Along the façade four metal casts of ancient statues are perched on the pedestals; these are the first works of the Keller brothers. Two giant Medici **vases★** representing *War* (by Coysevox) and *Peace* (by Tuby) stand under the windows of the War Salon and the Peace Salon located at either end of the Hall of Mirrors.
Statues of Apollo and Diana, surrounded by the Months of the Year, top the central building of the palace where the royal family lived.

D. Hée/MICHELIN

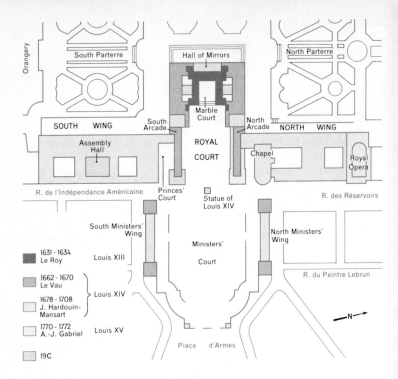

INTERIOR

Tour of the Grands Appartements and the Chapelle Royale from 09.00 to 18.30 (17.30 from 1 October to 30 April); 40F. Guided tours of the Appartements du Roi and the Opéra Royal from 09.30 to 16.00; 25F.

From the visitors' entrance go though the vestibule which houses the ticket office and up by the circular staircase to the Chapel Room (a) on the first floor.

★★★ Chapelle Royale (Chapel)

This two-storey palatine chapel with a royal gallery is dedicated to St Louis. It was constructed by Jules Hardouin-Mansart, and finished in 1710 by his brother-in-law Robert de Cotte. The ceiling is the work of the painters Jouvent, Coypel and La Fosse. The marble altar sculpted by Van Clève is decorated in front with a gilded bronze low relief representing a *Pietà* by Vassé.

Grands Appartements (State Apartments)

These consist of the reception rooms – the Salon d'Hercule, the Grand Appartement and the Galerie des Glaces – and the living quarters, of which the most interesting are the royal bedrooms.

★★ Salon d'Hercule (Hercules' Salon)

This room, begun in 1712 and completed in 1736, owes its name to the ceiling painted by Lemoyne. The artist needed three arduous years to cover the 315sq m - 3 390sq ft ceiling with a painting of *Hercules entering the Kingdom of the Gods*. The artist committed suicide in 1737 shortly after finishing it. Two Veronese canvases occupy their original places: **Christ at the House of Simon the Pharisee★, Eliezer and Rebecca.**

★★★ Grand Appartement (Grand Apartment)

The six-room suite with decoration by Le Brun was the King's apartment from 1673 to 1682. Then Louis XIV took up residence definitively at Versailles and had a new apartment designed around the Marble Court. Three times a week on Mondays, Wednesdays and Thursdays from 18.00 to 22.00 the king held court in the Grand Apartment.

One entered the rooms through the Royal Court by the Ambassadors' Staircase, sumptuously designed to impress visitors, but which was torn down by Louis XV in 1752.

Salon d'Abondance (Abundance Salon) (b) – When the king held court during the time of Louis XIV there were three buffets, one for hot drinks and two for cold. The ceiling painted by Houasse represents royal magnificence and the gold ware collections of Louis XIV in *trompe-l'œil*.

Salon de Vénus (Venus Salon) (c) – The ceiling was painted by Houasse and like the ceilings of the following rooms, it features decorated panels with gilt stucco borders.

Salon de Diane (Diana Salon) (d) – Billiard room under Louis XIV. Notice the **bust of Louis XIV** by Bernini (1665), a stunning example of baroque workmanship. Paintings by La Fosse and Blanchard.

Salon de Mars (Mars Salon) (e) – Guard room before 1682, this room was later used by Louis XIV for balls, games and music.
Two paintings have been restored to their 18C places: *Darius' Tent* by Le Brun and *The Pilgrims of Emmaüs* after Veronese. On the side walls, Louis XV by Rigaud and Maria Leczczynska by Van Loo occupy their original places. The ceiling with its martial scenes is by Audran, Jouvenet and Houasse. Above the fireplace hangs one of Louis XIV's favourites, *King David* by Domenichino in which he is pictured playing the harp. It originally hung in the king's bedchamber.

Salon de Mercure (Mercury Salon) (f) – Formerly the antechamber, kings occasionally lay in state in this room. In 1715 Louis XIV lay in state for a week, with 72 ecclesiastics keeping vigil to ensure that four masses could be said simultaneously every day from five in the morning until noon without interruption. The ceiling is the work of J.B. de Champaigne.

Salon d'Apollon (Apollo Salon) or Salle du Trône (Throne Room) (g) – The throne stood on a central platform beneath a large canopy. One can see the three hooks which supported the canopy.
Ambassadors were received here. This room was used for dancing and concerts when the king held court. The ceiling features *Apollo in a Sun Chariot* by La Fosse.
The Grand Apartment ends here. The entire front of the palace overlooking the gardens is occupied by the Hall of Mirrors and its two wings, the Salons de Guerre et de la Paix.
Crossing the **Salon de Guerre★** (War Salon), which links the Grand Apartment and the Hall of Mirrors, notice the large oval low-relief by Coysevox representing Louis XIV triumphing over his enemies.

★★★Galerie des Glaces (Hall of Mirrors)

Designed by Jules Hardouin-Mansart in 1687, the Hall of Mirrors was the show piece under Louis XIV where court celebrations and elaborate receptions for foreign potentates took place.
The hall is 75m - 246ft long, 10m - 33ft wide, and 12m - 40ft high, and it is illuminated by seventeen large windows echoing seventeen glass panels on the opposite wall. The 578 mirrors of glass which compose these panels are the largest that could be manufactured at that time. The hall enjoys the last rays of the setting sun.
On the ceiling Le Brun executed the most important cycle of his career as the King's chief painter. The cycle illustrates the life of Louis XIV and his military victories until the Treaty of Nijmegen in 1678.
The Hall of Mirrors was abundantly decorated with solid silver furniture cast under Louis XIV.
The German Empire was proclaimed in this room on 18 January 1871 and the Treaty of Versailles was signed on 28 June 1919.
From the central windows one has a good **view★★★** of the Grand Perspective. Entrance to the Queen's Suite is through the **Salon de la Paix★** (Peace Salon) which is decorated with a canvas by Lemoyne of *Louis XV presenting peace to Europe.*

★★Appartement de la reine (Queen's Suite)

The suite was constructed for Louis XIV's wife Queen Marie-Thérèse who died here in 1683.

Chambre de la Reine (Queen's Bedroom) (h) – Le Brun's original decoration for Marie-Thérèse was redone for Queen Maria Leczczynska between 1729 and 1735. The white and gold woodwork, the greyish tones of the ceiling by Boucher, and the doors decorated by Natoire and de Troy demonstrate the inclination towards the rococo under Louis XV. Marie-Antoinette had other renovations made in 1770: the two-headed eagle and the portraits of the house of Austria recall the Queen's origins. The floral wall hangings were rewoven to the original pattern in Lyon matching exactly the original hanging of the Queen's summer furnishings of 1786.
In France, royal births were public events: in this room nineteen children of France were born, among them Louis XV and Philip V of Spain.

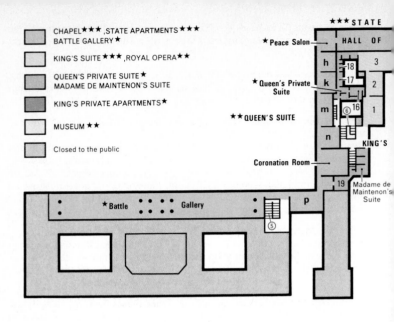

Legend:
- CHAPEL★★★ ,STATE APARTMENTS ★★★ BATTLE GALLERY ★
- KING'S SUITE ★★★ ,ROYAL OPERA ★★
- QUEEN'S PRIVATE SUITE ★ MADAME DE MAINTENON'S SUITE
- KING'S PRIVATE APARTMENTS ★
- MUSEUM ★★
- Closed to the public

★★★ STATE

HALL OF

★ Peace Salon

★ Queen's Private Suite

★★ QUEEN'S SUITE

Coronation Room

KING'S

Madame de Maintenon's Suite

★ Battle   Gallery

Salon des Nobles de la Reine (Peers' Salon) (k) – In this one-time antechamber presentations to the Queen took place. This room was also where queens and dauphines of France lay in state. The room has been restored to the way it looked in 1789.

In the **Antechamber (m)** note the painting by Madame Vigée-Lebrun of Marie-Antoinette and her children (1787). The **Salle de gardes de la Reine** (Queen's Guardroom) **(n)** protected against intrusions such as that which occurred on the morning of 6 October 1789, when a rioting mob tried to invade the Queen's Suite and had to be fought off by the royal guard in a prolonged and bloody scuffle.

Salle du sacre (Coronation Room)

Initially used as a chapel from 1676 to 1682, this large guardroom housed the sessions of Parliament which passed laws here. Louis-Philippe had the room altered to accommodate three enormous paintings: *Murat at the Battle of Aboukir* by Gros, *Champ de Mars Eagles* and *The Consecration of Napoleon* by David.

When it is open the visitor may see the **Galerie des Batailles★** (Battle Gallery) which occupies the south wing. Designed in 1836 for Louis-Philippe by the architects Fontaine and Nepveu, it created a sensation. The thirty-three vast pictures evoke France's greatest military victories and include works by Horace Vernet, Eugène Delacroix and Baron Gérard.

★★★Appartement du roi (King's Suite or Louis XIV's Suite)

The king's suite stretches around the Marble Court. Designed between 1682 and 1701 by Mansart in Louis XIII's château, the decoration marks a clear break in the evolution of Louis XIV style. The ceilings are not coffered but painted white; the white and gold panelling replaces the marble tiling; large mirrors adorn the fireplaces.

The **Escalier de la Reine** (The Queen's Staircase) ⑥ was the normal entrance to this apartment at the end of the Ancien Régime.
After the guard room **(1)** an antechamber **(2)** leads to the **Salon de l'Œil de bœuf** (Bull's Eye Salon) **(3)**. Here gentlemen attended the King's rising and retiring. The decoration marks the first flowering of Louis XV style.

Chambre du Roi (King's Bedroom) (4) – This was the bedroom of Louis XIV from 1701 and it was here that he died.
Above the bed, the alcove decoration represents "France watching over the sleeping King" and was sculpted by Coustou. The wall hangings are faithful reproductions of the summer furnishings of 1705. The paintings belonged to the King's personal collection.

Grand Cabinet du Roi ou du Conseil (Council Chamber) (5) – Characteristic of rococo, this room was created under Louis XV by uniting two rooms. In this room decisions were made that involved the destiny of France, among them the decision to participate in the American War of Independence.

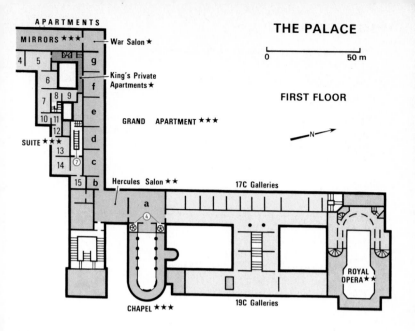

APARTMENTS
MIRRORS ★★★
War Salon ★
King's Private Apartments ★
GRAND APARTMENT ★★★
SUITE ★★★
Hercules Salon ★★
17C Galleries
ROYAL OPERA ★★
CHAPEL ★★★
19C Galleries
0   50 m

★★★ Appartement Privé du Roi (King's Private Suite)

These are the private apartments of Louis XV, reserved for those closest to him. Here the king removed himself from the constraints of the Court. The rooms were designed by Gabriel and are decorated with carvings by Verberckt: shells, foliated scrolls and rococo flower motifs are scattered everywhere.

Chambre à coucher (King's Bedroom) (6) – Louis XV, and then Louis XVI, retired here after they had "performed" the rising and retiring ceremonies which took place in the Grand Apartment. It was here that Louis XV died of smallpox on 10 May 1774.

Cabinet de la Pendule (Clock Cabinet) (7) – This was the gaming room when the king held court. Until 1769 it owed its name to the astronomical clock whose works were built by Passemant and Dauthiau with bronze embellishments by Caffiéri. Cross the **Antichambre des chiens** (Dog's Antechamber) **(8)** (Louis XIV panelling). In the dining room called **Retours de chasse** (Hunters' Dining Hall) **(9)** Louis XV gave private dinners on hunting days.

Cabinet intérieur du Roi (Corner Room) (10) – This became a work room in 1753. As an example of Verberckt's rococo style, the furniture is remarkable; the medal cabinet is by Gaudreaux (1739), corner cupboards by Joubert (1755), a **roll-top desk★** by Oeben and Riesener (1769).

Salles neuves (New rooms) – They were designed under Louis XV on the site of the Ambassadors' Staircase. In **Cabinet de Mme. Adélaïde** (Madame Adélaïde's Cabinet) **(12)**, the child Mozart played the harpsichord. The medal cabinet by Benneman is a masterpiece. The following rooms, the **Louis XVI's Library (13)** and the **China Salon (14)** show the evolution of Versailles style towards the sober under neo-classicism. The most notable is the **Salon des Jeux** (Louis XVI's Gaming Room) **(15)** as it appeared in 1775; corner cupboards by Riesener (1774), chairs by Boulard, gouache landscapes by Van Blarenberghe.

Go down the Louis-Philippe staircase ⑦ to leave via the north gallery.

★★ Opéra Royal (Royal Opera)

The opera house begun by Gabriel in 1768 was inaugurated in 1770 for the marriage celebrations of the dauphin, the future Louis XVI, and Marie-Antoinette. The first oval hall in France, it received other exceptional technical touches from the machinist Arnoult: for festivals the floor of the stalls and circle could be raised to the level of the stage.

The balconies' low-reliefs, executed by Pajou, represent the gods of Olympus (dress circle) and the children and their signs of the zodiac (upper circle).

Initially reserved for the court, the opera housed sumptuous receptions on the occasion of the King of Sweden's visit in 1784, of Emperor Joseph II in 1777 and 1781, and of Queen Victoria in 1855. The National Assembly held session here from 1871 through 1875. On 30 January 1875 the adoption of the Wallon Amendment here laid the foundation of the Third Republic. A reception for Queen Elizabeth II of England in 1957 coincided with completion of the final restoration.

★★★PARK AND GARDENS

The fountains play to background music every Sunday from early May to early October at 15.30; ☎ *39 50 36 22.*

Laid out principally by Le Nôtre during the years 1660 to 1670, the park and gardens are masterpieces of the art of French landscape gardening in which nature is ordered geometrically according to the principles of classicism.

The basins, fountains and statues are perfectly integrated with nature. The grand perspective or east-west axis symbolically retraces the path of the sun, from the **Latona Basin**★ and fountain to the **Apollo Basin**★, continuing along the **Grand Canal**★★.

On both sides of the axis flower beds, hedgerows and sculptures are to be found.

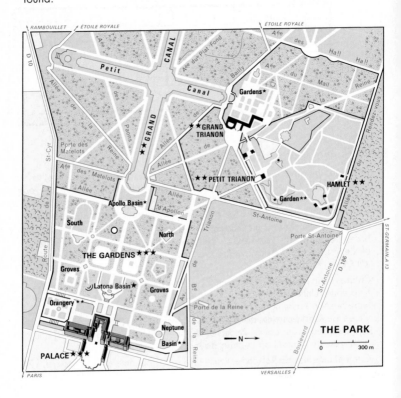

Index